WHERE YOU'RE AT

WHERE YOU'RE AT

Notes from the Frontline of a Hip Hop Planet

PATRICK NEATE

BLOOMSBURY

First published 2003
This paperback edition published 2004

Copyright © 2003 by Patrick Neate

The moral right of the author has been asserted

Bloomsbury Publishing Plc, 38 Soho Square, London WID 3HB

A CIP catalogue record for this book is available from the British Library

ISBN 07475 6389 6

10 9 8 7 6 5 4 3 2 1

All papers used by Bloomsbury Publishing are natural,
recyclable products made from wood grown in
well-managed forests. The manufacturing processes
conform to the environmental regulations of the
country of origin.

Typeset by Hewer Text Ltd, Edinburgh
Printed by Clays Ltd, St Ives plc

www.bloomsbury.com/patrickneate

This book would never have got written without a whole lot of people's love, support and advice. So, in no particular order, thanks to Tom Rowley (still eating crazy cheese like you'd think he's from Paris), Dan and Tania (for bed and burgers), Claude Grunitzky, Siany Sian (the bridge is, like, so over), Rainer Lampkins-Fielder, Sandra Klopper, Forzanah Badscha, Sky 189, Rachel and Alistair (for bed and boerwors), Papa Joe Sciorra, Indo Aminata (Guinea's greatest gift), José Junior, Def Yuri and Renata Hotbutt.

Even in London, a lot of people were cool. They included Anna@Abstrakt, Shane@Universal, Sam and the other Darlings, Marie-Agnes@the French Music Bureau, Austin and Snowy@-Woah, Will@Big Dada and Vez@Ninja. Who else? Bandit from MSI, Burhan, Charlie Dark and Mike Ladd (the original renaissance men), Ils (because lemonade was a popular drink and it still is), Francesca, Drew and Sacha (TV? You *are* joking). Much love, too, to Gez and Feels (a.k.a. Tha Godsunz), Lil' Meems and Gusta Gus.

Most humble thanks, however, go to those who have forgotten more about this and other cultures than I'll ever know and still had the grace to share their wisdom. Kenyatta Belcher (peace to you, my friend; we'll hook up soon), Jeff (a.k.a. Peanut Butter Fly), Yuko Asanuma, Carlo Schilir, Dylan Lloyd and Luke Dowdney. Incidentally, if you're reading this with a heavy wallet, check out Luke's work at www.vivario.org.br for a useful way to splash your cash. The good fight's the only one worth fighting and Luke knows that better than anyone.

Finally, acknowledgements aren't acknowledgements without offering gratitude to the man upstairs for his unfailing help: Mike Jones, my editor.

For Kanyasu. Thank you.

CONTENTS

Intro
Straight Outta The Jungle[1]

'We call him Yella/He is the best/He rocks the house on the DMX/ When he's on the beatbox, he cannot miss/So listen to the beat as he rocks like this.'

How far can you get from the ghetto? Not much further than a village ten miles from Chippenham, Gloucestershire, UK.

So when are we talking? Let me check the vinyl. OK. The album's called *Street Sounds Electro Volume 9*. The track is 'World Class' by the World Class Wreckin' Crew. 1985.

It must have been my friend's fourteenth birthday then. Joss. And, yes, he was posh. Posh Joss. His parents owned a rambling country pile and a whole gang of us had bussed out there from the South London burbs. The sound system was set up in the garage (his dad's Jag had been moved on to the gravel drive) and the girls danced in gaggles, nervously sipping cans of Heineken, while the boys lit cigarettes from ten-packs of JPS and argued over the tapes.

The music was diverse, unified only by its '80s mediocrity: a fair dose of Wham and Duran Duran, a dash of Meatloaf, a pinch of the Clash, a sprinkling of Siouxie and the odd soul tune. So what were we wearing? Like I say, this was the '80s and, the way I remember it, youth culture was uniquely unfocused; so scrawny metallers in Iron Maiden T-shirts rubbed shoulders with fey new romantics, pallid goths, wedge-haired casuals, boys dressed like Madonna and girls dressed like Boy George. We're talking lots of post-Fame

[1] *Straight Outta The Jungle*, The Jungle Brothers, 1988, Warlock.

leg-warmers and pristine Nike trainers (in the days before the swoosh ruled the world); hairspray and black eyeliner gone mad.

As for me, I was confused. My Sunday football team was strictly casual and for the last couple of years I'd been listening to soul-boy anthems by the likes of Shakatak and the Fatback Band. But the hip kids at my school were all, believe it or not, into 'psychobilly' (think Huey Lewis goes thrash) and if that's not a sign of lacking focus I don't know what is. That lot liked nothing more than a night of seedy abandon at the Clarendon on Hammersmith Broadway. It's about ten years since the Clarendon was finally and inevitably swallowed by an identikit mall but, back then, there was little to beat a weekend spent moshing to the Meteors or Guana Batz. So my uniform wedge haircut (bleached white at the front, of course) probably topped off a faux-American baseball jacket (twenty quid from Camden market), secondhand 501s and a pair of Doc Marten boots. Very cool in a '*Breakfast Club* meets the National Front' kind of way.

It was a big night for me. A year after my first snog, I'd just enjoyed numbers two and three (a pair of pubescent blondes whose names have faded despite vivid memories of smell and touch) and I was high on a cocktail of warm lager and half-fulfilled sexual frustration. Then someone – God knows who; romo, goth or casual – dropped in a tape of . . . of what? Rap, electro, *hip hop*.

I'm listening to it now, that same compilation that I rushed out and bought the following week. *Street Sounds Electro Volume 9*. It's hard to figure its appeal. Maybe it was the nascent electronica that sounded so much more advanced than John Taylor's bass, or maybe its urgency and aggression tapped into the aspirational psychobilly in me. Whatever. I tugged the unwilling blonde (number three) into the middle of the garage dancefloor and began to move with all the grace and rhythm of a moth around a lightbulb.

The memory makes me squirm with embarrassment. But it probably makes DJ Yella (the one who 'rocks the house on the DMX') squirm too. Back then, the World Class Wreckin' Crew were a bizarre LA outfit who wore shiny suits and their hair in jheri curls. But it was only a couple of years later that Yella graduated to the gangsta-lifestyle, ghetto-celebrity attitude of hip hop legends

NWA. By then hip hop had changed, Yella had changed and I had changed too.

But I will always remember that first night. It was the night I vowed to be the first B-Boy in London. I thought hip hop was totally new and didn't realise that, like me, the genre was just entering awkward adolescence.

In the fifteen years plus since Joss's party, I've met all kinds of B-Boys from all over the world – from hip hop legends to wannabes, LA gangstas to ghetto-fabulous New Yorkers, Johannesburg township kids to Tokyo hipsters – and they often talk about their conversion to hip hop in almost epiphanic terms. They mention the first time they heard Kool Herc play at a block party or their first DJ Quik mixtape or 'Fight The Power'[2] on the sound system after Mandela was freed or the release of *Breakin' 2: Electric Boogaloo*. But me? To paraphrase the great Ice Cube[3] (rapper, actor, Nigga With Attitude, voice of disenfranchised black America, that kind of thing): 'Straight outta Chippenham, crazy muthafucka called Patrick.' Yeah, right.

Genres of popular music come and go; some swell as others contract, some evolve and others simply disappear (psychobilly, anyone?). The most long-lived and successful tend to be those that encompass more than music alone; perhaps a style of dress, attitude or dynamic of consumption. Any record-company man will tell you that if you want to shift units, you have to sell to the kids. And what do the kids want? Symbols they can appropriate as tools of their growing identity. It's obvious stuff.

Marilyn Manson is not a modern American icon thanks to the quaint power chords of his faux-goth rock but because he flirts with images of androgyny, satanism and alienation and spawns reams of angst-ridden teen poetry. Little wonder that the Brits don't get him. Oasis don't stand or fall by their sub-Beatles meandering but by their Madchester, mad-for-it, proto-lad pronouncements. Little wonder that the Yanks have never got them.

Hip hop, though, is different. It certainly sells to the kids but it's

---

[2] 'Fight The Power', Public Enemy, 1989, Def Jam.
[3] 'Straight Outta Compton', NWA, 1988, EMD/Priority.

also one of the few musical forms that can be followed by the word 'culture'. What is hip hop? It's always been hard to explain and these days it's harder than ever. KRS One, that old-school colossus, once said: 'I am hip hop.'[4] And he's right. The visceral rap polemicist Chuck D (of Public Enemy) has described hip hop as 'just black people's creativity'.[5] And he's right, too. But hip hop is much more (and sometimes much less) than both these definitions.

Hip hop is now both the biggest-selling musical form in the USA and the voice of alienated, disenfranchised urban youth – a cultural dialectic that takes quite some explaining.

When heads refer reverentially to 'hip hop culture', they generally mean the four core skills of the B-Boy: as emcee, DJ, graffiti artist and breakdancer (and sometimes they chuck in a fifth element, the nebulous 'consciousness'). But even this definition starts more arguments than it finishes as the ubiquity of 'rap music' (as opposed to 'hip hop') engulfs popular culture. '*I'm* hip hop,' brags one cat. 'No, I'm the *real* hip hop,' retorts another. And the kids in the Sean John denim and fresh Nikes look on and wonder who gives a shit.

Reality is an issue that has both dogged and defined hip hop since the beginning. For all its new-found dominance, hip hop has remained to some extent insular, exclusive and hostile (which in part explains why it manages to be so successful and so cool all at once). This can be a huge hassle. In preparing this book, I contacted a prominent London hip hop critic for some advice. He sent me an e-mail: 'There are only two hip hop writers in England who I respect. I'm one of them and you're not the other.' But outside our front doors, hip hop has hijacked mainstream culture (or do I mean this the other way round?) and become all-encompassing, influential and global. It is the worldwide urban soundtrack; from New York to Nairobi, the Rio *favelas* to the townships of South Africa.

Off the top of my head, then, some hip hop symbols, thematic and stylistic (and in no particular order): race, politics, religion, alienation, slavery, sex, partying, materialism, slang, violence, crime, philosophy, clothes, haircuts, trainers, boots . . . I could go on for

---

[4] *The Source*, January 1994.
[5] *The Hip Hop Years*; Alex Ogg, 1999, Channel 4 Books.

ever. You speak the B-Boy language? You're speaking Ebonics.
You want hip hop champagne? Cristal. A watch? Rolex – platinum,
of course. Gun? Desert Eagle. Car? Used to be an Oldsmobile, then
a Lexus, now a Bentley (I think; I might be behind the times). Hip
hop has its own movies, art and literature. It's a subculture with its
own subcultures. It has a history of wars and revolutions, civil wars
and colonial conquests. It has its own missionaries, martyrs and,
above all, mythology.

But, for me, when I started working on this book, the essence of
hip hop had always been something intuitive and visceral; an
inexplicable concept that sat on the very tip of the tip of my
tongue. Hip hop matters to me and now, I think, it matters to
everyone else too. You see, some people may not have noticed and
some people may not like it, but the truth is we're living on a hip
hop planet.

It's 1992 and I'm sitting in a bar in Harare, Zimbabwe, when a
guy walks in wearing a Lakers vest and Chipie jeans; his hair is neatly
dreaded and he walks with the rolling ease of the B-Boy swagger.
He clocks my Karl Kanis and second pair of Air Jordans (the
originals were nicked in South Africa; long story) and comes straight
over. 'Yo, my brother, wassup?'

Dressed the way I was, sitting the way I was, blunted the way I
was . . . Taurayi thought I was an American and I made the same
mistake by return. Turned out, despite his accent and his attitude,
he was a born-and-bred, never-left-the-country Zimbabwean.

Taurayi and I got talking. We had nothing in common except
hip hop but that was enough to be going on with. Here were a
Zimbabwean black kid and an English white kid, each utilising the
most poignant and pointed imagery of modern African-American
identity for his own ends. It's a small world indeed.[6] And it's only
getting smaller.

These days I'm never surprised to buy sushi in Playa Del Carmen

---

[6] An aside: I recently met New York emcee, poet, lecturer in English literature
and all-round renaissance man Mike Ladd and we discovered that, for that
summer a decade ago, we both DJ'd hip hop in Harare nightclubs; him at
Archipelagos and me at Harpers. That's ever-decreasing hip hop circles for you.

or a Coke in the Cambodian bush. But when a Tokyo teenager greets me with 'Word up, dog' or I stumble across a white Afrikaaner rapping in a suit and tie, it still catches me unaware. It shouldn't. Hip hop may be the most elemental expression of contemporary America but it is also, in its essence, universal.

The end of the twentieth century was increasingly identified by platitudes about our global village. But if the events of the last five years – CNN-authenticated horrors from Bosnia to the West Bank to New York – have taught us anything, it's that the utopian village of our imagination is in fact more of a city with all the rootlessness, alienation, materialism, violence and inequality associated with the word. And, of course, there's no more urban music than hip hop.

So no wonder it's a hip hop planet. And I ought to get used to it. Or, better than that, understand it. Or, better than that, write a book about it.

Hip hop, both as music and culture, often inspires remarkable devotion among its followers. Not me. Since 1985, I've spent large tracts of my life trying to ignore it, during, for example, the vacuous years of gangsta rap or my brief flirtations with acid house and ecstasy. Generally I've felt it's not really *me*; unsurprising when you consider inescapable facts of race, nationality, class and, increasingly and depressingly, age. But hip hop was my first love and, like any youthful romance, it still holds me in its thrall and can beckon a seductive finger whenever faced with the competition of some or other pretender. For better or worse, and as foolish as I think it sounds, hip hop is a part of who I am.

What follows, therefore, is a tale of our small planet, with hip hop, in all its multifarious forms, as my central character. Of all musical styles, hip hop (easily identified by beats and rhymes) is perhaps the most easily stereotyped. Maybe that's why it's so frequently pigeonholed and dismissed even as it becomes all-pervasive. But, as it globalises, so both the music itself and under-standings of it are reinvented and re-understood; internationally, locally and individually. *Where You're At*, therefore, is hip hop's story of how it conquered the globe and nobody noticed. It is my pilgrimage in search of the essence and the answer to a fifteen-year-old question.

I make no claim that this is a definitive analysis of worldwide hip hop; rather it's a snapshot of where we're at that inevitably omits more than it shows. What's more, I know I talk subjectively about all sorts of different places, cultures and people and you're bound to get vexed at some point or other. I guess I'll have to live with that because you can't say anything about hip hop without vexing somebody; it's the nature of the beast. But I hope you'll trust that I'm writing with complete love and honesty because I'm writing this for all of you who are open-minded enough to recognise the most intriguing, bizarre and downright important manifestation of popular culture of our times.

I dedicate this book, of course, to hip hop heads the world over. Because ask any B-boy or B-girl and they'll tell you the same as the greatest-ever emcee told them. Like Rakim says, 'Even other states come right and exact; it ain't where you're from, it's where you're at.'[7] Word.[8]

---

[7] *Where You're At*. The title of this book is taken from a lyric in Eric B and Rakim's classic 'I Know You Got Soul' (1987). The full lyric, 'It ain't where you're from/It's where you're at', has also been used as the title of an essay by eminent black British critic Paul Gilroy. In my understanding, Gilroy uses this line to express both the unity and diversity of black identity. My appropriation of this lyric, on the other hand, expands the meaning to include London's white middle-class. This thought makes me laugh. As for Rakim? His probable intention was simply to express unity in a hip hop movement that was, by 1987, increasingly fractious. Hip hop meanings are ever-flexible.

[8] A note on the notes: it's been tricky deciding which tracks, names, slang and other cultural arcana merit a note or reference so I have simply done as I see fit. Similarly, I recognise that my use of language lurches between hip hop slang, local slang and, occasionally, academic verbosity. If I'm going to write honestly and in my own voice, I guess that's the way it has to be. At first I thought this was a weakness but now I figure it's a clear and important reflection of the absolutely personal way in which this global culture is processed.

Part One: New York
It's All About The Benjamins[1]

So I'm in New York without a plan. This could be a mistake. Everybody in New York has a plan so I'm just plain getting in the way; standing on the top of the subway steps in Union Square and trying to decide where to go.

My girlfriend, Kanyasu, is getting impatient. She's a few steps below me, dodging suits and waiting for me to make a decision. But I don't want a plan. I've been to this city maybe twenty times and every single visit's been an in-and-out job; duck in for a couple of days and interview this emcee or that producer and catch the red-eye back to London. This time it's different. This time it's a pilgrimage and a pilgrimage is sometimes more about the journey than the getting there. Sometimes, I reckon, when you get where you're going, it's not all it's cracked up to be. So let me just stand here for a moment.

This is where it all began. Not in Union Square, of course, let alone on this step. But here in New York city. It's almost thirty years since a young Jamaican called Clive Campbell (nicknamed 'Hercules', on account of his size, and then 'Kool Herc') began to DJ in the Bronx. The more he played, the more he realised that the dancers thrived on the portions of a track when the song faded out and the rhythm section kicked in (unsurprising when you consider he was brought up on the Jamaican sound systems and their use of dub plates). So he began to play two of the same record back to

[1] 'It's All About The Benjamins', Puff Daddy and The Family, 1997, BMG/ Arista/Bad Boy Entertainment.

back, keeping the rhythm running and the dancefloor busy. And so the breakbeat was born and, with it, hip hop.

Like following the subway map with my finger, I can trace a line from Herc through the stations of the other founding fathers (DJs all – Marley Marl, Grandmaster Flash and Afrika Bambaata) to the first commercial rap hit (the Chic-driven disco of 'Rappers Delight').[2] From there, I sidestep to KRS One and Run DMC and the founding of Def Jam. Then there's the black radicalism of Public Enemy giving white America the bum rush and terrifying it in the process – a nation of millions couldn't hold them back – and then a leap across country to the laid-back menace of Ice T and the burgeoning production genius of Dr Dre.

I've got double vision as I recall hip hop's parallel development: NWA and gangsta rap in LA, and New York's brief golden age in the hands of Quest, Black Sheep, De La, EPMD . . . When are we talking? Early '90s.

Now I tilt my head back to look at the Manhattan skyline and I find myself picturing the two great empires that rose out of Babylon. To my left is Death Row Records, steepling over the West Coast in the clumsy hands of former hired muscle Marion 'Suge' Knight and personified by Tupac Shakur, the New York-born son of a Black Panther. To my right is Bad Boy Entertainment, the brainchild of middle-class college kid Sean Combs whose original 'Puffy' nickname suits him a whole lot more than P.Diddy. I think about Bad Boy's frontman, Christopher Wallace a.k.a. the Notorious B.I.G. (or Biggie Smalls), a larger-than-life ex-crack-dealer from Brooklyn. I think about how these two empires traded units and traded insults until Tupac was shot dead in Las Vegas in September '96 and Biggie met the same fate six months later in LA.

In the fall-out after Biggie and Pac, the horrified American media made much of hip hop's East–West rivalry and it's no coincidence that both artists have shifted many more CDs after death than they ever did alive. But as I stand stock still amid the downtown bustle, I find the chorus of 'Warning', a seminal Biggie track (from the

---

[2] 'Rappers Delight', the Sugarhill Gang, 1979, Sugarhill.

prophetic *Ready To Die* album)[3], running around my head: 'Damn! Niggaz wanna stick me for my paper.'[4] Because it was probably as simple and as complicated as that.

After the collapse of these twin Babels (literal for Death Row; metaphorical for Bad Boy, which continues to rake it in while unable to escape Big's considerable shadow), hip hop blew up nationwide as emcees and producers stepped out of the wings from every US town and city: Common from Chicago, Masta P from New Orleans, Missy from Portsmouth, Virginia, Nelly from St Louis, Bubba Sparxxx from rural Georgia and, of course, Eminem from Detroit. Hip hop had become as all-American as baseball. Or perhaps jazz.

Maybe it's memories of Biggie and Pac because, in spite of myself, I find my thoughts wandering over news footage from Columbine High School after the infamous 'massacre' in 1999. On the slide show of my mind's eye, my attention is grabbed not by the images of the two gunmen, nor by the stereotypes of the 'trenchcoat mafia', but by the snapshots of their fellow students. Whatever alienation motivated the killers to attack the mainstream, there's one association I can't escape. The mainstream was wearing Hilfiger. And listening to hip hop, I'm sure. All this from Herc's first breakbeat.

And now my daydreaming is broken as some burly kid, maybe sixteen, pushes past me. He's white, with Eminem blond hair and a sparse Fred Durst goatee. When he turns to meet my eye, I'm smiling for no apparent reason. He looks me up and down and his face twists in a sneer. 'Bitch,' he says before turning and disappearing into the shadows underground. I still don't have a plan but I follow him down.

The 'underground'. It's always been an important hip hop construct.

---

[3] *Ready To Die*, the Notorious B.I.G., 1994, BMG/Arista/Bad Boy Entertainment.

[4] 'Paper' is slang for money. Perhaps unsurprisingly, hip hop has a lot of words for money: Benjamins, paper, papes, cheddar, cheese, green, dead presidents, cream . . .

Back in the day, of course, all hip hop was underground. Then it became a distinction from – time to sneer – 'crossover' (when L.L. Cool J crossed over with the smooch rap 'I Need Love'[5] back in 1987, it charted worldwide. And almost finished his career). But as hip hop became more of a commercial proposition, so the underground became the nursery of future stars: The Notorious B.I.G., Jay-Z and Eminem were all underground emcees at some point. Once upon a time, the term, 'underground' even expressed something about the quality of the music, distinguishing it from the slick mainstream. It was harder and dirtier and the lyrics were brash and uncompromising. But these days, for the industry at least, the distinction is both simpler and more complex as the mainstream's got ever dirtier and the underground does slick as well as anyone. So in contemporary hip hop, an underground artist is one who doesn't shift many units. So there you go.

Nonetheless, underground hip hop still matters to some consumers. I mean, if you're a 'real' 'hip hop' 'head',[6] you might pick up the odd banging track by pop stars like Jay-Z, Ja Rule or Ludacris, but the underground's your passion; because it's stuff that nobody else has heard of that sets you apart, and for me that means tracking down the independent labels.

The offices of Bronx Science are not what I was expecting. For a start, they don't even live up to the name, located as they are in Hell's Kitchen on the Lower West Side. They're kind of cheap, too. I guess I knew they'd be cheap but I imagined the gritty cheapness of a garage operation (preferably in the Bronx) rather than this low-cost functionality of Formica desks and chipboard partitions.

For the last couple of years, this record company has been sending me underground vinyl by the likes of Apathy, Louis Logik and K-Otix. It's amazing stuff: urgent rhymes and raw beats that hark back to hip hop's zenith a decade ago. So every fortnight or so, when a

---

[5] 'I Need Love', L.L. Cool J, 1987, Def Jam.

[6] 'Head' is slang for a true hip hop lover. It's almost certainly derived from '60s campus slang for a drug user (e.g. 'acid head'), which is appropriate considering the obsessive devotion of hip hop fans. In fact, rap lyrics have long used the metaphor of hip hop as a drug.

package drops on to my mat in Shepherd's Bush, I open it with some reverence, conjuring images of an urban hideout where guys make great music, just for the love. So I'm in New York without a plan and this label seemed like a good place to start.

Dave Walis, head honcho of Bronx Science, its sister label, Fully Blown, and Buds Distribution, is talking about his business. Next to him, Celph Titled – his top artist-cum-A&R-cum-all-round-right-hand-man – is nodding along. These two aren't what I was expecting, either. Dave is thirty-ish, white and earnest in that New Yorker 'I'm so busy I'm still living yesterday' kind of way. Celph is a jowly twenty-two-year-old with a Florida twang to his accent.

Dave very quickly gets frustrated by my questioning: 'Look. Hip hop in New York is what you hear on the radio, period. If you walk down the street and meet a so-called hip hop head, do you really think they've ever heard of Bronx Science? No way. If you start talking to them about underground artists, they don't know who they are and they don't want to know. Bronx Science is kind of popular in Europe and Japan but no one cares about us here. Most of the records we sell are shipped overseas. Most of our income's from you guys.'

I find myself shaking my head. I feel like the last kid in the class to stop believing in Santa.

How does a hip hop artist make it big in New York? Maybe it goes, as they say, a little something like this: MC – what shall we call him? – Lyrix starts dropping rhymes on a street corner until he's spotted by some would-be producer who adds beats and texture and they start doing local shows. They put out a couple of tracks on white label or a small independent which receive the head nod of approval from the underground *cognoscenti*: now Lyrix has got a rep. Then an A&R man sees them perform and gives them his card. 'Yo, kid. I like what you guys are doing. It's really –' he looks a little embarrassed at this point – '*fresh*. You wanna be famous?' His card says Hank Berkowitz (or similar) and they give him a demo tape. Hank's people are 'real excited' so they meet with Lyrix's people (probably his Uncle Reggie and his cousin Akino Kunte) to cut a deal. Six months later, MTV goes crazy about Lyrix's debut (called, say, 'N****s Need Lyrix') and they put it on heavy rotation. It debuts at number 16 in the national chart and it's the number-one most requested record in Oshkosh, Wisconsin. Lyrix, Reggie, Akino and even Hank are bling-blinging it all the way to the bank. It's about cream rising to the surface, it's about success from adversity; it's the American dream, right? Wrong.

To be honest, an alt-country rock band from Oshkosh have got more chance of making it in music than an underground emcee in New York. The hip hop scene that burst out of the African-American community (for the most part) in a rush of spontaneous creativity in the late '70s is now, in its city of origin, a closed shop.

These days hip hop is big business, and, as with other big businesses, outsiders find themselves banging their heads against a glass ceiling. Back in the day, independent labels like Profile and Sleeping Bag could shift tens of thousands of records by word of mouth alone. But the power of the major labels (in association with their buddies in MTV and the print media) has long since squeezed them out of the equation.

The majors have had their fingers burned enough times to know that they don't understand hip hop, so they set up their stars with their own record labels and employ prominent hip hop DJs, producers and rappers as 'cool hunters': it's the Puffy (Bad Boy), Jay-Z (Roc-A-Fella), Missy Elliott (Gold Mind) model. Consequently, every new star has a mentor – he's somebody's cousin or somebody's 'boy' from back in the day – and that's the only way to get hooked up. So Beanie Sigel got to Jay-Z through a friend of a friend and sells units on Jay-Z's label (Roc-A-Fella) with Shawn Carter (a.k.a. Jay-Z) as executive producer. So, at this specific moment in time, New York's latest rap superstar is Fabolous, brought through by the influential DJ Clue (who was brought through by Jay-Z). So Puffy stood trial alongside his nineteen-year-old protégé, Shyne, on weapons charges. And Puffy walked away while Shyne was sent down for ten years. Hip hop is big business and it's just as dirty. And the 'rap game' – the term favoured by Jay-Z – knows it.

Writing in *The New Yorker*, Kelefah Sanneh has it about right: 'Fifteen years ago, a rapper might have called himself a "microphone controller" or a "rhyme animal" – epithets that called attention to lyrical skill. Today, rappers distract listeners from the fact that there's any rapping going on at all, claiming to be pimps and thugs and cocaine dealers and businessmen and leaders and commodities.[7]

Fully Blown is Dave Walis's commercial rap label. For the last couple of years, it's been releasing tunes by Big Scoob, a minor star a decade ago, known mostly for his association with old-school veteran Big Daddy Kane. He's arguably Dave's most saleable asset.

'We made a video for Big Scoob,' Celph explains. 'It was a good, commercially viable track and a tight video. You think MTV took any notice? They didn't even want to watch it. Hip hop's like a private club where everything's bought. I would love K-Otix or Scoob to sell but we're not Universal or EMI and we can't buy ads on MTV or pay them any money so we don't get the airplay. It's been hard for me to swallow but that's the truth.'

The conversation turns to Rawkus – the only New York independent to break through to the big time in the last five years, with hit records by the likes of Mos Def and Talib Kweli.[8] Celph points to a gold record hanging on the wall. It's *The Big Picture*[9] by Harlem emcee Big L (distributed by Buds).

'That gold record? No disrespect to Big L but that was bought. Rawkus sold that record to the stores and then bought it back so they'd have a hit and get the clout with MTV.'

Dave agrees: 'The philosophy is that you build a brand until it's big enough that you can turn round and sell it for a lot of money.'

My head is beginning to swim. There's a macabre, unspoken irony in this. Big L was shot dead a couple of blocks from his home a year before *The Big Picture* was released. Now he's a brand with a gold record.

---

[7] 'Getting Paid – Jay-Z and the rise of corporate rap', Kelefah Sanneh, *The New Yorker*, 20 & 27 August 2001.

[8] More to the point, since Rawkus was co-founded by a certain James Murdoch, it benefited from a sizable injection of News Corporation money. This backing has since been withdrawn, forcing Rawkus to lay off the majority of its staff and throw itself on the mercy of MCA.

[9] *The Big Picture*, Big L, 2000, EMD/Priority/Rawkus.

I'm finding it hard to ignore the conclusion that a dead emcee, from the industry point of view, is an incomparably fine brand. He's not going to piss his percentage up a wall or lose his temper with a hotel's soft furnishings or find solace in hard drugs. A dead emcee is both fully formed and eminently flexible. After 'recognition' (which is ensured by a gold record) these are arguably the two primary qualities of brand identity and there's money to be made. How did it go? 'Damn! Niggaz wanna stick me for my paper.'

Celph is telling the story of another Bronx Science artist, Louis Logik: 'Louis has been flown out to California for discussions with majors. He's one of the most talented emcees on the underground and a lot of people wanted to sign him. But then they give him the run around. He said his meetings were really weird. Because he's intelligent, when he's talking to the head person of A&R or whatever? He can't even do it. The A&R wants him to be real ignorant.' Celph adopts a slurring, thugged-out tone. ' "Yeah, yeah. No doubt, baby, we gonna sell a mill." And everyone was, like, "You made a mistake going in there yourself. You should have had a manager represent you." So because he's a smart guy, they don't want to sign him. He's not marketable.'

Celph is shaking his head and I realise I've been shaking mine for, like, ten minutes.

Drop in on Bronx Science on a weekday afternoon and you might get lucky. Around four p.m., once or twice a week, you'll find an impromptu gathering of thirtysomething old-school cats who come to hang out with their man Big Scoob and shoot the breeze. Some of these guys are legends – Daryl MacDaniel from Run DMC, Das EFX, Fu Schnickens, King Sun and MC Shan[10] – and they tell their stories like Vietnam vets; of their gold records and how they used to sell out this or that venue.

---

[10] Aside from one-time superstar DMC, Das EFX are best known for the tongue-twisting rhymes of their gold-selling debut *Dead Serious* in 1992 (East-West). The Fu Schnickens briefly hit the limelight a couple of years earlier with their ragga-infused classic 'Ring The Alarm' (BMG/Jive/Waterstone). In 1987, MC Shan released 'The Bridge' (Cold Chillin'), arguably the first great diss track.

Sometimes they talk bitterly of how fucked up the scene is right now. These guys were the founders but they were never paid like the superstars of today; often tied into exploitative contracts, they didn't 'get' the business like a Jay-Z or a Puffy. They talk about making comebacks and they don't understand that their brands are long played out. DMC isn't DMC any more; he's just plain Daryl. He's not marketable either.

Unsurprisingly, Dave Walis seems jaded and depressed by the state of the game. I want to cheer him up a bit. 'Look,' I say. 'What you're doing is great music. It's the best thing coming out of New York right now.'

'Thanks,' he says. But he looks grim. 'That's good to know. Because you're my target market.'

He doesn't add 'ageing', 'old school' or 'European' (or even 'white'). He doesn't have to.

'Hip hop is dead'.

This is a bad start to my book and an ironic statement to make about the best-selling form of popular music in the USA. Besides, in more than fifteen years of listening to the music, reading the magazines and buying the T-shirts, I've learned that real hip hop heads are always likely to tell you two things: first, 'hip hop was better back in the day', and second, 'hip hop is dead'. They said it when Run DMC first 'walked this way',[11] they said it when the world was forced to 'stop, collaborate and listen'[12] to Vanilla Ice, they said it after Tupac and Biggie were killed and they're still saying it now.

Trouble is, this time it's my friend Claude Grunitzky, editor of respected New York magazine *Trace*, speaking. 'Hip hop is dead,' he says. 'These days it's all about money. That's all it is.'

I find myself trying to puzzle it through and I suddenly realise that I am utterly unsurprised by hip hop's growth and success. If it really is now just big business, then it's not an accident. Once upon a time, sure enough, hip hop was no more than the voice of minorities of

---

[11] 'Walk This Way', Run DMC, 1986, BMG/Arista.
[12] 'Ice Ice Baby', Vanilla Ice, 1990, SBK.

minority communities but – and this is the key – it has proved itself to be unfailingly and intuitively modern.

Practically, hip hop was the first musical genre to rely exclusively on technology, in its use of turntables and mixer, drum machine and sampler. It paved the way for all the varieties of dance music that now monopolise (and monotonise) club culture. Conceptually, hip hop has always understood postmodern irony; sampling the best beats and hooks from everything from old soul tunes to kids' TV themes and kitsch musicals. This was long before Tarantino began to dip into expired cinematic genres or fashionistas began to talk about '60s, '70s, '80s or even '90s revivals. And what about the content? Whether talking politics or partying, hip hop has always known that a good soundbite is worth more than a dozen reasoned arguments (whether it's 'fight the power' or 'let's get butt-naked and fuck').[13]

However, it's in its grasp of modern commercialism that hip hop seems to come into its own. It has, for example, a bizarre and masochistic tendency towards built-in obsolescence that would put even your household appliances to shame. Rappers insist on locating their lyrics in a specific place in time. 'This is '98!' they exclaim. Or 'Comin' atcha in the Y2K!' And they consequently ensure that the track is soon past its fashion sell-by date, often in less than six months.

More to the point, though, long before Nike's celebrated and castigated (depending on which side of the Free Trade Zone fence you're sitting) CEO, Phil Knight, decided that his company was about brand rather than product[14] (and exported the production base to Asia), hip hop had taken this idea on board with seemingly instinctive enthusiasm. There are famous examples of this: as in the Run DMC track 'My Adidas',[15] which scored the 'kings of Queens' a $1.5 million sponsorship deal, or when preppie clothes designer Tommy Hilfiger saw the former Brand Nubian emcee Grand Puba

---

[13] 'Girls LGBNAF' from *The Power*, Ice T, 1988, Sire.

[14] See *Just Do It: The Nike Spirit in the Corporate World*, Donald Katz, 1994, Holbrook: Adams Media Corporation.

[15] 'My Adidas', Run DMC, 1986, BMG/Arista.

clad head to toe in his label and put two and two together to come up with a whole new market. But hip hop's grasp of the modern brand expands beyond deals cut with fashion companies (and even deals cut for rappers' own clothing lines).

Hip hop has always been about brands. Can you think of any other pop music where not just the group but its members too have one, two, three or more branded identities? Look at the Wu-Tang Clan; a platinum-selling loose collective of more than a dozen emcees. Wu-Tang's mastermind, the Rza, also releases albums under the names Bobby Digital and the Gravediggaz and watches his fellow band members release their own solo projects on as many different labels. And who are actually the members of Wu-Tang? It's a tricky call and it doesn't matter so long as the trademark Wu logo is stamped on each release. Hip hop is its own best promotion.

A couple of years ago, discussing new art, John Seabrook wrote, 'The artists of the next generation will make their art with an internal marketing barometer already in place. The auteur as marketer, the artist in a suit of his own: the ultimate in vertical integration.'[16] Whatever the truth of the next generation of fine artists, both present and past generations of hip hop have long lived out this prophecy. Think about the times you've caught a generic rock track by a generic rock band on generic rock radio. If you missed the DJ's announcement, you might never know the band's name. But a generic hip hop track by a generic rapper on generic rap radio? Within eight bars, MC Lyrix will have name-checked himself, his crew and probably the street where he grew up. Like I say, hip hop – in spite of (maybe even because of) the soundbites – understands modern commercialism and it's little wonder that mainstream businesses have embraced hip hop so wholeheartedly.

When I was a kid, one reason I got into hip hop was because of the alienation expressed in so many of the lyrics. Of course, hip hop alienation was about economics, politics and race, whereas mine had more to do with the prosaic realities of being sixteen. But that didn't stop me seeing connections, however tenuous.

At my school, the real outsiders listened to gloomy angst like the

---

[16] 'The Big Sellout', John Seabrook, *The New Yorker*, 20 & 27 October 1997.

Smiths, mooched around the corridors in monosyllabic packs and wrote bad poetry. But, as for me, I wasn't particularly miserable or particularly socially inept; I was just alienated and angry about it in a typically adolescent way. So I listened to hip hop and wrote bad rap lyrics.

In fact, themes of alienation could reasonably be my final example of hip hop's modernity. Hip hop was originally the music of racial minorities (mostly black but Hispanic too) and, by its nature, often expressed alienation from 'mainstream' society. These days, however, we frequently discuss the 'mainstream' itself in the same terms: we are alienated from our families by the breakdown of the nuclear unit, from our neighbourhoods by fear of crime, from relationships by our fetish for electronic communication, from representation by the end of meaningful politics. So is it any surprise that adolescents, who are only too eager for a little cultural estrangement, consume hip hop as an expression of what they are (and what they are not)?

African-American writer W.E.B. Du Bois's key concept was of 'double consciousness';[17] that black people in the USA are ever caught in the double bind of being 'in' but not 'of' American society and suffer all the alienation implied therein. Perhaps these days such double consciousness is not exclusive to African-Americans but is an endemic symptom of the modern Western world.

When I put the phone down on Claude, I turn on the TV for a little cultural anaesthetic.

Channel surfing, I am quickly disquieted. I've switched on to escape hip hop but I'm beginning to realise that in New York that's not an option. Hip hop has become the prime brand of cool that is used to sell everything: from Fugee refugee Wyclef Jean in a Pepsi commercial to the Gap girl who says she loves 'boys who scratch'. And it's not just the adverts. I pause for a moment on some daytime chat only to discover it's *Latifah* the talk show. That's Latifah as in Queen Latifah, as in 'Ladies First',[18] as in the butch lesbian in African-American chick-flick *Set It Off*; so it's one-time under-

[17] See *The Souls of Black Folk*, W.E.B. Du Bois, 1903, reprinted by Bantam, 1989.
[18] 'Ladies First', Queen Latifah, 1989, Tommy Boy.

ground emcee to pulp-TV host in three short steps. I flip to coverage of the US Tennis Open but even here I find Lil' Bow Wow, fourteen-year-old rap sensation, performing at the opening ceremony. I guess I knew hip hop had gone mainstream and I shouldn't be surprised. But there's frankly something bizarre about seeing America's embrace of a subculture that once stood toe to toe with the norm.

In the end I settle on a channel that at first sight has nothing to do with hip hop. The show's called *Moral Court*, with the only-in-America tagline 'Where it pays to be right'. The principle is simple: two bods with some or other minor disagreement appear before a 'judge' (Larry Elder, an African-American former attorney and talk-radio host, the self-styled 'sage of South Central') to present each side of the argument. Then Larry makes his ruling, delivers a few platitudinous *bon mots* and awards the winner up to $2,000. Today, Kiyosha, a thirtysomething African-American single parent, is in dispute with her daughter, Clarissa.

Clarissa, her mother complains, acts too white. She used to live with her father in a white neighbourhood and now she has white friends and she doesn't understand black slang and she doesn't take care when she walks past the local drug dealers. Kiyosha shows herself to be a concerned if overbearing parent; Clarissa is an intelligent if insecure teen. Kiyosha mouths off, Clarissa cries, they finally embrace and Larry awards the daughter a grand on the sliding scale of 'rightness'.

I'm bewildered by what I'm watching. To be honest, in *Moral Court* it doesn't really 'pay to be right', it just pays to be on the show. Whatever their problems, mother and daughter clearly have one thing in common: they're TV naturals who can slide from sound-bite to soundbite as smoothly as the slinkiest spin doctor and can drop in every media stereotype from every angle of the race argument. Their conflict is one steeped in subtleties – of African-American diversity and pigeonholing and victimisation and victimism – but every nuance is lost beneath truisms, the odd falsism and the stench of hard cash. Maybe I'm just unlucky to catch this particular episode (after all, other shows include a row about the merits of 'dwarf tossing') but for now I can't help making precisely the connections that I'd turned on the TV to avoid; connections with the state of hip hop in New York and, indeed, the USA as a whole.

It's less than forty years since the race debate was about marching and demonstrating; even dying, if you had to. Now, despite its continuing currency, it's played out for a meagre grand on daytime telly. This is not a victory. It's less than twenty years since hip hop was the voice of the urban excluded (a diffuse and non-specific voice, sure, but a voice nonetheless); now, despite its continuing currency, it's played out for vast sums of money at the US Tennis Open, on talk shows, on MTV. This is not a victory either. I find myself remembering an African proverb I once read in Chinua Achebe: 'Until the lions produce their own historian, the story of the hunt will only glorify the hunter.'[19] I'm sure hip hop used to be full of the lions' perspective. But these days it's ever harder to tell the lions and the hunters apart.

The hard fact is that perceptions of hip hop identity and alienated urban identity (in particular African-American identity) are now so intertwined as to be almost synonymous. This is, in fact, a defeat. Or, as Snoop Dogg put it so cynically in the title of his album in '98: *Da Game Is To Be Sold & Not To Be Told*.[20] Because, sure enough, it is and it isn't.

Of course, this appropriation of hip hop by mainstream culture is hardly unique either to New York or the US. France, for example, is the world's second-largest hip hop market and both the similarities and contrasts in the culture's development there make for an intriguing comparison.

Between, roughly, the mid-'80s and the early '90s, French hip hop was a strictly underground movement. It had a public face in the media-friendly MC Solaar whose facility for wordplay and relatively unconfrontational stance appealed to left-wing intelligentsia worldwide (he certainly had a place on a lot of London

---

[19] *Home And Exile*, Chinua Achebe, 2000, Oxford University Press.
[20] *Da Game Is To Be Sold & Not To Be Told*, Snoop Dogg, 1998, No Limit/Priority.

coffee tables). But the substance of the French scene was largely hidden in the ignored Parisian *banlieues*[21] and the multi-ethnic communities of Marseille. In Paris these included outfits like Assassins, Ministère AMER (the bitter ministry) and especially Suprême NTM (usually just NTM), comprising Kool Shen (of Portuguese descent) and Joey Star (whose ancestry is Antillaise). In the best traditions of US hip hop, the name NTM has dual meanings; either Nique Ta Mere (Fuck Your Mother) or Le Nord Transmet Le Message (Message from the North – a reference to their St-Denis background in opposition to rival suburbs from southern Paris). In Marseille the underground's loudest voice was IAM, a seven-man collective whose name is similarly multi-faceted: Imperial Asiatic Men, *Indépendantistes Autonome Marseillaise* or simply 'I am'; take your pick.

Lyrical content for all these crews was overtly political as they sought to articulate the difficulties and complexities of post-colonial ethnicity in France. For IAM, this meant combining continual references to their mythologised connection to ancient Egypt with unusually astute lyricism, ever expressing a view of themselves (as a multiracial group) within a global context. The track 'J'aurais Pu Croire' ('I Might Have Believed'),[22] for example, includes the following line: '*J'aurais pu croire en l'Occident si tout ces pays n'avaient pas eu des colonies*' ('I might have believed in the West if all these countries hadn't had colonies').

NTM, on the other hand, took a far more revolutionary line which sparked national debate in November 1996. Following a performance at an anti-racism festival in Toulon (a municipality governed by the right-wing extremists of le Front National [FN]), NTM were sentenced to six months in prison (three custodial), fined 50,000 francs and given a six-month ban on performing for comments they made on stage against the police. The charge was brought by the local judiciary for a bizarre and archaic offence

---

[21] *Banlieues*: suburbs. Whereas in, say, the UK the phrase 'inner city' conjures up images of urban deprivation, in Paris the reverse is true, with the suburbs bearing the brunt of unemployment and poverty.

[22] 'J'Aurais Pu Croire' from *Ombre Est Lumière*, IAM, 1993, Delabel.

known as Outrages Parparoles (outrages through words). Though the sentence was reduced on appeal, it spawned enormous amounts of media coverage: conservative affront and leftist soul-searching about the racialised nature of censorship. It also ensured that NTM sold records by the truckload.

Somewhere around this time, however, something in French hip hop must have changed. Because these days the music, almost exclusively local, shifts units like never before and dominates the airwaves on mainstream radio like Skyrock. But the once vibrant underground culture seems to have largely evaporated, even in the *banlieues*.

On a recent trip to Paris, I was taken to St-Denis by a local hip hop head who called herself MC. As we communicated in a mixture of schoolgirl English and schoolboy French, she pointed out this and that location saying things like 'This is where we had good parties' and 'There used to be pirate radio here'. But every time I asked her about now she just laughed and said, 'There is nothing now.' Clubs? 'No clubs for five years.' Radio? 'Only Skyrock. That's all.' So where do you find hip hop? 'I go to my friends. We have some mixtapes.'

We went to La Défense, the architecturally magnificent business district on the western outskirts of Paris where the monumental arch looks down over the city, and Les Halles, the massive shopping complex right by the Pompidou Centre. I remembered both these places as meeting points for breakers where crews would work through their moves or battle or just hang out. 'Sometimes you still see them,' MC said. 'For the tourists.' By now she'd perfected her Gallic shrug.

I hooked up with Solo, one of the original line-up of Assassins, outside the Pigalle studio where he was producing some new material. A stocky dude in jeans and a Next T-shirt, he was disparaging about the state of French hip hop: 'There's no such thing as hip hop culture here any more. You might as well talk about "girl power" as "culture".' And then, 'This is what happens when there's too much money. Exactly like America.'

In fact, though, the movement of French hip hop into the mainstream and its subsequent commercialisation is, I think, a little more complicated than that. It is about money, sure, and it is like America. But it also reflects long-standing French attitudes to ethnic difference which stress integration (i.e., 'becoming French') over multiculturalism.

One aspect of this attitude is the notorious protectionism of the French language, which in 1991 culminated in Le Loi Toubon,[23] which sought to replace Anglicisms like *le weekend* with French equivalents. In 1994 this extended to the provision that French radio stations had to comply with a forty per cent quota of Francophone output. It could be argued that this law was in part intended to attack hip hop and the perceived Americanisation of French through its slang. However, somewhat ironically, the new law actually gave an extraordinary commercial fillip to the local hip hop crews.

Malik, one of the emcees with Strasbourg's N.A.P. (New African Poets), gave me a concise and articulate explanation of what he regarded as the decline of hip hop culture in opposition to the explosion of what he termed 'French rap music': 'There was one moment when it happened, though I didn't see it at the time. It was when the law came into force in 1994. Radio stations like Skyrock were in a panic because they didn't know what they were going to play. But there was a very popular IAM record at the time called 'Je Danse Le Mia'[24] so they all caught on to that and started playing hip hop. So now? Rap music is very successful everywhere. But you'll never make progress if you're not on Skyrock's playlist and you generally don't get on the playlist unless you're hooked up with one of two or three camps.'

The comparison with the sentiments expressed by Celph Titled and others is all too obvious.

However, perhaps the biggest irony in all this is the way in which French hip hop has been appropriated not just by mainstream culture but even, to a degree, by the state. For example, to me, as a British person, the French Music Bureau seems an extraordinary

---

[23] Le Loi Toubon takes its name from the former French Minister for Culture Jacques Toubon.

[24] 'Je Danse Le Mia', IAM, 1993, Delabel.

institution. Part government- and part industry-funded, its directive is to promote French music sales overseas and a large slice of that work now revolves around hip hop. Talking to someone in their London office about the success of French hip hop, I was told it was partly because 'France has never had racial problems like England or the States'. This seemed like a bizarre opinion even at the time, let alone in the subsequent light of five million votes cast in the presidential election for the racist Jean-Marie Le Pen. But it articulates something of France's schizophrenic attitude towards race. Just as many of the five million FN voters undoubtedly cheer the notably multiracial French football team, so hip hop has become a new national representation of the ethos of '*black, blanc, beur*' (black, white and Arab – a multi-ethnic update of the French tricolore). But this process has also stripped hip hop of its oppositional resonance for its original core constituencies among the *banlieusards* as much of the revolutionary content has given way to ghetto-fabulous bragging worthy of their American counterparts.

This is neatly expressed in the N.A.P. track 'La Crise':[25] '*Depuis plus de dix ans le rap était ma cause / Quelle déception quand c'est d'venu un taff*' ('Rap's been my cause for ten years / What a let-down when it became a sham'). In other words, the game has been sold and not told or perhaps, as NTM would have it, '*L'argent pourrit les gens / J'en ai le sentiment*' – 'Money rots people / That's just the way it goes'.[26]

The Roots 'intergenerational celebration of hip hop culture' is taking place in a small venue just south of Canal. Kenyatta, one of the 'teaching artists' and half of politically conscious Brooklyn hip hop crew Black L.I.B. (that's 'Black Liberation: Let It Begin'), gave me directions but I can't remember the name of the street. So we're pacing the Tribeca grid from Broadway to Franklin to Church to White and Broadway again. I ask a couple of street hawkers if they've heard of Roots but they haven't.

[25] 'La Crise' from *A L'Interieur De Nous*, N.A.P., 2000, BMG France.
[26] 'L'Argent Pourrit Les Gens' from *Authentik*, Suprême NTM, 1991, Sony France.

A bunch of kids in identical white T-shirts run past. They're laughing and shouting and handing out leaflets: 'Free show! Come to the free show!' The guy selling fake Louis Vuitton and me, we shake our heads and don't look up. It's Kanyasu who points after them and says, 'I think we should just follow them.'

Roots is one of the arts programmes organised in association with the University Settlement House. Founded in 1886 by Stanton Coit, University was the first 'settlement' in the USA but there are now more than 150 nationwide. They are neighbourhood projects offering adult education, legal advice, counselling, artistic workshops and so on. Originally derived from the social thinking of liberal Brits, they were called settlements because the idea was that wealthy people of conscience and students might settle in poverty-stricken neighbourhoods to provide social services and improve quality of life. But it's now more than half a century since the settlement houses were last residential.

It's a summer evening and on entering the claustrophobic 'space' on Walker Street the heat immediately wraps you up like a damp blanket. It's jam-packed with, I'm guessing, friends and family of the kids on stage and the advertised air-con is no more than a couple of feeble fans. But it's not going to dampen the enthusiasm of either performers or audience. The show – a multimedia affair encompassing theatre, film, dance, music and poetry – is kind of chaotic: the acoustics are terrible, so it's hard to hear what the actors, poets and rappers are saying, and the stage is so small that all the dancers can barely fit. But the vibe is undeniable as proud parents cheer on and boys whoop at the sexy teen performing the dance solo. Kanyasu 'excuse-me's her way into the main body of the room but I'm happy to skulk at the back; near the door with its vague, unkept promise of fresh air.

From this position I notice something that makes me feel uncomfortable. The performers are almost exclusively black and Latino and the audience is almost exclusively black and Latino but those hanging out near the door are almost exclusively white. A well-dressed, middle-aged white couple come in and the woman immediately starts to fan herself with her programme. I wonder how they fit in. The guy on the door offers them two bottles of water from the stock behind the counter and the woman offers him a $10 bill.

The guy shakes his head: 'It's free.'

'But I just wanted to make a contribution,' the woman says. She is smiling and she presses him to accept the note. Eventually he takes it with a shrug.

I glance between this exchange and the action on stage and I duck out of the door and into the muggy dusk.

There are some kids hanging out in the street: four boys showing off in front of a girl who pretends she's not interested. I can't tell their ages. They could be anything between thirteen and eighteen; maybe younger, maybe older. One of them, a string bean with a starter moustache, sleeveless Nike T-shirt and yellow bandanna, asks me for a light. By return, I ask him if they're involved in the show inside. He eyes me cautiously and drags on his cigarette: 'Sure,' he says. 'They all my people.'

I explain to him about the book I'm writing and the others begin to gather round. It's not like they're really interested but it's not like they were doing anything anyway; just hanging out. They all listen to hip hop – the usual suspects from Jay-Z to Jadakiss, M.O.P. to Mobb Deep. The girl, Mary-Ann, says she likes Ja Rule and N'Sync best of all. The boys pack up laughing.

I ask them what they think of the Roots project. Anthony, a lanky mixed-race boy with wide eyes and an extraordinary translucent complexion as flawless as the pristine white leather of his Nike trainers, takes the lead: 'It's all good. It's positivity. People come together from the community to achieve something positive. Before I got into this? I was cutting school and running with the wrong people in my locality. But now my grades are good and I feel good about myself. It's all positive.'

There's something about Anthony that throws me. Maybe it's because he's pretty enough for TV or maybe his repeated use of the word 'positive' sounds like something he picked up from the small screen, something he thinks I want to hear. Anthony looks and sounds like he could be on *Oprah* or *Rikki* or *Jerry*. Or a witness in *Moral Court*.

Back inside, Roots is concluded by a short set from Black L.I.B. Despite the unprepossessing venue and increasingly viscous heat, Kenyatta and his partner Reggie throw themselves into their performance in their rap personas of Kahnobi and Love Born Saviour. It's an object lesson in how to rock a crowd as they spit out the lyrics, clear and true, and move seamlessly between stage and audience. I'm thinking this is what hip hop in New York used to be, free form and democratic, back in the day. As they hit their last joint, kids, friends and parents alike all join in: 'Play my shit, nigga, play that shit / Play my shit, nigga, do that shit.' And that's surely the chorus of every underground emcee in this city.

Everyone files out on a high and the performers mill around in the street, excitedly dissecting the show and congratulating one another. For some reason, I'm still kind of troubled by what Anthony said about twenty minutes ago so I start bugging different kids for their impressions of the Roots project. Many of them are shy and those who do want to talk sound no different from Anthony: a lot of truisms about 'positivity' and 'consciousness' and 'community' are flying around and there's not a personal story to be heard.

Eventually Kenyatta appears, bathed in sweat and knackered. I ask him about what the kids have been saying and he offers a tired shrug. 'But it *is* positive,' he says. He asks who I was talking to and I point out Anthony and his mates. He shakes his head: 'Never seen them before.' So they weren't even part of the Roots project? It didn't stop them knowing the soundbites.

If you accept that hip hop and by extension issues of social exclusion (poverty, race, crime and so on) have been appropriated as brands, then their discussion has been reduced to no more than soundbites and slogans that work a treat in media whose wages are paid by said brands. The globalisation debate has long anguished over the effects of the uber-brands on the economies of 'developing' nations. But the effects are also felt closer to home and they're about not just economics but basic issues of identity too. The dumbed-down language of the TV strips us of our capacity even to describe our experience in any meaningful way.

'Dumbed down' is such a perfect phrase because it's about dumbness from the top down – and perhaps, for all its modernity, hip hop was once also anti-modern. Because it was a grassroots, bottom-up expression of who you were and where you came from and its language was arcane and inaccessible to the mainstream. But now? Now hip hop *is* the mainstream and its language (both figuratively and literally) is the language of marketing and media. So Anthony says, 'It's all positive.' But he might as well say, 'Fight the power' or 'Let's get butt-naked and fuck' or 'Just do it'.

In 1996, the Oakland school board passed a resolution stating that African-American schoolchildren did not, in fact, speak English but a separate language called Ebonics. They should be taught, therefore, in the bilingual educational structure offered to other students with English as a second language. Unsurprisingly, this resolution caused a media ruckus that sparked debate across the political and academic spectrum. Unsurprisingly too, the shenanigans had little impact in London and my only real memory of the fuss was an e-mail that was doing the rounds. It was a 'winning entry' in a spoof Oakland public schools translation competition. The 'assignment' was to translate the Biggie track 'One More Chance'[27] into standard English. Here's a snippet:

Original lyrics:
First things first, I, Poppa, freaks all the honeys
Dummies – Playboy bunnies, those wantin' money
Those the ones I like 'cause they don't get nathan'
But penetration, unless it smells like sanitation –
Garbage, I turn like doorknobs
Heart-throb, never, black and ugly as ever –
However, I stay Coogi-ed down to the socks
Rings and watch filled with rocks

---

[27] 'One More Chance', the Notorious B.I.G., 1994, BMG/Arista/Bad Boy Entertainment.

Translation:

As a general rule, I perform deviant sexual acts with women of all kinds, including but not limited to those with limited intellect, nude magazine models, and prostitutes. I particularly enjoy sexual encounters with the latter group as they are generally disappointed in the fact that they only receive penetrative intercourse and nothing more, unless of course they douche on a consistent basis. Although I am extremely unattractive, I am able to engage in these types of sexual acts regularly. Perhaps my sexuality is somehow related to my fancy clothes and expensive jewelry.

The Oakland resolution arose from a desire to explain continuing underachievement by African-Americans in school. Black students, the argument went, were disadvantaged by the need to learn standard English that differed from the dialect they spoke at home. The merits (or otherwise) of this argument have been thoroughly picked over elsewhere.[28] It's hip hop's role in the dissemination of Ebonics (both in its perceived definition as 'black slang' and as a full dialect) and the consequences for hip hop identity that are of interest here.

Whether it's the white kid who calls me a 'bitch' as he pushes past me into the subway or the thirtysomething white record exec who once greeted me with the exclamation 'Yo, dog!' the cultural dynamic is obvious as white people appropriate black slang for some nuance of black cool. Of course this phenomenon is as old as pop culture itself,[29] but the growing ubiquity of hip hop culture (and language) and the consequent impact this appropriation has on African-American youth is new and bizarre. As cultural critic Jonathan Rutherford points out, 'Capital has fallen in love with difference: advertising thrives on selling us things that will enhance our uniqueness and individuality.'[30] It is this that explains the

[28] See, for example, *Losing The Race*, John McWhorter, 2000, The Free Press.
[29] See, for example, *After The White Negro*, Norman Mailer, 1982 (new edition), Little, Brown & Company.
[30] 'A Place Called Home: Identity and the Cultural Politics of Difference', Jonathan Rutherford in *Identity*, Ed. Jonathan Rutherford, 1990, Lawrence & Wishart.

misconceived white use of Ebonics; hip hop slang is perceived as culturally valuable. It is ironic, therefore, that an urban black kid's use of this language might be precisely what holds him back. Ebonics can grant a white person cultural value within mainstream society at the same time as it stops a black person from entering such society. 'Yo, dog!' says the white thirtysomething and he's down with alienation. 'Yo, dog!' says the black kid and he's down and alienated.

And so I come back to hip hop is dead . . . Well, dying. If so, it's attempting suicide. Perhaps Ebonics is just symptomatic of a wider pattern: where hip hop was once a voice of urban exclusion, it is often now a catalyst for the very same. An African-American friend of mine was complaining about changes in black slang. 'Black people used to call each other brother, then it became cuz, then nigger. Now it's dog. So we've gone from seeing each other as immediate family to seeing each other as no better than animals.'[31] As alienation has become a commodity to be sold, so alienation continues apace.

It's hard to keep up with Kenyatta as he strides down Fulton Street, Brooklyn's main drag. The street is teeming with shoppers and he's a whistlestop guide, pointing out this, that and the other local landmark until I'm spinning on the spot.

'I heard ten million dollars a day are spent on this stretch,' he says. 'Ten million dollars spent by some of the poorest people in this city. How do you explain that?'

We walk past two great cathedrals of hip hop gear, their windows decked out in the primary colours of Sean John and Fubu and Roc-A-Wear. There's something weird going on in hip hop fashion right now as the labels branch out into strange two-piece creations that look part English shellsuit and part Mafiosi lounging: think a Brummie Al Pacino walking through the Bull Ring *circa* 1985. 'These two stores are owned by this rich Israeli. He knows people

---

[31] This echoes a Talib Kweli lyric from his track 'For Women' from *Reflection Eternal*, 2000, Rawkus. 'She lived from nigger to Negro to coloured to black to Afro then African-American and right back to nigger.'

buy any shit these days,' Kenyatta says over his shoulder. 'Long as it's got the logo.'

Besides the clothes stores, you could easily believe every second shop sells gold; Christmas-cracker pendants and chains and rings. 'All these jewellery stores?' Kenyatta says. 'All owned by one guy. From Yemen. I only found out when I tried to get them to stock the Black L.I.B. mixtapes and in every single one I was told I needed to speak to the same man.'

I remember something Biggie said once, talking about his Versace clothes and Rolex watch: 'Kids who like my shit know that it ain't beyond their reach. I showed them they could have all that good shit if they try.'[32] Of course, Big grew up round here; straight up Fulton and on to St James.

We head downstairs at Beat Street records on the corner of the garish Fulton Mall and I'm like a child choosing chocolate. Beat Street is legend in hip hop; this is where every one of Brooklyn's finest from Biggie to Jay-Z came to sell their first pressings. I've never been here before and as I walk past the walls of mixtapes, CDs and then kung-fu flicks to the feast of vinyl at the back, I catch my breath. Beat Street is one essence of hip hop, no doubt, and I flick through the racks of 12s with increasing excitement. Hip hop obsession (especially the 'underground') has always had a touch of the trainspotter about it, of course, and I'm finding tunes that I haven't seen or heard of for more than a decade and they're only three to five dollars a pop. Kenyatta checks my reverie and laughs: 'You never been here before?'

'No.'

I'm barely listening. I can't believe I've found a copy of 'Strong Island' by JVC Force.[33] Mine was broken by a clumsy foot at a college party in about 1991 and here it is in mint condition.

'You never been to Brooklyn before?' Kenyatta asks incredulously and I look up.

'Course I have,' I say. And I have. But even as I say so, I find myself scanning back over my numerous previous visits to New

---

[32] 'Young, Rich And Deadly', *The Source*, July 1995.
[33] 'Strong Island', JVC Force, 1988, B Boy Records.

York on behalf of this magazine or that paper. So I've been to Brooklyn several times but mostly when I've been driven in by corporate limo to check out the housing projects where such and such a rapper grew up. Because it's these trips that lent my stories the heady spice of credibility and allowed me to write things like 'Jay-Z grew up on the mean streets of Marcy' with the unwritten parenthesis that says 'and I know because I've been there and seen it through a car window'.

Skirting Fort Green, an area Kenyatta dismisses as 'full of buppies and bohemian shit', we're discussing the state of hip hop. Kenyatta is forthright in his opinions. 'Jay-Z's top of the tree, man. That's just the way it is. Since Big passed, Jay-Z's the king of New York. Ask anybody and they'll tell you the same.'

Really? I don't like that thought because Jay-Z's so . . . So what? Slack and simplistic and poptastic and *jiggy*.

'So who's better, then?'

I find myself mumbling. 'I dunno. I like stuff like Mos Def, Talib Kweli and Common Sense.'

Kenyatta laughs and points a finger across the street. 'That's where they belong, man. Fort Green. Common even lives there. Y'know, I've known Mos since time and I give him respect but all that stuff is so . . .' This time it's his turn to struggle for words.

'Fort Green?'

'Exactly.'

I try to figure through this distinction with Mos Def on one side and Jay-Z on the other. I know what Kenyatta's getting at but it's hard to put into words. Mos has blown up in the last couple of years with his intelligent rhymes and musical production, while Jay-Z's brand of populism controls the nation's dancefloors. I think back to similar distinctions in hip hop; between, say, Public Enemy and Slick Rick. Although their content was different (righteous indignation on the one hand and thugged-out party music on the other), they sold similar quantities of records to the same market. But now Jay-Z churns out multiplatinum disc after multiplatinum disc. And Mos? Well. I saw him pack out a London venue a couple of months back and it was bursting with students, *Guardian* readers and all the self-consciously politically conscious. So maybe that's the distinction (albeit a very jaded and subjective one). Public Enemy debated alienation for the alienated while Mos, through no fault of his own, sells the *idea* of alienation to the culturally literate. Or maybe I'm thinking about this too hard because Kenyatta's explanation is a whole lot easier. 'Look,' he says. 'Jay-Z's the best because he sells the most records and he's not wack.' Right. As simple as that.

We're sitting in the backyard of Kenyatta's apartment on a quiet street near the junction of Flatbush and Atlantic. Opposite him live an African-American couple, both doctors; on one side is the fortified household of Hispanic crack dealers, on the other a stars-and-stripes flies proudly above the door. Welcome to the multiculture that makes up modern Brooklyn.

Kenyatta is animated. But then Kenyatta's always animated; just give him some hip-hop-related stimulus and he's off and suddenly he's a hip hop twitcher, reeling off stats and opinions and laughing – everything from the best posse cuts and collabos to the most underrated artist, even his favourite rap metaphor. And which emcee would he choose to rhyme for his life? He goes for Redman.

Kenyatta starts to analyse the skill of the emcee: how to say what you want in a way that people understand. 'Like Jay-Z. On his first record, people didn't catch a lot of what he was saying because it was too complex. So now? Every Jay-Z rhyme has the same formula. He sets up an idea and then undercuts it; like with a punchline or a laugh or something.[34] It's simple but it's clever too. In fact, it's clever *because* it's simple. I learned a lot from that.

'Like I wrote one verse and I played it to my boys and they were all, "That shit's too deep." So I re-recorded it and didn't change a thing; just added "my nigga" at the end of each line and then they were all, like, "OK. *Now* I'm feeling you." It's crazy but you've gotta give people some kind of hook.'

Hot 97, New York's premier hip hop station, is on in the

---

[34] Kenyatta's right. Even a cursory listen to Jay-Z's lyrics reveals a repeated reliance on a simple four-rhyme structure in which the last line offers a linguistic, thematic or aural twist.

background and Kenyatta's suddenly zoned into the track. It's a big tune, 'I Don't Do Much'[35] by Jay-Z's protégé Beanie Sigel; an arrogant strut through all the things he doesn't do because he's too busy getting high, counting his money and 'fucking bitches'. Kenyatta packs up laughing and turns up the volume.

'This shit's hilarious!' he exclaims and he begins to pick out lyrics. ' "You don't want me duct tapin' your mouth / You don't want me smackin' up your kids." What the fuck's he talking about? You gonna come and tape up my mouth and beat on my kids? Of course I don't want that. "You don't want me layin' up in your trash." What's he *talking* about? What's he doing in my trash? Shit! I've got Beanie Sigel in my trash!' Kenyatta's laughing so hard his eyes are popping. 'That's what people forget, man. Hip hop's funny. It's self-parody. I don't care whether Beanie Sigel means it or not. It's fucking hilarious.'

Part of hip hop's tension has always lain in the taut line strung out between realism and fantasy. Public Enemy used to take to the stage flanked by the S1Ws (Security of the First World), a crew in combat fatigues who marched about the stage brandishing uzis and performing strange and, in retrospect, high-camp dance routines; kind of like drum majorettes meet the territorial army. But in the audience, you never suspected the S1Ws would actually use their guns any more than you doubted the veracity of Chuck D's lyrics. As far back as 1993, the De La Soul classic 'Ego Trippin' '[36] poked fun at emcees who bragged about being this or that, while the video showed the absurdity of rappers hiring in busty models, fancy cars and a plush crib for three minutes of MTV promo. But now the balance between realism and fantasy has finally tipped in the latter direction as emcees describe themselves as larger-than-life cartoon characters who drink Cristal (hip hop's champagne of choice – probably because it is both readily available and enormously expensive) like it was spinach and drip platinum like Lex Luther drops kryptonite.

Back in the day, hip hop's content used to express the exclusion of those it represented and the fantasies (lived out or played out) were

[35] 'I Don't Do Much', Beanie Sigel, 2001, Universal/Def Jam.
[36] 'Ego Trippin' ', De La Soul, 1993, Tommy Boy.

no more than the spoils of war. Back in the day, Wu-Tang Clan christened their Staten Island projects 'Shaolin' and their adoption of kung-fu personas spoke metaphorical volumes of alienation. Back in the day, rappers characterised their work as 'reality' and that gave hip hop a democracy which allowed Chuck D to describe it as 'black people's CNN'. But today? Today rappers are more likely to use words like 'episode' and 'drama', and, in doing so, they remove hip hop from collective experience to describe a lifestyle that's individualistic, aspirational and exclusive; more like 'black people's QVC'. Can the kids of Marcy and St James really get, as Biggie put it, 'all that good shit if they try'? Frankly they're more likely to find Beanie Sigel layin' up in their trash.

Ameachi, the head of Ozone, has just launched a new independent label, Def Jux. It's in partnership with El-P (formerly of Company Flow)[37] and I heard about it back in England where the style press picked up on acts like Cannibal Ox and Aesop Rock. To be honest, the sound isn't exactly hip hop as I know it; it's dark and grungy and claustrophobic with little of the typical hip hop swagger. This time I'm not surprised when Ameachi tells me their main markets are college kids and overseas.

Ozone's offices on the corner of Lafayette and Broome are busy. They're about to fly out to Japan for a couple of promo shows and the Def Jux artists are lounging around, killing time. El-P, a squat gingernut, is snoozing in a chair while Aesop, a lanky kid who kind of looks more hick than hip hop, is proudly checking the artwork of his latest CD.

Ameachi's sitting in his glass-walled office, shooting the breeze. He has a similar take on the state of hip hop as Dave Walis but, being part English and part Nigerian, he has little of the New Yorker's cynicism. 'Hip hop's a bubble, sure, and maybe it will burst and maybe it won't, but it doesn't bother us. What you need to understand is there are a lot of different markets right now and we're not competing in the same market as most hip hop. Ozone

---

[37] Company Flow's *Funcrusher Plus* was the album that solidified Rawkus's reputation as the leading New York independent label in 1997.

and Def Jux is just people doing it for the love of the art form and there'll always be an audience for that.'

El-P idles in. For a couple of minutes he listens and he looks eager to join the conversation. But he'd rather make use of the sofa. He smokes a cigarette and then falls asleep.

Ameachi continues: 'Part of what El-P and I are doing is about ethical business practices. We don't have a whole lot of money but we treat our artists with respect and we respect hip hop. Let me explain something to you. Say you compare Puffy and Master P? Now, personally, I don't like either of their music. But, while Puffy moves upstate, at least Master P has stayed in his community in New Orleans and is bringing jobs and money into that community. That's a model I can respect.'

Master P is an extraordinary hip hop success story. Coming out of New Orleans' Calliope projects in the early '90s, he set up No Limit records and the first two releases, 'The Ghetto's Tryin' To Kill Me' and '99 Ways To Die', sold 100,000 and 200,000 units respectively, with no major-label distribution.

Hip hop has always had a powerful sense of place as emcees frequently define themselves by locality (a fact that has spurred many of hip hop's most notorious beefs) and Master P tapped this ethos to engage phenomenal local support. Unsurprisingly, several majors offered him a deal but, when P finally signed with Priority in 1995, it was a simple pressing-and-distribution deal that ensured his continuing control of the music, the business and, above all, the lion's share of the profits. In 1998, Master P was listed for the first time in the Forbes Top 40 of America's richest entertainers.

The No Limit model (from local sales to national exposure, if not the retention of commercial control) has since been continually repeated. Outside of New York, anyway. It's a no-brainer for the major labels when local popularity guarantees profitable sales and the potential for an act to blow up nationally, even globally. It's precisely this dynamic that saw the likes of Nelly, a kid from St Louis, appear as if from nowhere with the multiplatinum *Country Grammar*.[38] But it doesn't work in New York.

---

[38] *Country Grammar*, Nelly, 2000, Universal.

As Ameachi puts it, 'In St Louis, Nelly and his boys are probably the only crew in town. But New York? Everyone's a rapper and they're all cynical. That's why there's no "New York sound" any more. You hear a record from New Orleans and Florida and you know where it comes from straight away. But New York? It's lost its identity.'

El-P wakes up just as I'm leaving. He shakes my hand and smiles. 'What was it you said you were doing?'

'Just looking for what's going on in New York hip hop at the moment.'

He raises his eyebrows ironically. 'Good luck, man. We're New York hip hop right here. And we're flying to Japan tonight. Guess you may as well go home.'

Cheetah, a downtown nightclub on West 21st, is Friday-night rammed and a good-time crowd is getting down to a mixed bag of dirty-south hip hop by the likes of Mystikal and Ludacris. Maybe Ameachi's right, because there's barely a New York tune to be heard. The crowd is predominantly black, exclusively well-dressed and altogether exclusive: braided honeys are poured into body-paint dresses and dapper guys wear shirtsleeves and smart boots and only the loose cut of their chinos nods to the streets. I'm sure the gargantuan bouncers only let my scruffy self through the door on the strength of my dumb-foreigner act. Despite the music, this doesn't feel very hip hop and yet it's one of the biggest hip hop nights in town. It's also one of the only hip hop nights in town.

Mayor Giuliani's war on clubland is in full effect. Once regarded by most as a vibrant part of New York life, club culture has been successfully demonised by the city administration as a prime source of antisocial behaviour. Though every kind of music and every kind of venue is suffering, in this climate a hip hop night is an especially risky venture. There's Fridays at Cheetah and Funkmaster Flex's notorious Sundays at the Tunnel . . . and that's about it. In the city of its birth, hip hop is *persona non grata* and it's turned away from club doors for wearing its colours or its cap or its $100 sneakers.

In some ways it's fair enough, isn't it? When there's a shooting in Cheetah or the Tunnel is blamed for the murder of a sixteen-year-old in the nearby streets (after a fight inside[39]) it's little wonder that the city takes offence. But it's nonetheless a sad fact that hip hop has been spatially (as much as conceptually) taken away from its core audience. As journalist Frank Owen pointed out, 'The irony is that if you're white, or a black person projecting a bourgeois or trendy image, it's relatively easy to hear hip hop at Manhattan clubs.'[40] Hovering by the bar in Cheetah, I order a Scotch on the rocks and wait for my change. I'm in for a long wait. These days, hip hop in New York comes at a premium.

We're eating with a couple of Kenyatta's friends and fellow teaching artists from the Roots project. Andre and Roy are both kind of intense; wiry African-American intellectuals with opinions that must burn calories. Andre is talking about the companies who still send 'cool hunters' to the basketball courts of Brooklyn and the Bronx in search of the latest 'black cool'. 'The players on those courts have more cultural capital than anybody on earth,' he says. 'And less actual power than anybody on earth, too.'

Roy agrees: 'The trouble is that kids, whether they're smart or dumb, it's difficult for them to have the breadth of perspective. *I* can say that a guy buying Nikes is pretty much paying for the privilege of marketing the corporation's product, but it's something like a conundrum. Because you have to be outside the loop to see the loop. But once you're outside the loop it becomes a whole lot harder to affect it.

'If you're talking about race then it's a complex situation and it's only getting more complex. There's been progress, for sure. But if you want to talk about present discriminations then they're far more subtle than they used to be and therefore harder to identify. Look at slavery. That was simple oppression backed by the threat of coercion. Now, of course, coercion is outlawed so there are more

---

[39] Terrence Davis was murdered on the corner of 30th Street and 10th Avenue on 9 April 2001.

[40] 'Hip Hop Under Heavy Manners', Frank Owen, *The Village Voice*, 23–29 May 2001.

subtle forms of oppression. They're conscious and subconscious on the part of both oppressors and oppressed. They've been going on so long that they've become part of the structure and therefore difficult to see. You have to spread knowledge to kids but that's hard when the structures themselves mitigate against acceptance of that knowledge.'

Kenyatta is laughing. 'That's America, man!' he exclaims. 'You talk to a kid like that and he'll be all, like, "What you saying, dog? My sneakers are dope!" It's America all over. We live in a culture of ignorance and people are proud of it. Look who we elected president: George W. Bush, a man who's proud that he doesn't read any books! You say to people, "What? You don't know *that*?" And they're, like, "Damn skippy I don't know *that*! Come to think of it, I don't know *shit*!" Real proud.'

Everybody cracks up but Roy's comments are as disturbing as they are unsurprising.

More than sixty years ago, in his impassioned plea for solidarity among colonised people (and provoked by his time as a student in the States), Kwame Nkrumah wrote: 'Imperialism knows no law beyond its own interest.'[41] It seems that, these days, the empire – Roy's 'structure' – is the free market and its only interest is profit. That's why hip hop in New York is a closed shop. Major players may be fast-tracked through the industry but they're still in thrall to a system that appropriates their art form and exploits the very people they claim to represent.

As an outsider, I find myself considering the representations of African-American identity that are produced by this system and are most familiar to me. It's hard not to conclude that the decades since the triumphs of the civil-rights movement have actually seen a slip back to the most negative stereotypes of an earlier era. In the Mexico City Olympics of 1968, Tommie Smith and John Carlos were stripped of their medals for their Black Power salutes on the winners' rostrums. Compare that with the way the all-black American relay team were pilloried by the media for their show-off celebrations at Sydney 2000. Which of these is to be

[41] *Towards Colonial Freedom*, Kwame Nkrumah, 1945, Panaf Books.

regarded as the most negative stereotype of a black identity? And hip hop is probably the worst culprit in the promotion of these caricatures. Consider the uncanny similarity in appearance between many rappers and the traditional 'black faces' of minstrelsy. In the '30s, historian Carl Wittke wrote, 'The plantation type which got into minstrelsy apparently was calculated to give the impression that all Negroes were lazy, shiftless fellows . . . he dressed in gaudy colors and in a flashy style . . . the Negro's alleged love for the grand manner led him to use words so long that he not only did not understand their meaning, but twisted the syllables in the most ludicrous fashion in his futile efforts to pronounce them.'[42] Couldn't he be writing about, say, Beanie Seigel's 'I Don't Do Much'? Frankly, no postmodern arguments about the reclamation of negative identities for new ends are going to convince me that this is in any way progress.

Eventually it's Kenyatta who interrupts my thoughts: 'You want to see real, underground hip hop in New York? I know one place I've got to take you.'

'Where?'

'I'm not telling you. But this place you've got to see. It's a surprise.'

I'm talking to Bobbito Garcia, one of the most celebrated underground hip hop DJs in New York. Bobbito, with his partner Lord Sear, is the host of *CM Famalam* on WKCR but best known for his show with Stretch Armstrong that just about spanned the '90s between WKCR and Hot 97. A member of the Rock Steady Crew (*the* original B-Boy crew), in his time Bobbito has been a professional basketball player (in Puerto Rico), a journalist for the likes of *Vibe* and *The Source* and head of the respected Fondle 'Em label; and he's a DJ who's in demand the world over.

'Look,' he sighs. 'When people say hip hop is dead it just shows they're not in touch. People talk about the elements of hip hop culture but, I tell you, in any period of hip hop, the best stuff always

---

[42] *Tambo and Bones: A History of the American Minstrel Stage*, Carl Wittke, 1930, reprinted by Greenwood, 1971.

had to be searched for. That's why I say that search and discovery is the most neglected element of hip hop.'

But these days hip hop is a global business . . .

'So? Just because hip hop is accessible globally, that doesn't make it good. But people can always find a way to hear good music. I can't tell you the number of places I've gone where they know my show; through the Internet or their friends making tapes or whatever. It's just about good music. If people want to listen to Jay-Z, they can. If people want to listen to my show, they can. Everybody has choices and nobody has to listen to anything they don't want to.'

For some reason I'm disquieted by what Bobbito's said. Perhaps it's the idea that hip hop is 'just about good music', because it's always been about more than that for me; even if I can't quite put my finger on exactly what I mean. Or maybe it's because everything seems to lead me back to Jay-Z, the 'king of New York', and I vaguely remember something Kenyatta said ('Like Jay-Z. On his first record, people didn't catch a lot of what he was saying because it was too complex') and something Jay himself said to me five years ago.

It takes two hours of scrabbling through attic boxes before I find the tape I'm looking for. This was late 1997, just before the release of *In My Lifetime, Vol. 1.* Jay had always claimed that he'd only put out one album. But this was number two. His first album, *Reasonable Doubt*, was an underground smash and the sales changed his mind. *In My Lifetime, Vol. 1* was the first in a deluge that currently stands at seven (or is it eight?) albums in five years. This interview was also about six months after Biggie's murder. At the time of his death, Big was New York's undisputed hip hop champion and on *Reasonable Doubt* he guested on a track called 'Brooklyn's Finest'. Of course I didn't know it at the time, but *In My Lifetime, Vol. 1* probably marked the passing of the East Coast rap baton. It also signified Jay's crossover into the mainstream (in his own mind if not in sales) since it coincided with his multimillion-dollar deal with Def Jam, the launch of Roc-A-Wear clothes and Roc-A-Fella Films. Perhaps, therefore, this was the birth of what Kelefah Sanneh has called 'corporate rap'.

You have to picture me chasing him round this Harlem football field while he's shooting an MTV intro. I'm holding my microphone at arm's length, trotting after him like an irritating kid brother, and you can hear my plaintive little voice going, 'Umm . . . Jay . . . just one more question . . . Umm . . . selling out . . . umm . . . some people have said you . . . umm . . .'

'Selling out?' He's talking to me over his shoulder. 'I don't particularly understand that. That's why I made "Can't Knock The Hustle",[43] know what I mean? If drugs was my hustle then you can't knock that; because hustling is my life. Now rap's my hustle and I give people what they want to hear because rap's my way up out of here.

'With myself, I was hustling before rap so I knew that lifestyle before I even recorded my first record. So it's a little different for me from any other artist. Before my first album was out, I already had four cars, know what I mean? So I understand the hustle and I understand the business. If someone's not from where you're from and can't understand what you're saying, then you'd better take it slow. Because you want to shift your product, right? Selling out? *That's* the hustle.'

And he's off across the football field again. And there's me in the background, 'Great . . . interesting . . . Umm . . . Jay . . . one more question . . .'

Bobbito says, 'Everybody has choices and nobody has to listen to anything they don't want to.' I wonder how right he is. In 1972, French social theorist Michel Foucault wrote: 'We know perfectly well that we are not free to say just anything, that we simply cannot speak on anything, when we like, or where we like.'[44] And that was in 1972. In Western society these days, we define ourselves as much by what we consume as by what we say and the actual restrictions on our consumer desires are at least as stringent as the social restrictions on our speech. In 1991, zeitgeist curator Douglas Coupland coined the phrase 'option paralysis' to mean 'the ten-

---

[43] 'Can't Knock The Hustle', Jay-Z, 1996, Roc-A-Fella.
[44] *The Archaeology Of Knowledge And The Discourse On Language*, Michel Foucault, 1972, Abacus.

dency, when given unlimited choices, to make none'.[45] But in the last decade a lot's changed as choices are increasingly made way above the level of the individual consumer. Back in the day, hip hop culture lived in New York's poorest neighbourhoods: its music was corner-shop business, its fashions ebbed and flowed like any street fads and its identity was expressive and revolutionary and constantly reinvented. Now you can find hip hop music and fashions in the chainstores of, say, Oshkosh, Wisconsin. And in New York? Well you can certainly find the same major-label releases in Tower Records and you can buy any sneakers you want in Niketown. As long as they're Nike. So hip hop identity has become one dimensional and codified and is pumped out with evangelical zeal on MTV; from New York to Oshkosh.

If hip hop is 'just about good music,' of course it doesn't matter. It's just another pop craze that will grow and shrink with the vagaries of marketing and consumer taste (in that order). But hip hop isn't just about good music and I don't believe Bobbito actually thinks that any more than I do.

Hip hop was once a voice of the excluded and, as such, it was appropriated, cut to size and packaged as a prime resource of 'black cool' or 'urban cool' or 'alienated cool' or whatever you want to call it. This process was so successful that it is now the prime (only, even) mainstream signifier of black or urban or alienated identity. So now, in its city of origin, the voice of the excluded does little but reinforce their exclusion. Worse still, the success of mainstream hip hop actually deprives the excluded of the choice to express themselves or to hear beyond the appropriated exclusion that has become a bizarre kind of norm. If you picture hip hop as a drug, then the progress of a handful of street fiends to New Jersey mansions only ensures the continuation of a cycle. If hip hop is a drug then its dealers don't have to worry about their addicts; they're pretty much a captive audience who'll take any shit they're given, no matter what it's cut with. Do you buy that? I do. And it matters.

In My Lifetime, Vol. 1 is booming from my speakers. It's a track

---

[45] *Generation X*, Douglas Coupland, 1991, Abacus.

called 'Rap Game/Crack Game' and Jay's laid-back drawl slides seductively into my consciousness as he describes how, as an emcee, he built a hardcore audience while biding his time to explode on to the commercial market. And the hook, sampled from Nas, kicks in: 'Somehow the rap game reminds me of the crack game.'

By the time we reach Kenyatta's surprise venue, I've kind of given up. I'm searching for the essence of a culture I love and, in the city of its birth, I find that hip hop is everywhere. But nowhere, too. I'm disheartened; I've walked the walk, talked the talk and bought the T-shirt but all that's just ephemera.

The Izzy Bar is on 1st and 10th. The Lower East Side used to be a rough neighbourhood but, post-Giuliani, it's a gentrified sort of place with restaurants and bars where young Uptowners come out to play. These days, then, perhaps it's a perfect hip hop setting.

We head into the basement and it's already pretty packed with old-school B-Boys and a sprinkling of white girls who look more Manhattan glam than anything street. A tiny stage is fully loaded with turntables, rhythm section, keyboards, guitars and three or four mics. The punters huddle around small tables or lounge against the bar. It's candlelit and smoky and nervously expectant.

The Real Live Show, broadcast live online and to no more than sixty people at the Izzy Bar, is hosted by Malik, a.k.a. Dionysos, alongside his crew, the Eclectic Regiment. Kenyatta is smiling at me; like he knows a secret.

The band take their places and launch, with no ceremony, into an easy rolling funk break, embellished with scratches and the occasional improvised snatch of melody. Dionysos takes a mic and assumes the master-of-ceremonies persona like it's a second skin. He's stalking from the stage about the room and the atmosphere is suddenly charged.

'When I say "real", you say "live",' he exhorts. 'Real!' And everyone shouts back with one voice, 'Live!' 'Real!' 'Live!' He drops into a freestyle rap, an introduction to the show. He's vibing off the rhythms and the words are improvised from what he sees. A pretty blonde emerges from the audience and starts to gyrate in front of him and he raps at her, hitting on her in rhyme, one hand on her hip and the other gripping the mic. The room cheers his every lyric; his expertise is astounding. Gradually other emcees emerge from the audience and the microphones are passed from hand to hand as words and ideas bounce from lip to lip and around the room: 'Easily I approach / The microphone / 'Cause I ain't no joke.'

For two hours, the band doesn't stop. They slide between rhythms at the drummer's signal, as emcee after emcee takes their turn to drop a verse. Some are awesome – lyrically dextrous and witty, pulling words apart and reassembling them like Plasticene shapes – but every emcee is cheered just the same and the walls are sweating. I remember what Ameachi said about New York: 'Everyone's a rapper and they're all cynical.' And the truth of the former is as apparent as the absence of the latter. Behind me a sax has appeared from nowhere and some older dude is blowing for all he's worth, a melody that soars above the band; and now the emcee slips into a supporting role, like some kind of lyrical snare. Now there's a guy with a bongo and he's snapping out a new rhythm that beckons the band in its wake. And all the while Dionysos prowls the room, calling for more from the emcees and from the band and from the punters whose heads jerk up and down in unified rhythm.

Dionysos. Malik chose his emcee name well, as *The Real Live Show* reeks of Bacchanalia; like a pagan ritual in its free-form democracy. And suddenly I'm drunk on the essence of hip hop that first caught me fifteen years ago. I don't want it to end because I can't explain it. I want to package it and take it home and show it to my mum so she can see for herself and understand what I've been talking about for all this time.

After the show, I'm hanging upstairs with Malik and Dana, the drummer, a jazz head who runs the band and used to play with Branford Marsalis. Malik talks about his love of hip hop, his confidence in what he's doing and how he's expecting big things for their show. Dana talks about his love of jazz, the thrill of working with live emcees and how he's expecting big things for their show. They're both intrigued by my book but more by the idea that I might be able to hook them up with, like, a promoter in London. 'Hook me up' and 'play my shit': the new slogans of underground hip hop, New York style. And in the meantime, Malik organises and hosts rap competitions around the state. It's all part of some promotional work. For Sprite.

Kenyatta and Reggie (his partner from Black L.I.B.) join us and the conversation takes a different if equally familiar tack: hip hop is dead. 'I'm gonna have that printed up on a T-shirt,' Kenyatta says.

We start talking about hip hop worldwide; how maybe there are more possibilities internationally than in the States. Reggie says, 'I hear that when you go to Japan, if you're a rapper, women just throw themselves at you. Like, just for being an emcee! That's where I wanna go!'

'Right,' Kenyatta laughs. 'That's what's gonna be on my T-shirt. "Hip hop is dead". Right across the front. And on the back, "Let's go to Japan".'

They all pack up laughing, clink their glasses and start to check out and discuss the assembled talent in the bar. But me? I know where I'm heading next. Hip hop is dead. Let's go to Japan.

Part Two: Tokyo
A Watcher's Point Of View (Don't 'Cha Think)[1]

'Reality used to be a friend of mine.'[2]

There aren't many times that I turn to the lyrics of P.M. Dawn. In the early '90s, just as Native Tongues[3] acts like De La Soul seemed to have made the so-called 'hip hop daisy age' credible, along came P.M. Dawn with their African beads, powder-puff melodies and pussyfooting, abstract lyrics. And suddenly, despite some critical praise, that whole hippy vibe was seriously wack. So, like I say, there aren't many times I turn to the lyrics of P.M. Dawn. But this is one of them.

We're walking through the fashionable Tokyo district of Shibuya and my eyes are on stalks. It's the wash of red and yellow lights. In most cities you could spot, for example, the golden arches from streets away, iconic and unmissable. But here? Even that famous trademark is lost in the lava of fluorescence that bubbles beneath the two enormous TV screens that tower over Shibuya station. From the electronic stores to the sex stores to the gadget stores to the electronic-sex-gadget stores, this is neon homogeny so you'd best know which is which before you order a Big Mac. It's the restaurants. From KFC to the 'American' diners to the 'Japanese' noodle bars, you choose your food that looks like plastic from a

---

[1] 'A Watcher's Point Of View (Don't 'Cha Think)', P.M. Dawn, 1991, BMG/Gee Street.

[2] 'Reality Used To Be A Friend Of Mine', P.M. Dawn, 1991, BMG/Gee Street.

[3] The Native Tongues was a late '80s East Coast collective that included classic hip hop acts like A Tribe Called Quest, Black Sheep, Jungle Brothers and, of course, De La Soul.

photograph of a plastic representation of your food. This is eating as alienation. It's the people. There are '80s goths and foppish glam boys and women dressed like schoolgirls and schoolgirls dressed like hookers and endless Lil' Kim coochies in blonde wigs and crop-tops that bear obtuse English phrases like 'Sexy Kitty' or 'Culture Style' and their eyes are manga wide and their make-up is as thick and as solid as cement. It's the superficiality. Because if the neon bulbs popped and the food was broken down into its constituent parts and the make-up was chiselled away, what would you be left with?

The atmosphere is muggy thick and the narrow streets are packed. Kanyasu is striding ahead, unbothered, but I feel claustrophobic and neurotic and like I desperately need to scratch.

How do you find out about hip hop in Tokyo? Maybe you would think to look on the Web. You would think. But every Google search seems to bring up the same message: 'This page contains some characters that cannot be displayed'; and your every click reveals only snakes of commas and question marks as the poor browser tries to unravel the mysteries of the Japanese alphabet. Even if you could read them, you can't access the characters.

But I did eventually find an English-language Web site – blacktokyo.com – and we're heading to meet its editor, an African-American who goes by the name of Craig Nine. I called him earlier in the day and told him about the book I'm writing. He said it shouldn't be too difficult to meet some people. 'There aren't many black guys out here,' he explained. 'So brothers look out for each other.' I felt like I should say something about my race.

We agreed to meet outside Shibuya's mammoth HMV. I asked him how we would recognise one another and he laughed and said it wouldn't be a problem. 'OK', I said. And then, 'Well. Kanyasu's black with braids and I'm white and scruffy.'

Craig is short and skinny with unruly dreadlocks and almond eyes that almost make him look Japanese. His girlfriend is Japanese; dark-skinned and dolly beautiful. He doesn't introduce her and she doesn't introduce herself.

We sit on plastic bucket-seats to drink coffee and eat sandwiches from disposable place mats on easy-wipe tables in a diner lit like a hospital. Craig has been in Tokyo for almost four years. He got a job as a Web designer but now he's getting more into acting. He has no plans to go home.

'There are so many more opportunities out here for someone like me,' he confesses. 'In school I guess I was what you might call a geek but here I can be an actor. I get a lot of work on TV. I'm famous. You see how everyone's staring? That's because most of the people in here know who I am. They're very polite, the Japanese.'

I scope the room but I can't see anybody staring. Maybe they're just too polite.

Craig suggests that Kanyasu and I check out Harlem, Tokyo's premier hip hop club, as our first port of call. It's only just up the road. 'What day is it today?' he says. 'Friday? It's a night called Daddy's House. Harlem will be hot tonight.'

We part company outside the diner. When Craig's girlfriend says goodbye, it seems she speaks fluent English. For the last hour she hasn't spoken a word. I still don't know her name.

It's approaching midnight but, as we cut through Shibuya, the streets are as busy as ever and the crowds are making me feel itchy all over again. So it's a relief when, following Craig's directions, we take a left up Maruyama-cho. The steep street is lined with bars and clubs and it immediately feels more . . . more *real*.

Club Harlem is just about at the top of the hill and outside the next-door convenience store gaggles of B-Boys are fronting with testosterone on tap. They've got corn-rowed hair and thick cigars and Raiders shirts and Fubu jeans and a well-honed B-Boy swagger. I like the way they're checking each other out; a raised eyebrow and a slight jerk of the head. I like the way they're checking me out; a high chin and a glance through an imaginary target at the end of the nose. I like the way they're checking Kanyasu out; a brief bob of the neck and a coy sideways scrutiny. On the door, I like the bullshit from the Italian-American bouncer. He thinks my ballpoint is a knife and makes me write my name to prove otherwise. I like all this. It has a gritty seaminess that is familiar and welcome, a real antidote to the trendy ephemera that swarms a street or two away.

Inside, Harlem is dark and smoky and beginning to fill up. The dancefloor is already busy and when the beats rumble my belly I feel that customary adrenaline rush. The music is jiggy US hip hop – not my bag – but, in the half-light, the way people move, the way people are dressed, you could be in any hip hop club in the world. I feel like a whisky to set me up.

The bar area is pretty much deserted. I signal to the barman and he looks faintly surprised. I order a large bourbon and the bill surprises me right back. At these prices, no wonder the punters steer clear. Taking a sip, I glance to the far end of the counter where maybe twenty young men are neatly lined up against the wall. I'm sure they're staring at me and I begin to feel a bit uneasy. Kanyasu comes over and I ask her, 'What do you think they're doing?'

She's laughing at me: 'They're in the queue for the bar.'

I look again and, sure enough, the guy at the front is paying for a couple of beers from beneath his Kangol hat. I'm a little embarrassed and I throw what I think is a polyglot shrug along the length of the line. Nobody responds, though a couple of people look away. I've just jumped the queue to the bar and all I've provoked is the odd look of disapproval. I suddenly realise that this isn't like any hip hop club I've ever been to.

It's B-Boy Park, Tokyo's annual hip hop festival in Yoyogi Koen. You walk up from the station along the dual carriageway that bisects the park. On your left you pass the large tented village that houses hundreds of Tokyo's homeless. An old man is pottering outside his tarpaulin shelter. He looks up at you curiously for a moment. On your right, there are streams of kids heading up their side of the road. You need to cross over. You hear the first pulse of distant music and see the footbridge up ahead. As you approach, the repetitive hip hop break is joined by another screeching sound. There's a rock band set up by the bridge and their guitars are screaming for all they're worth. Yoyogi Koen has always been a place where Tokyo's musicians come to play at weekends but this band's choice of location seems perverse. Squared off against the huge speakers on the other side of the road, they're rock Davids against hip hop Goliaths. The frontman is singing wholeheartedly, hunched over a microphone, his face concealed by a mop of bleached hair. His tight T-shirt cuts an inch or two above the waist of his sagging jeans. He has the look and posture of an oriental Kurt Cobain.

From the top of the bridge there's a decent view of the whole park. To your left, the road stretches towards Shinjuku, the heart of modern Tokyo, where skyscrapers and department stores tower over love hotels and hostess bars, and down to Shibuya on your right. Behind you a landscaped walkway leads to a fountain where young parents are watching their children play and old women weave their fingers and look on impassively. To a depth of around twenty metres, the orderly ribbon of homelessness clings to the roadside while, right beneath you, Kurt Cobain is still wailing as if his life depended on it. In the middle of the bridge, you pause for a moment. Ahead of you is the hip hop festival and a couple of thousand kids are milling in knotty clusters.

The beats from the distant stage are getting louder as a small figure, swamped by his American football shirt, stalks on to riotous cheers. He shouts into the microphone: 'How you feeling? How you feel? Make some noise!' The tide of people heaves towards the stage. On one side, gifted writers are halfway through a glorious, colourful piece proclaiming 'B-Boy Park'. They have their own set of fans. Another swell is circling the stalls, run by black men, that sell bootleg T-shirts bearing the labels Hilfiger and Triple 5 Soul. By now, you've reached the far end of the footbridge and there are B-Boys hanging from the railings, trying to get a view of the elastic breakers who battle it out just below to the cuts and scratches of two adept turntablists. Emcees, graffiti artists, breakers and DJs; you've found hip hop culture in all its prime forms.

We've been here for about an hour and it's not panning out like I'd hoped. Of course I want to talk to people, to get a little local perspective, but it's proving tricky. There's this enormous guy with a shaved head and eyes hidden behind wraparound shades. He's bare-chested with muscles like bags of potatoes and one rippling arm slung around the shoulder of a bijou glamour puss in a skirt shorter than her implausible high heels. As he passes, I spot the glorious tattoo on his back and shoulders. An elaborate angel is framed with the words 'Los Angeles' and 'Trust No Man'. I chase after him and ask if he speaks English. His girlfriend is gigging shyly but he smiles, 'Word up, dog.'

Great. Could I ask him a few questions about the Tokyo hip hop scene?

'Word.'

'Sorry. But *do* you speak English?' I can see my reflection in his mirror glasses and his smile is uncomprehending. 'Never mind,' I say. 'Thanks anyway. Peace.' I raise my clenched fist. He does the same and we touch knuckles.

'Peace,' he says.

I'm harassing a gaggle of kids. They speak fluent English but language isn't my only problem. They are reluctant to talk. At first I think they're shy but then one of them says, 'You should talk to other guys. We are not hip hop fans.' Fair enough. But I'm checking out their Ruff Ryders chains, Roc-A-Wear jeans, Sean John jackets and Wu T-shirts. So what about the clothes, then? The same kid shrugs, 'Just fashion.'

I'm talking to a guy called Taro. He's a stringy cat in combats and a Yankees baseball shirt. His fine Japanese hair has been crimped into a bizarre haystack effect with an Afro comb wedged right in the middle. He's trying to be cool but he's irrepressibly excitable and the words seem to jump out of his mouth like popcorn from a hot pan. 'We're just representing on this side, man,' he says. 'Just representing ourselves, you know? Here, you find real hip hop, no doubt. We're representing and keeping it real.'

I point to the emcee on stage and ask him who it is. He doesn't know. I ask him what he's rapping about. Taro stops for a moment and his face is studied concentration. Then he shrugs. 'He's just saying you gotta keep it real.'

'Keep what real?'

'You know. You gotta represent.'

Represent what? I'm bemused by his answers and, when Taro returns to the heart of the bouncing crowd, I say as much to Kanyasu. But she shrugs. 'They're just kids,' she says. 'What do you expect? You could ask any kids in the world why they were in to hip hop and they'd say the same thing. Why does it have to be any deeper than that?'

At that moment, a girl wearing an official badge taps me on the shoulder and points to the bottle top I've just dropped. She smiles sweetly and gestures towards the recycling bins manned by B-Boys in aprons. Such good citizenship isn't very hip hop, is it? Obediently I drop my bottle top and empty water bottle into one of the bins. The nearest pinnied B-Boy wordlessly retrieves my bottle, strips off the paper sticker and deposits it in a separate container.

Aside from Kanyasu and me, most of the other *gaijin*[4] at B-Boy Park are average-Joe tourists with snapping cameras and guide books. But I spot a couple of guys, one white and one black, scooting through the crowds on those low-rider bikes that seem to be trendy over here. Oliver is a graphic designer from Baltimore with a pencil beard and an easy manner. Kobe is a car designer from DC with piled dreadlocks, goggle shades and supercool wariness. They've both been working in Tokyo for a couple of years.

'When I first got here,' Oliver complains. 'I was, like, "This place is amazing." I saw all these kids B-Boying all over the place and it was, like, so cool. But it's all bullshit. Scratch the surface and you'll find nothing. It's empty.'

Kobe agrees: 'Hip hop here? It's like they read it from a book. They go to DJ school, emcee school, graffiti school. There's no spontaneity, no creativity. Check out the spray-can styles? Copied from the States. DJ styles? Copied from the States. That's Japanese culture all over; it's the culture of appropriation.'

'Exactly, man,' Oliver nods. 'It's superficial. It doesn't mean shit.'

Kobe leans forward to add his final word. 'Let me tell you something else,' he says. 'What you need to understand about Tokyo; everyone here is straight-up racist or bigoted or at the very least ignorant. Believe me, man. That's just the way it is.'

I say, 'Right.'

'It's true, man. You'll see.'

By one a.m. Harlem is peaking and the DJ launches into his classics set: old-school tunes by the likes of Mark the 45 King, Biz and Quest that have me mouthing along in silent karaoke. They're

---

[4] *Gaijin*: foreigner.

skilfully chopped together all right but I find myself somehow suspicious because, to me, even the DJ's seamless mixing sounds a little too clinical. I'm shaking my head and sipping whisky three-or-is-it-four. Maybe it's just me.

Looking around the crowd, I'm beginning to realise it's a funny mixture. Aside from the Japanese, there's a smattering of *gaijin* men but Kanyasu is the only foreign woman I can see. A couple of gangs of white youngsters in high-school-typical football shirts, baggy jeans and Tims are getting raucous. They're a healthy American size and tower over most of the Japanese, dancing in demarcated, post-adolescent circles and swigging bottled beer. But it's the black guys who interest me; prowling the periphery, alone or in pairs, or taking centre stage on the dancefloor, surrounded by gaggles of Japanese women who seem to take their turn for each funky step, cock of pelvis and jerk of hip. These girls are dressed in different uniforms of cool but the theme is consistent: accurate pastiche of African-American fashion. There's one of Destiny's Children in knee-length boots and a dress that clings to bust and butt, there's a sloppy B-Girl whose Hilfiger underwear protrudes at the waist of her oversized jeans and there's an Afrocentric chick, her head festooned in a wrap *à la* Erykah Badu. Some of them wear their hair in dreadlocks. Japanese hair is so fine that locks require a serious effort of will and wallet; hours in the hairdresser's chair at more than US\$1,000 a time. Many of them have darkened their skin with hard hours on the sunbed. I've heard about these girls. They're known as 'blackfacers' or *kokujo* – (Japanese women who like black men).

Before arriving in Japan, I came across a back issue of *Transition* magazine with an article by an African-American called Joe Wood who travelled to Japan in search of the blackfacers. It's a brilliant read – introspective and disturbed. He writes: 'The sexualized "cool" that Japanese attribute to blackness doesn't leave much space for black humanity.'[5] And I'm sure he's got a point. But somehow, as I watch a petite *kokujo* arse grind into a sturdy African-American thigh, I feel more dismayed than disquieted. It's a little like watching one of those home-video blooper shows when you

[5] 'The Yellow Negro', Joe Wood, *Transition*, Issue 73.

find yourself laughing while part of you cringes with vicarious embarrassment. I guess it's because I'm not the one being fetishised but, to me, the complex cultural dance being choreographed to a hip hop break just looks so crass, so *wack*. It can't seem threatening or dangerous because it's so obviously daft. Besides, I figure the 'sexualized "cool" ' must work both ways – geisha on one hand, black sexuality on the other – and, as a white outsider, I can't help thinking that both sides look kind of exotic to me.

I get talking to a girl called Kioko. She's nineteen and strikingly beautiful, with copper-coloured skin and stacked braids pulled back so tight that they seem to tug her eyes into unwilling shapes. She doesn't look black, of course, but she doesn't really look Japanese either. If anything, she could pass for one of the Hispanic girls at the Roots project we went to in New York. I ask her why she likes hip hop and she shrugs. 'Because it's cool.' I ask her why she likes black men and she corrects me. 'Just black Americans,' she says. They are, she claims, 'more romantic than Japanese'.

As for the objects of her affection, they're not so keen to talk but, after half an hour of 'no's, I eventually find a couple of friends who chat easily enough. One is a tall, monosyllabic, blue-black Franco-phone African whose high-waisted jeans are around the level of my chin. He plays for a football team over here. His friend is an American; a short, tub-shaped ex-serviceman with chunky ankles poking out beneath his baggy shorts and a visor on his head that just about keeps the beginnings of a picky Afro in check. When I tell them what I'm working on, they get a little coy and refuse to give me their names.

The ex-serviceman does most of the talking. He used to be stationed in Okinawa and, after leaving the forces, decided to give it a go in Tokyo. His voice is incongruously thin and high-pitched and barely audible above the booming basslines.

'So what do you do now?' I ask and his reply drowns beneath the waves of sound. 'I'm sorry?'

'I'm a track maker.'

'A what?'

'A track maker. I make tracks.'

I'm confused. 'What kind of tracks?'

'Y'know. Like, music tracks.'

'You're a producer?'

He nods enthusiastically, like this is just the word he's been looking for all his life. 'Yeah. Right. A producer.' He touches his friend on the arm. 'And he's a rapper.'

'A rapper?'

'Sure,' the tall guy says. 'I play football and I rap.'

'What kind of rap do you like?'

'Gangsta rap. Gangsta shit. I love gangsta shit.'

'Gangsta shit,' I say. 'Right.' I'm feeling more than a little bemused. These two make quite a double act. 'So what do you make of the women out here?'

'Real nice,' says ex-serviceman. 'They're all real friendly, you know what I'm sayin'?'

'Do you think it's odd that they want to look black?' I try. But he doesn't seem to understand what I'm getting at so I point to a nearby girl with a typical charred complexion and lovingly tangled dreads.

'I never noticed that,' he shrugs.

Later, I catch sight of the pair at the side of the dancefloor. Ex-serviceman is leaning in to a conversation with a tiny woman in bootylicious shorts and a tight T. Footballer has his back to a pillar with his body locked in a hip hop posture. Shoulders sloped and arms wrapped around his chest, it's a kind of gangsta vogue. Scoping round, I check out the Japanese B-Boys queuing for the bar and I feel the friction as two cultures rub up against one another (literally and metaphorically).

Kobe told me that everyone in Japan was 'straight-up racist or bigoted or at the very least ignorant'. I remember my first visit to Tokyo. I was working as a journalist, chasing some British drum 'n' bass DJ, and I ended up getting drunk with his Japanese representative, a cool young guy called Nave. The drunker we got, the more morose Nave became until he launched into a full-scale rant about the frustrations of being a Japanese man. He said he'd just read some article in which the nationalities of the world were rated for their attractiveness. Japanese women were apparently riding high at number three while their male counterparts failed to make the top forty. The memory then leaps forward five years to tonight when

Kioko tells me that African-American men are 'more romantic than Japanese'. Then this thought makes way for the memory of Kenyatta, Malik and the rest sitting in the Izzy Bar and shooting the breeze. What was it Reggie said? 'I hear that when you go to Japan, if you're a rapper, women just throw themselves at you. Like, just for being an emcee!'

The whisky's kicking in and I'm so confused that, despite the Ummah's[6] bassline and Q-Tip's trademark flow, I can't hear much beyond P.M. Dawn. Because, from a watcher's point of view, the relations here between black people and Japanese are contaminated with such a bewildering array of brutal stereotypes that it is hard to even guess where my friend Reality might have hidden, let alone how to go about finding him. But I've got a feeling that these questions of race are fundamentally important and that the ways the Japanese see black people probably give a decent insight into a Japanese mind . . . or a Japanese hip hop fan's mind, anyway.

There is a fifty-year-old story from a village called Katsuyama on Okinawa. It goes like this. In 1945, in the midst of the vicious battle for the island (in which 200,000 Japanese were killed), three US marines used to come to Katsuyama every week and rape the defenceless local women. Okinawa, designated as Japan's last stand, had by this time descended into lawless chaos as civilians fled for any place of safety in the jungles and hill caves and the three marines felt they could do pretty much as they pleased.

It didn't take long for the marines to get cocky and reckless and, one day, a group of male refugees sheltering in the village saw their opportunity and murdered the Americans and hid their bodies in a cave. A month later, the atom bombs were dropped on Hiroshima and Nagasaki and, with the war abruptly ended, nobody thought too much about the three missing marines. Pfc. John M. Smith, Pvt. Isaac Stokes and Pfc. James D. Robinson were declared first as deserters and then as missing in action and that was that. But, in Katsuyama, the story lived on.

---

[6] The Ummah is the production collective made up of Q-Tip and Ali Shaheed Muhammad (from A Tribe Called Quest) and Jay-Dee (of Slum Village).

In 1998 a local guide who takes hikers around old war sites found the cave and the marines' remains. They were returned to the American military and flown home for burial. It was only in April of 2000, however, that a Japanese paper made the connection between the bodies and the Katsuyama folklore. This was a couple of months before the G8 summit in Nago and there were brief fears that the story might overshadow President Clinton's visit to Okinawa. But the Japanese police decided not to pursue the case since all statutes of limitation (even for murder) had long since expired. Similarly, American military officials (who had begun to investigate) were more than happy to let the matter rest. The Katsuyama locals called the Americans' tomb Kurombo Gama. This roughly translates as 'nigger cave'. The three marines were black.

There is also a story from a shopping mall known as American Village in Chatan Town on Okinawa. This one's from the beginning of July 2001. A young 'blackface' Japanese girl was seen leaving the 3F bar and nightclub with a tall black man. Nobody took much notice. The 3F is a hip hop joint and a favourite of the African-American servicemen among the 25,000 stationed on Okinawa so it's hardly surprising it attracts the local *kokujo*. A little while later, a marine friend of the girl who was supposed to drive her home went to look for her outside. He saw her bent double over a car bonnet with the tall black man having sex with her from behind. When the marine called out, the man stopped and jumped into a car that sped away. It was a military vehicle. The girl claimed that she'd been raped and on 6 July, twenty-four-year-old Air Force Staff Sergeant Timothy Woodland was arrested and charged. He insists it was consensual sex.

Two stories of rapes of Japanese women by African-American servicemen on the island of Okinawa . . . I repeat them not to stress the miserable similarities but because of the disproportionate media and public attention they have received in Japan. What's more, these two incidents frame half a century in which Japanese attitudes to race have in some ways changed extraordinarily and in others stagnated. You see, I'm beginning to realise that to understand the ways the Japanese look at hip hop requires understanding the ways they look at race (the black races in particular). What's more, to understand the ways the Japanese look at race requires an understanding, within an historical context, of the ways they look at themselves.

Chatting at B-Boy Park, Kobe, an African-American, is convinced that the Japanese are inherently racist. Aside from personal, nuanced experiences with B-Boys and *kokujo*, his opinion is hardly surprising when you consider that, for example, only fifteen years ago, the then prime minister, Yasuhiro Nakasone, ascribed America's declining competitiveness in the world market to the low intelligence of its black and Hispanic peoples. And yet? And yet prominent African-American thinkers once considered Japan as a blueprint for 'coloured' progress: Langston Hughes derived inspiration from Japanese intellectuals in the '30s while Elijah Muhammed, the leader of the Nation of Islam, was imprisoned during the Second World War for urging African-Americans not to fight against fellow non-whites in the Pacific war. So the question troubling me is singular and simple. What changed? What changed in the ways Japanese see black people? What changed in the ways Japanese see themselves?

Before the Second World War, imperial Japan's relationship with the wider world was consistent only in its awkwardness. Compelled by nineteenth-century Western governments (that of the US in particular) to open its ports to ensure their trading routes, the response was the 1889 Meiji Constitution, which codified a new understanding of Japanese identity as 'the land of one people'. Shinto was adopted as the state religion (with the emperor as god on earth), the Imperial Rescript on Education formalised the individual's loyalty to the state and, with the motto of 'strong army, rich country', the role of the military was given new prominence.

By the turn of the century, therefore, the West was forced to recognise Japanese potential both militarily (after the wars with China and Russia) and culturally (as European sideboards creaked beneath Japanese *objets*). Indeed, after siding with Britain in the First World War, Japan was one of the 'big five' at the Paris Peace

Conference and a founder member of the League of Nations. Notably, however, the Japanese desire to have a declaration of racial equality included in the League's Charter was frustrated by Americans, Australians and British alike. There was already evidence, therefore, of Japan's uneasy relationship with the West (and, indeed, vice-versa).

The '30s saw economic slump accompanied by a predictable rise in the power of the army. This meant first a treaty with Germany against any hostile intentions of the Soviet Union (the 1936 Anti-Comintern Pact), then the full-scale invasion of China the following year and, finally, entry into the Second World War, proclaimed as an opportunity for the 'Greater East Asia Co-Prosperity Sphere' to finally rid itself of Western colonialism under Japan's enlightened guidance. However, such declared intention took no account of Japan's own ambitions nor, more to the point, the burgeoning racism towards its neighbours.

When Emperor Hirohito finally surrendered on 15 August 1945, a broken nation was in shock (not least to hear the voice of a living god broadcast over the radio). Japan had never before suffered military defeat. Under the auspices of the 'American Shogun', General MacArthur (Supreme Commander of the Allied Forces), the Japanese constitution was hurriedly rewritten to an approximate US blueprint.

The occupation officially lasted until 1952 but, in practice, America has been culturally, economically and politically entwined with Japan ever since. The Treaty of Mutual Co-operation and Security ensured the continued presence of US troops on Japanese soil; and in 1955 American intelligence funded the coalition of the Liberal Democratic Party, which went on to oversee the economic triumph of 'Japan, Inc'[7] and almost four decades of growth and prosperity. It was 1998 before Japan finally had to admit that it was in recession as unemployment rose to 5 per cent and the value of the yen tumbled. And it was against this background that a more vocal

---

[7] 'Japan, Inc' is a term (often used with a sneer) that characterises the complex of relationships between individual, family, government and business in post-war Japan.

questioning of received cultural knowledge began: of familial and business hierarchies, of cultural homogeny, of gender stereotypes and of race.

Now the briefest sketch of modern Japanese history hardly merits sweeping social conclusions. But, frankly and as already said, if I'm going to understand hip hop in Japan then I'm going to have to put it into some kind of context even if the subsequent opinions are subjective and personal.

Japan's recent history is located in the cultural no-man's-land between the West and the rest. Colonial and neo-colonial governments quickly recognised that they ignored Japan at their (other yellow) peril but they also wanted to avoid dealing with it on any kind of level playing field. It seems inarguable that Japan was patronised and courted and dismantled and patronised and courted and . . .

Japan reinvented itself after 1945. But as is necessary for all such successful reinventions, it did so with a selective memory in which America was complicit. So a definitive history of the American occupation is still unwritten half a century after its end, the truth buried somewhere in the social subconscious. So Katsuyama's extraordinary history (or myth) of three African-American rapists (or victims) is quickly brushed aside by Japanese and Americans alike. Because why open old wounds when there are new ones that need attention? Like the case of Air Force Staff Sergeant Timothy Woodland.

The mighty American presence on Okinawa has always been a cause of tension. Despite the statistics suggesting otherwise,[8] it is perhaps unsurprising that Okinawans should regard the American military as the source of most of the island's crime. But it is the negative perception of African-Americans that is most intriguing. Of course, it is understandable in the light of the 1995 gang rape of a twelve-year-old girl by African-American servicemen. However, as Lisa Takeuchi Cullen put it, referring to this obscenity in *Time Asia*: '. . . the crimes committed by blacks are particularly noted and

---

[8] Between 1972 and 2001, US military personnel were responsible for 1.7 per cent of crime in Okinawa despite making up 4 per cent of the population.

remembered, and . . . no-one seemed surprised when the three servicemen . . . turned out to be black.'[9]

As for the Woodland case, whether he is guilty or not its context is full of disturbing ironies. For example, the Japanese government boasts an extraordinarily high conviction rate in the prosecution of sexual crimes. However, the proportion of reported crimes that make it to court is, conversely, extremely low. This is at least in part because a woman's sexual history and proclivities are admissible as evidence in a Japanese rape trial. So imagine this fact applied to the Woodland case: a *kokujo*, with a known taste for black men, leaves a bar hand in hand with an African-American and an hour later cries rape? There is little doubt that, were Woodland Japanese, he would never have been charged. But he's not Japanese, he's American. And he's black.

The sad fact is that contemporary Japanese attitudes towards black people are schizophrenic and Woodland, rapist or not, has certainly looked squarely into both faces. People of African origin are hardly the only ones to feel the brunt of bigotry in Japan (just ask the numerous naturalised Koreans or descendants of the traditionally 'unclean' *burakumin* caste)[10]; however, no other race inspires such mixed emotions.

What changed? That was my earlier question. What changed in the Japanese regard for black people after the '30s? And to that question we'd better add another: where's it at now?

The Second World War shattered Japanese confidence until it regrouped within its most trusted and basic form of nationalism, a nationalism that emphasised homogeny and the relationship between the individual and the state. In this context 'blackness' that was once a potential (junior) partner against the arrogant white world was soon simply a threat to this new tribalism and even, worse still, representative of reinforced Western dominance.

---

[9] 'Okinawa Nights', Lisa Takeuchi Cullen, *Time Asia*, 13 August 2001.

[10] The Buraku people can be traced back to the Middle Ages of Japanese history; an 'unclean' designation imposed on occupations like butchers, tanners and, ironically (in the light of modern Japanese society) entertainers. The Buraku Liberation League estimates there are three million Buraku people in Japan.

The 'bubble economy' of post-war Japan is a well-trodden history. However, it is worth pointing out that this astonishing economic growth was built on the selective memory and reinvention (of workplace, education, aspiration and identity) noted above. The Japanese bubble, therefore, may be best seen as a double-layered phenomenon; like, say, – in the light of the Japanese-South Korean World Cup – a football, in which the fragile epidermis of the economy was stretched over an altogether hardier pig's bladder of culture.

Even as Japan regrouped within this economic and cultural ball, so it swelled with pride throughout the '60s, '70s and '80s and gave a front-row view of the rest of the world (with all the engagement and its lack suggested in such a phrase). The economy enabled Japanese companies and products and people to reach out to every corner of the globe while the culture ensured that their identity remained immutable and interaction was acquisitive rather than mutual.

Of course, the economy burst in the '90s. But the tougher pig's bladder merely punctured and the hissing effects of this rupture are still being processed. Japanese identity – from national to individual – is facing new and tricky questions that require more than the immediate and internal logic of changing markets to answer. And when recession hit, so this long-drawn-out moment coincided with the international appropriation of African-American identity. It is, unsurprisingly, the young Japanese who have necessarily (and, arguably, happily) confronted the questioning and they have done so in the context of Jordan on every court, Bonds on every diamond, Tyrese in every commercial and Boyz in every hood. And, of course, hip hop is on worldwide MTV – twenty-four, seven, fifty-two. It is no wonder that identity has become a courtroom battle with race a fundamental (if often crass) argument and hip hop and broader African-American identity two of the key witnesses.

I guess what I'm trying to point out is that hip hop is interpreted not just locally but also time specifically; so the boom of Japanese hip hop coincides with a particular moment in culture (or rather, perhaps, moments in cultures). There is, I reckon, a touch of societal alchemy about this; i.e., hip hop emerges from a mysterious recipe of social ingredients.

One of the main catalysts for hip hop's growth in a specific place surely has to be the existence of alienated urban youth. However, for hip hop to thrive beyond mere imitation, young people also require self-consciousness and this is often derived from a specific set of circumstances. In fact, if those circumstances change (certainly if that consciousness is lost), so hip hop's strength can begin to fail.

Recently, for example, I went to Rome in search of an Italian scene. I had read numerous bits and bobs – academic papers, newspaper articles, Web sites[11] – about the emergence of hip hop in Italy and it sounded way too fascinating to pass up.

In the late '70s and early '80s, *centri sociali* started to spring up in cities all over Italy. These were semi-legal, cooperative squats (roughly modelled on the Communist Party's *case di lavoro*)[12] that took over disused buildings to become focal points for young people. Raising funds through proto-rave parties and the like, they acted as drop-in centres for addicts, gave legal advice and offered medical care to immigrants; that sort of thing. They were also heartbeats of militant political protest, anarchic and left wing, and, by the late '80s, breeding grounds for Italian hip hop too.

I got talking to a guy called Stefano Piccoli, a journalist and long-time B-Boy who edited the Italian hip hop mag *Biz* until it went bust in January 2001. He recalled those days in the *centri sociali* with undisguised nostalgia.

'Every nation has social problems,' he said. 'In the US or France, it's racial tension. But that's not true in Italy; not yet anyway. The only traditional arguments in Italy are political; we're a nation of partisans. So, in the early '90s, rap was the weapon for militant politicos who had something to shout about. It was a great time around La Pantera as university students and activists squatted in schools and workplaces. Hip hop was at the centre of that with

---

[11] For an excellent (English) introduction to Italian hip hop, see Joe Sciorra's Web site: www.italianrap.com

[12] *Case di lavoro:* community centres.

militant rap groups like 99 Posse and Assalti Frontali [Frontline Assault]. But now?'

Stefano shook his head.

La Pantera, named after an escaped panther loose in the city at the time, was the Roman movement organised from the *centri sociali* against the threatened privatisation of Italian universities. The anthem of La Pantera was provided by the Onda Rossa Posse (the Red Wave, the forerunner of Assalti Frontali) from the *centro sociale* at Forte Prenestino. Their self-produced track 'Batti II Tuo Tempo'[13] with its chorus '*Batti il tuo tempo / Per fottere il potere*' ('Beat your own tempo / Fuck the power') became the battle-cry for the movement. And there were similar posses initiating similar movements in *centri sociali* throughout Italy. Hip hop was, then, specifically located within a particular kind of (and, indeed, time of) leftist protest.

Commercially, though, it was the mid-'90s before Italian hip hop reached its peak. I'll let Stefano explain: 'Even if it worked outside the record industry, militant rap was economically great. Assalti Frontali sold 20,000 units without any mainstream support. It took the Italian major labels a while to catch on but, by 1994/1995, they were all desperate for rappers, and guys like Articolo 31, Neffa, Sottotono[14] and Frankie Hi NRG – even 99 Posse – all signed deals. Some of the records sold very well. Articolo 31, for example, had an album that sold 600,000;[15] that's six times platinum! A lot of these guys were dissed by the underground but of course it was very important for Italian hip hop.

'Unfortunately, in retrospect it happened much too fast and reached a point of saturation. Every artist was rushing into contracts, the quality dropped and sales dropped too. I don't think Italian hip hop has collapsed but – how would I say it? – it's cracking.'

Certainly for the last couple of years Italian hip hop has been standing on a precipice. At a commercial level, this has meant bankruptcy for Good Stuff (Italy's premier hip hop distributor), the collapse of labels (Neffa's Jackpot imprint, for instance) and

---

[13] 'Batti Il Tuo Tempo', Onda Rossa Posse, 1990, Assalti Frontali.

[14] Sottotono: low tone.

[15] *Cosi Com'è* (How It Goes), Articolo 31, 1996, BMG.

the closure of both of Italy's specialist magazines (*AL* as well as *Biz*).

Perhaps, within the parameters of hip hop mythology, the 'underground' shouldn't care about this lack of mainstream success. However, it is hard to ignore the changing subject matter of Italian hip hop too. Where once the form articulated local social protest, some crews now seem to indulge in little more than pastiche of American gangsta rap. Bands like Flaminio Maphia,[16] for example, talk up their ghetto roots and posture like would-be gang-bangers. Similarly, my friend Carlo (who now works alongside Stefano on the Web site www.blackmusic.it) described an ongoing beef between two of Rome's biggest posses: Robba Coatta (Rough Stuff) and Rome Zoo. 'Once maybe it was about something,' he said. 'But now it's just bored kids who want to pretend to be hard men.'

Outside this imagined thug life, other emcees struggle to articulate something specifically Italian. Carlo and I hooked up with this guy Michael from a crew called la Squadra (the Team). Sixteen years old and hard at work on a new album, he had an interesting perspective: 'A lot of the old-school groups grew up with American hip hop and they tried to translate it. I don't do that because I grew up with Italian hip hop so that's where I live and die. Some people like to diss but my lyrics are just about problems of youth and school and my neighbourhood; everyday life. Will it work? I think so. We're passing through an evolution right now so we don't know where we'll end up.'

Intriguingly, Piotta (by Michael's terms, one of the 'old school') largely agreed. Interesting bloke, Piotta.[17] He was rhyming for years as part of the Robba Coatta crew before having a surprise nationwide hit at the end of 1999 with a track called 'Supercafone'[18] that satirised an ageing disco king. He has subsequently developed this bizarre pimp character, which mixes American hip hop stylings with visual elements from the '70s Italian film genre *commedia sexy* ('sexy

---

[16] Flaminio is a working-class district of Rome.

[17] *Piotta*: Roman slang for 100 lire.

[18] 'Supercafone', Piotta. 1998, Antibesmusic/Universo. *Cafone* means something like an old thug.

comedies': think the *Benny Hill* show with nipples). Unsurprisingly his image (and perhaps his success) provoked truckloads of criticism from the hip hop underground, even though the persona is comparable to the cartoonish creations of the likes of Wu-Tang, Eminem and Busta Rhymes. Whatever. It's undeniable that Piotta has bridged the underground and mainstream more successfully than most.

Piotta's a funny-looking dude, too; chubby with lank long hair, he couldn't look much less hip hop if he tried. But he talked about Italian hip hop with a disarming mixture of intelligence and bemusement.

'Honestly, I don't remember if choosing this character of Piotta was conscious or not,' he admitted. 'It just felt natural, using a mixture of American and Italian pop culture. I started off rapping for a small group of people and then, boom! It was for everyone. My music was appreciated by the underground first but, when the mainstream started listening to it, all of a sudden the B-Boys thought I was a traitor. It was a strange time.

'Of course hip hop needs roots but mainstream success means the flower is blooming; otherwise it's just a dog chasing its tail. I often say hip hop in this country has made two big mistakes: the underground dissing the mainstream and the mainstream dissing the underground.

'It's difficult. In the US, hip hop can stick with an aggressive attitude. The market is so big, they're will always be an audience for that. But in Italy? You need something different. There was left-wing, political rap here and that worked because all culture in Italy is left wing. But as for now, I'm not so sure. I think the only way to be recognised by the mainstream is to be honest and to find subjects that they can understand. It's difficult for a rapper to say "My girlfriend left me and I want to cry" but maybe that's exactly what we should be doing, because it's more Italian.

'There are two possibilities. Either Italian rap will stay like it is, small and disparate, or it will have its reawakening, its revenge, and I think that could be in mixing with other cultures. Asians and Africans can relate to hip hop and this cultural mixing is an important issue in Italy right now.'

Piotta's insight is, I think, astute. Speaking about the downturn in Italian hip hop in an interview in *Music & Media* in 2001, the president of Universal Italy, Piero La Falce, commented: 'I don't think there really was a hip hop boom in this country, so much as a period of fortunate popularity.'[19] While this opinion is understandable, I reckon the rise and subsequent stumbling of the culture requires more explanation than that.

Hip hop blossomed in Italy in the late '80s and early '90s, when the political content of American hip hop (Public Enemy, KRS One, X Clan and the rest) was at its peak. It was adopted as a tool of protest by self-conscious groups in specific locations and, importantly, at a specific time. The subsequent impact of major-label involvement and the music's movement into the mainstream should not be underestimated. However, nor should the election, in 1995, of Italy's first left-wing government for half a century. Frankly, it looks to me like the combination of new commercial pressures and the dilution of core agenda cut off the music's balls and left its artists – whether Flaminio Maphia, la Squadra or Piotta – scrabbling around for new subject matter or, rather, a new ethos. Stefano's parting comment was, 'Now is the moment of truth. Everybody who doesn't really care about hip hop will disappear and only the heads will remain.' And I'm sure he was spot on. But what will their ethos be?

Personally, I reckon Piotta had it right when he talked about 'mixing with other cultures'. Recent immigration from Eastern Europe and Francophone Africa has given Italy's cities a new multicultural aspect and the number of racist attacks has increased as surely as racist chants on Italian football terraces persist. Combine these factors with the re-election of Silvio Berlusconi's right-wing alliance in 2001 and the potential for a new consciousness (among immigrant youth and the like-minded) is at least a possibility.

However, whatever the future holds, I come back to the central point of all this: the fluctuations in hip hop's success in Italy demonstrate the subtle and complex way hip hop is appropriated by and interacts with local culture, time specifically. If alchemised

---

[19] 'Urban Music On A High In Europe', Thomas Gareth, *Music & Media*, 21 July 2001. Cited on www.italianrap.com

Italian hip hop has somewhat lost its lustre, what about Japan? Are the twin factors of an economy hit by recession and new questions of national and individual identity ingredients enough for the production of hip hop culture and, if so, what does it mean?

Harlem is getting sweaty and Kanyasu decides to dump her jacket in one of the provided lockers. She comes back to find me swaying drunkenly by the edge of the dancefloor and she's vexed. Apparently some fool just pinched her arse. 'Who?' I ask and I stand up a little straighter and try to locate a little muscle in the bottom of my glass. Before coming to Tokyo, one of my female friends warned me that she'd heard Japanese men liked to catch their freebies on the underground so, on the strength of such a testimony mixed with the strength of the whisky, I'm angry but not really surprised. But then Kanyasu points out some lanky black dude. He's way on the other side of the club and he's wearing a baseball cap so I can't see his face. I say, 'I'll go and have a word.'

But Kanyasu shakes her head. 'Don't bother.'

'No. I'll go and have a word. Cheeky fuck.'

'Really,' she says. 'Don't bother.'

'Really? You don't want me to say anything?'

'No. It's fine.'

'Because I'll have a word if you want me to . . .'

'Honestly. Let's forget about it.'

She's mad cool, Kanyasu; lets me keep some semblance of machismo without risking a scrap. Only trouble is I can't forget about it. It's the black guy trying it on with the white guy's black girlfriend in Harlem in Tokyo where Japanese girls who try to look like black girls hit on black guys while Japanese guys queue for a beer. It's a dizzying racial dance and, for some reason (be it anthropological interest or macho bravado) I want to find some kind of cultural truth.

Kanyasu isn't as interested in this debate as me and she tuts. 'African? American? Maybe he's just an arsehole.'

It's easy to find an African in Tokyo; just tough to find one who admits it. You can walk the streets of the populist nightlife district of

Roppongi and there are black guys handing out flyers for clubs that promise so many free drinks for so much of an entrance fee. They're wearing baggy jeans and have bandannas tied around their heads and, being paid in accordance with the number of customers they attract, they target the *gaijin* servicemen and tourists. Their language is unpinnable, an international dialect of sales pitch and hip hop cool, and they're none too keen to chat when there's work to be done.

I ask one bloke where he comes from and he shrugs.

'Just wondered,' I say. 'You American?'

'International,' he smiles and he takes me by the arm. 'Happy hour all night . . .'

It's the same in the record and clothes shops around Shibuya, which are staffed almost exclusively by young black men. I try my same question on a dreadlocked kid in the Triple 5 Soul store. 'From Brooklyn,' he says, unconvincing and unconvinced, and his accent's a whole lot more Mombasa than Marcy.

Finally one of the guys punting bootleg T-shirts at B-Boy Park admits he's Ethiopian. 'A lot of Africans say they are American here,' he acknowledges. 'Because that's what people want and it is easy to find a job.' He looks around the crowd and his eyes stop on my friend with the Los Angeles tattoo. 'The Japanese pretend to be American so why not us too?'

'Right,' I say. 'Thanks. Peace.' I offer him my knuckles at exactly the same moment as he offers me his hand. He shakes my fist awkwardly and looks at me like I'm weird.

It's the last day of B-Boy park and the Kick the Can Crew are on stage. Their mixture of catchy melodies and sing-song raps are vaguely familiar. In fact, close my eyes and I could swear I was listening to Arrested Development and my mind flits back to Kobe the previous day: 'Hip hop here? It's like they read it from a book.' Or watched it on MTV anyway.

The crowd is, well, crowded but there isn't much in the way of hype or energy. In my experience, live hip hop has always been more interaction than spectator sport (not least because slam dancing and shout-along choruses clumsily conceal most inadequacies in performance) but the throng at B-Boy Park, maybe six or seven hundred strong, might as well be watching opera for all their apparent involvement.

On stage the Crew are game enough and one emcee exhorts: 'Wave your hands in the air! Yeah! Wave your hands in the air!' The audience respond by raising their arms in synchronised, metronomic time. It's so regimented that it looks kind of funny, doesn't it? I remember that bit in *Life of Brian* when the reluctant Messiah tells the crowd, 'You are all individuals!' And the crowd responds with one voice: 'Yes! We are all individuals!'

I'm watching with Yuko Asanuma, editor of the underground Japanese hip hop magazine *Clue*. Unlike the majority of the masses, to look at Yuko you'd never dream she was into hip hop (any more than you'd ever dream the masses were into anything else). She's naturally light-skinned with natural short hair and simple jeans and a T-shirt. She was born in Japan but spent most of her childhood in Australia before moving back to Tokyo for university.

I don't know where to begin so I start with Kobe's comment that everyone in Tokyo is 'straight-up racist or bigoted or at the very least ignorant'.

Yuko shrugs charmingly: 'I'm sure he's right. People here are still very closed.' And, as if to illustrate the point, she doesn't go into it any deeper than that.

'Look,' she says. 'Hip hop here is mostly just imitation. Definitely. Hip hop is seen as something that's independent and a little bit anti-society so a lot of young kids get into it as something to identify with outside the mainstream. But there's nothing particularly Japanese about what they say.

'Some rappers are, like, wannabe gangsta and they rap about thug life in Japan. But there aren't any gangs here. There are teenage kids who fight and steal cars; they shoplift, stuff like that, but most of it's total fantasy. No doubt a lot of kids here are so influenced by the media that they don't have a critical view of magazines or music videos. They read stuff or see artists and they just take to it without any questions. My generation is probably the first to have a wider view of the world. But it's not necessarily a more critical view.

'But you need to understand that Japan doesn't have class problems or race problems.' I realise that she's echoing that Roman guy Stefano. 'Of course they are there but not so big as in London or the States and it doesn't make sense to rap about those. You say hip hop is just fashion but, in Japan, people identify themselves by how they look. It's very important. It's not just hip hop. Goth and glam rock are very big at the moment so you see a lot of guys wearing make-up and dresses. Young people identify themselves by how they are seen.'

'But that's not what hip hop's about.'

'Where?'

'Everywhere.'

'Why?'

'Because.'

'Because in Japan that's how it is,' Yuko says finally. Charming shrug. 'Here, hip hop is about representing, keeping it real.'

'Representing *what*?' I say. 'Keeping *what* real?'

'Representing yourself, keeping real to you as an individual. You laugh at me but here it is not so easy.'

Keep it real. The penny is beginning to drop. I've already noted that the power of hip hop's symbolism (be it language, clothing or mannerism) lies in its flexibility. But the strongest symbols in any sphere are those that manage to be flexible and specific all at once; symbols that seem to apply with pin-point accuracy to you as an individual. Discussing the nature of hip hop, DJ Krush has said, 'The philosophy of hip hop is more important than the form.' And, 'The outside form can be different, but the whole concept or philosophy of people doing these things connects. It's all about being . . . pure to yourself.'[20] Fair enough. But when a cat from Tokyo says he's 'keeping it real' he doesn't mean the same thing as a kid from the Bronx or, for that matter, some white geezer from London; even though the use of such a phrase denotes all three as, at some level, 'real hip hop heads'.

Ian Condry, an American anthropologist who has written extensively about hip hop in Japan, puts it like this: 'Analyses are likely

---

[20] Quoted in 'Zen And The Art Of Noise', an interview with Dom Phillips, the *Guardian*, 7 June 2001.

to begin with the notion that there are such entities as "Japanese culture" or "hip hop" and then set out to explore their interaction. But the images from American hip hop also contribute to Japanese youths' understanding of what Japan is . . .'[21]

Of course this idea should have been pretty damn obvious but it hasn't stopped me looking straight past it with my eyes on a personal prize. Because I thought I was searching for the essence of hip hop and it's taken time for me to realise that I am, in fact, only searching for *my* essence of hip hop.

And so I come back to the conversation I had with Tokyo-based Americans Oliver and Kobe.

'Scratch the surface and you'll find nothing,' Oliver said. 'It's empty.' And we all shook our heads and had a bonding moment over the fact that the Japanese understanding of hip hop didn't match our own. They didn't get it. Not like us. Kobe said. 'It's superficial.' And I'm still convinced that he's right but I reckon I need to remove the pejorative from that statement if I'm going to figure out the truth. 'It's superficial [*Booooo!*]' needs to be replaced with 'It's superficial [*Exactly!*]'

The interest of Japanese youth in Western popular culture is hardly something new, whether we're talking surf crazes in the '60s, bell-bottoms and air guitars in the '70s or the current fetish for foppish goth fashion. However, the symbiotic relationship between 'international hip hop culture' (whatever that means) and 'modern Japanese youth culture' (whatever that means) is of a substantively different order and can be understood within the broader context of economic crisis and consequent gradual cultural metamorphosis. While an economy may burst overnight (literally or figuratively), the social structures (of, for example, the education system and employment practices) and the social myths (of, say, racial and class homogeny) that support it cannot react nearly as quickly. These take a while to change.

The success of the post-war Japanese economy was built, at least

---

[21] 'The Social Production Of Difference: Imitation And Authenticity In Japanese Rap Music', Ian Condry *Transactions, Transgressions, and Transformations*, Heide Fehrenbach and Uta G. Poiger (eds), 2000, Berghan Books.

in part, on a regimented and enormously competitive education system. Japanese childhood is frequently a homogenising process – schoolyards, buildings and classrooms are of oppressive, uniform design – that puts little value on creativity or individualism. Of course a rapidly growing economy requires social stability and a capable workforce and this system certainly delivered. But the economic slump has created new and obvious kinds of pressures (within the job market and therefore within familial units) and the rigid education structure is not equipped to deal with them.

A similar argument can be made of employment practices. Traditionally, new graduates have been hired *en masse* each April and this has efficiently located them within the workplace. But the combination of recession and an ageing workforce has reduced the need for this recruitment drive and young people are left unemployed and, perhaps more importantly, alienated from the 'salary-man'[22] ethos on which the economy was built.

The generalised social effects of recession are obvious enough but it is plausible that, in a society built on the strengths of conformity, they might become more extreme. For those still 'lucky' enough to join the ranks of corporate Japan, the work pressures have undoubtedly intensified. In 2001, Japan's suicide tally topped 30,000 for the third year running. For starters, that's about three times the number of people killed in accidents on Japanese roads and, for dessert, almost one third of all recovered suicide notes cited economic struggle as a motive. What's more, it's hard to avoid a sense of 'only in Japan' when you discover that Japanese law can hold companies accountable for a phenomenon known as *karoshi* (death by overwork).

On the other side of the equation, the bursting of the bubble also generated a new group of young people known as 'freeters' (a combination of the English word 'free' and the German word for worker, *Arbeiter*). These are defined as men and women in their

---

[22] The term 'salaryman' refers to all white-collar employees of private companies. They are regarded as the men behind Japan's growth, men with absolute loyalty to the company ethos. It is also, however, sometimes used in a derogatory sense to describe imposed uniformity.

twenties or early thirties who work in part-time or casual jobs (*arubaito*) and generally still live with their parents. Such a description is certainly comparable with the generation X/slacker terminology of '90s America. However, the Japanese equivalent needs to be understood within the context of a more regimented society that has no experience of such a phenomenon. The number of so-called freeters doubled in the decade to 1997.

Of course the new freeter class can be easily explained away as a direct by-product of recession. But most analyses (including that of the Japanese Institute of Labour) accept that for a significant minority their status is a chosen one driven either by a desire to pursue other interests or merely to be non-conformist. It seems to me that economic crisis gradually led to increased questioning of both received wisdoms and the social structures that support them. This questioning may take the form of an Institute of Labour report or something like the brutal satire of the education system in the cult movie *Battle Royale*. And then, of course, there's hip hop.

Japanese hip hop boomed in the mid-'90s as the economic troubles bit and local artists (starting, perhaps, with East End X Yuri's 'Maicca',[23] which reached number three on the singles chart in 1995) began to shift serious units in the local market. If sales have since plateaued, no one doubts the continued potential of the genre. Generally the most successful artists make 'party rap' where lyrical content is secondary to a good pop hook and saleable image. It is true, however, that some emcees have addressed important issues from Japanese ethnicity to sexual exploitation to the education system. In 'Nippon Sei Jijyo' ('Laid In Japan'),[24] for example, Shing02 describes young girls prostituting themselves to afford the latest fashions while King Giddra (since disbanded into their constituent parts of emcees Zeebra and K Dub Shine) are notable for the consciousness of their lyrics on tracks like 'Shinjitsu No Dangan' ('Bullet of Truth'):[25] '*kodomo tachi no yume made hakai shite*

[23] 'Maicca', East End X Yuri, 1995, Epic/Sony.

[24] 'Nippon Sei Jijyo'; Shing02, 1996, Mary Joy.

[25] 'Shinjitsu No Dangan' from the album *Soro Kara No Chikara* (*Power from the Sky*); King Giddra, 1995, P-Vine/BluesInteractions.

kita gakureki-shakai umaku dekita kai?' ('Even the dreams of children have been crushed in our society built on qualifications / How well did you do?')

It seems to me, however, that such lyrical articulation of 'issues' is still the exception rather than the rule. For the vast majority of young people, hip hop remains a vague signifier of 'cool'. That said, I'm beginning to realise that such ephemera may not be so ephemeral after all.

As Yuko expressed it to me, 'Japanese society doesn't like uniqueness. The education system, the workplace, the whole society is like that. As a student, you can be punished for bleaching or dreading. And it's even hard for a man to find a job if he has long hair.'

Hip hop in Japan may have more to do with style than substance but there is a remarkable substance to the style. Choosing to dress in a certain way or wear your hair in a certain way or even burn your skin to a deeper colour may not be the most eloquent form of social debate. But at least the questions are beginning to be asked. It was easy for Oliver, Kobe and me to laugh at the superficiality of the Tokyo scene but I know that, personally, such a reaction told more about my own hip hop territory (demarcated and pissed around) than any wider truth.

I am talking to Rob Jordan, otherwise known as Quietstorm, a Tokyo-based DJ and producer who's worked with all the great innovators of Japanese hip hop from Krush to Kensei. He's American by birth and, I guess, Japanese by inclination, having spent the majority of his childhood and the whole of his adult life in Japan. Softly spoken with shaggy hair and burgeoning beard, he looks more hippy than hip hop and, when he begins to speak, at first he struggles with his English. He hasn't used it in a while.

'The way things are,' he says. 'I'll probably live in Japan my whole life with a Japanese wife and Japanese kids but I will never be completely accepted. I just don't think it's possible. I don't see it as negative, just the way it is. There are always some aspects and nuances that I will be excluded from. I don't think anybody really understands the Japanese.'

Then he turns to where I come from. 'A lot of people,' he observes quietly, 'say Japan and Britain are kind of alike: historical island nations, resistant to outsiders and change.'

As observations go, this isn't so cute. Despite the worst efforts of post-colonial nationalism, the Britain I know is a European multi-culture that puts many other European multicultures to shame. But Rob's comment still resonates for me as I remember the society in which I grew up.

One premise of this book is that hip hop is a global culture and, as such, finds expression both transnationally and locally. The globa-lisation of hip hop doesn't mean the homogenous consumption of a homogenous product but rather the diversification of a culture that is reinterpreted and/or reinvented internationally and nationally and by city, small group and individual. Condry (again) illustrates this elegantly in his discussion of the intro to Japanese emcee ECD's album *Big Youth*:[26] 'He . . . describes the arrival of hip hop in Japan as a flying spark (*tobihi*) that traveled from the Bronx across the ocean to light a fire. This image of a flying spark is important, for it reminds us that although popular music styles travel on the winds of global capitalism, they ultimately burn or die out on local fuel.'[27] However, just as the local fuel lights reinventions and reinterpreta-tions that promote transnational dialogue and understanding, so it can also combust misunderstandings and stereotypes.

Arjun Appadurai has written that '. . . electronic mediation and mass migration mark the world of the present not as technically new forces but as ones that seem to impel (and sometimes compel) the work of the imagination.'[28]

Contemporary Japan doesn't know much about mass migration even if the Japanese imagination has been given plenty of informa-tion to process by the electronic media. In this context, it is unsurprising that the collision of economic depression and the ubiquity of mass-media African-American imagery have given rise

---

[26] *Big Youth*, ECD, 1997, Cutting Edge.

[27] 'A History Of Japanese Hip Hop', Ian Condry, *Global Noise*, Tony Mitchell (ed.), 2001, Wesleyan University Press.

[28] *Modernity At Large*, Arjun Appadurai, 1996, University of Minnesota Press.

to crass interpretations of hip hop in particular and blackness in general.

In our globalised world, exoticisation has become both tool and luxury for the powerful. And this can be represented by tie-dye clubbers on the Goan trail, or pashmina-wrapped lunching ladies, or middle-class white kids dancing to a hip hop break. I finally feel that I have a decent snapshot of hip hop Japan but, unfortunately, I had to take a snapshot of myself too, and the personal prints in my fifteen-year-old photo album are none too flattering.

But none of this talk of crass exoticisation is meant to denigrate the 'realness' of Japanese hip hop culture. My initial assumption was that it simply articulated a view of the wider world (of black America in particular). And sure enough it does. But, just as my desire to find my essence of hip hop seems to force me to look at my reflection, so Japanese hip hop culture is a mirror to its society.

I asked the blackface girl Kioko why she liked hip hop. 'Because it's cool,' she said and I marvelled at such a vacuous answer. But now, for all my worries about appropriation, objectification and exoticisation, I can't ignore the idea that 'cool' matters in a city where 'cool' is a signifier for social change. I guess that, for Kioko, beauty is skin deep. But I guess that Japanese society may be changing from the outside in. And I guess that hip hop is probably the number-one cosmetic. And there's the cultural alchemy.

We're on our way out of Harlem. It's four a.m. but the club's still rocking. Maybe the Japanese really know how to party or maybe they're just waiting for the underground to open because they know (as I'm about to find out) that cabs in this city cost a fortune. Whatever. Even if Kanyasu wants to stay on the dancefloor, I need to get out of here. I'm drunk so I'm feeling confused. Or I'm confused so I'm feeling drunk. Definitely one of the two. Definitely.

Then, approaching the door, I see this black guy coming the other way and it's only the cheeky fuck who pinched Kanyasu's arse. His face is concealed by the brim of his baseball cap and I feel myself bristle. It's not like I really want a ruck but I want him to know that he can't go around treating women like that.

As he sidles past me, I drop my shoulder firmly into his and he spins round. I can see his face in the strobe light and he smiles. I see his mouth form the word 'sorry' but I can't hear anything or catch an accent. More to the point, he's just a kid, no more than sixteen, and all my ruminations about racial and cultural realities are suddenly thrown into an absurd and uncomfortable light. He's a kid, first and last, and I find myself looking around the club at the other kids' faces – black, white and Japanese – as they dance to the hip hop break and drink like morning never comes and hit on each other with varying degrees of confidence and competence. As Kanyasu said, 'They're just kids. What do you expect?' And what did I expect because, no disrespect to hip hop Japan, but I'm back to where I started, to P.M. Dawn. 'Reality used to be a friend of mine' and I need to get out of here. Or maybe a Japanese writer summed it up best: 'My reality seemed to have left me and now was wandering around nearby.'[29] I need to get out of here to find it.

[29] *The Wind-Up Bird Chronicle* Haruki Murakami, 1997, Vintage.

Part Three: Johannesburg
How Many Mics[1]

I've spent a lot of time in South Africa. But it's been a while. And, now I come to think of it, most of the more recent visits have been brief and specific; to do this or that job, to go to such and such a wedding or to visit so and so. I haven't been to South Africa *like this* – eyes open, wallet closed – for more than a decade.

It was 1990, just before Mandela was released from Robben Island, and I was teaching in Zimbabwe. I hitched down from Harare to Beit Bridge with an English friend – two eighteen-year-olds with bedraggled hair, knee-length shorts and flip-flops. I remember we had some minor hassle at the border where an Afrikaans immigration officer didn't like the look of us and locked us in an interview room for a couple of hours. Just because he could, I thought.

In retrospect I wonder if it had something to do with my mate's tie-dye T-shirt with the slogan 'Samora Machel – Aluta Continua!' pasted across the front. At the time, I hardly knew who Samora Machel was, let alone the 'struggle' that 'continued' and I barely acknowledged that the Mozambican civil war was tailspinning to a bloody conclusion no more than 300 miles away. I probably just thought, Cool T-shirt.

We caught a combi from Beit Bridge that arrived in Johannesburg just before sunset. My friend was going to stay with a relative and he was picked up from the downtown Holiday Inn. I didn't really know where I was or what I was doing so I found a dirt-cheap

[1] 'How Many Mics' from *The Score*, the Fugees, 1996, Columbia.

hotel room in Hillbrow. That evening I pulled on jeans and trainers and went out exploring on my own. A stone's throw from the hotel, I was stopped by two guys who demanded my wallet. I handed it over without a murmur. Then they demanded my trainers; a two-year-old pair of Jordans, my pride and joy. I slipped them off, wandered back to the hotel room in my socks, locked the door and went to bed. I wonder if they knew they'd consigned me to a month's travelling in flip-flops. I don't suppose they cared. They probably just thought, Cool *tackies*.[2]

We're driving through downtown Jo'burg in a clapped-out Golf with Dylan Lloyd. Dylan's a dreadlocked white Zimbabwean who shoots music documentaries and local hip hop videos and he's agreed to show us around. A decade ago in Harare, Dylan used to rhyme with two emcees I knew called Tendayi and Herb. I don't think I met Dylan back then but we must have hung out in the same clubs and bars, no more than one handshake apart (me and Dylan and Mike Ladd too, I guess). These days Herb is putting out tunes in Germany under the name Metaphysics. And Tendayi? He teaches forensic psychology at the University of Kent. Of course he does. But it wasn't actually Tendayi or Herb who hooked me up with Dylan. That was through Tam, an Anglo-Indian friend of mine (and another film-maker) who knew Dylan through Appleseed, a black Zimbabwean who used to be part of Bongo Maffin, one of the first and most successful kwaito crews. Kwaito? We'll come back to that. But the point of all this is that it's a small and shrinking hip hop planet.

Kanyasu's excited to be back in Jo'burg. She lived here for six months a few years ago and she's leaning forward from the back seat and asking question after question. But I barely register what she's saying because driving through the city centre makes me feel like Kurt Russell in *Escape from New York*; i.e., a stranger in a treacherous neighbourhood, only without the muscles and guns and Holly-wood immortality. These days downtown is a dingy place of

---

[2] *Tackies* is South African slang for trainers; sorry, sneakers. I find it strange and somehow quaint that, despite international hip hop slang, global footwear nonetheless seems to be locally identified.

crumbling buildings, street hustling and crime as the vast majority of big companies have jumped ship for high-security fortresses in affluent suburbs like Sandton. I pull my baseball cap low and slump in my seat as I peer out of the window and ponder memorised South African statistics: like a 34 per cent rise in violent crime between 1994 and 2000, like 1 in 3 crimes being violent in nature (in the UK it's 1 in 20) and a murder rate of 59 per 100,000 in 1998 (compared to just 9 per 100,000 in neighbouring Zimbabwe that year).

I feign a yawn and my stretching arm just happens to snap down the lock on the passenger door. If Dylan doesn't notice that, he's certainly figured I'm spooked because he starts telling me how Jo'burg's not nearly as bad as everybody says. He claims that white South Africans in particular seem to take a perverse pleasure from their stories of how a friend of a friend was jackrolled[3] or murdered in their beds or shot for their mobile phone. Dylan then stalls the Golf at a junction and, while I chew my knuckles and he tries to restart the engine, he notes the happy coincidence that we seem to have stopped right at the spot where he was jumped at knife-point the previous year. Dylan thinks this is funny. I can't help but think that I've seen few urban realities as gritty and as grim as this.

Reality. One aeroplane step from Tokyo, one day in Jo'burg and I'm already back to that word and beginning to feel like the search for my essence of hip hop is perhaps more of a search for some kind of reality. But what do I mean in my use of the word? In New York, for example, I found myself questioning the fantastical narratives of the current crop of emcees and their use of the language of fiction, like 'episode' and 'drama'. In Tokyo, on the other hand, I was turned off by the appropriation of hip hop symbolism to express realities that just weren't 'real enough' for me. So what exactly is the reality I'm after? I'm coming to understand that it is only a reality of my imagination, a reality that I have experienced vicariously

---

[3] 'Jackrolled' is South African slang meaning the forceful abduction of women. It became commonplace in the late '80s, taken from a gang of kidnappers called the Jackrollers who operated in the Diepkloof area of Soweto.

through hip hop music for the past fifteen years, an imagined urban reality of discrimination, alienation and ghetto-isation.

One of the buzz words of our era is 'glocalisation'. Wheeled out ad nauseam by hip cultural critics, it frequently seems to defy definition. However, in its most obvious meaning – the concurrent process of globalisation and localisation – it can evidently be applied to all aspects of popular culture but hip hop more than any. And vicarious experience of reality is one of glocalisation's chief effects: authenticity is no longer necessarily an inherent part of culture but can be ascribed by its consumers.

Take hip hop's number-one pariah, Vanilla Ice. In the early '90s, he was dissed and dismissed as 'fake'. Sure, his music was the paradigm of wack, but it is inarguable that he floundered as much on his own success and the subsequent publicity given to his middle-class background. It is easy to forget that Robert Van Winkle was regarded as a competent emcee before Capitol's marketing guys got their hands on him; just as it is easy to forget that other credible artists (Gangstarr's Guru, for example) come from similarly 'un-ghetto' backgrounds. Of course Vanilla Ice didn't help himself with his pseudo-gangsta posturing but he didn't fade from the limelight because he was wack nor because the rest of hip hop said he was wack. No. He faded from the limelight because the ten million kids who bought *To The Extreme*[4] decided he was wack. And it's a fair assumption (even without the benefit of stats) that the vast majority of these kids were not from the poor neighbourhoods of urban America and were probably pretty wack themselves.

I never figured I'd be defending the Ice Man. But, like I've said all along, key hip hop language is flexible in its meaning and it is this flexibility that goes part of the way to explain the global hip hop phenomenon.

Glocalised consumption has ensured that hip hop themes (of 'wackness', say, or 'reality') find their meanings on the canvases of countless teenage imaginations. So I find myself experiencing a city that reminds me of a film rather than a film that reminds me of a city

---

[4] *To The Extreme*, Vanilla Ice, 1990, Capitol.

(and personal fiction outweighs objective fact). So I find that the hip hop reality I'm after – black and urban and rough – is, for me at least, little more than a personal invention. So I find myself driving through downtown Jo'burg, an environment that suits my criteria better than most, and here I am snapping down locks, shrinking into my seat and waiting for the engine to turn over so we can get the fuck out of here.

We're sitting in Rosebank mall with Mizchif, one of the stalwarts of the Johannesburg scene. At first, the setting seems inappropriate for such a meeting. Relaxing outside a coffee house called the Tribeca Café on the pristine flagstones of an air-conned suburban mall, it's hardly very hip hop and this homogenised urban experience could be anywhere in the world. Then again, maybe that's the point. Besides, it seemed the easiest place to catch up since it's the location for the show Mizchif's presenting on Channel O;[5] a hip hop show called, wait for it, *Where Ya At* (nice spelling).

An easy-going character in combats, cable-knit black jumper and a camouflage cap, he's got that strange Creole accent that's commonplace among young urbanites from English-speaking Africa. It's hard to characterise: a very proper use of the language undercut by a mixture of African-American and local inflections and slang. If the source of such an accent can sometimes seem arcane, in Mizchif's case it's fully explained by his transient upbringing. Another Zimbabwean by birth, his dad is an academic (a theologian) who relocated the family to the States when Mizchif was in his early teens to complete a PhD at Syracuse University in upstate New York. Later, they moved to the city following a job offer at NYU and lived first in Brooklyn and then Southern Boulevard in the Bronx.

'I won't lie,' Mizchif explains. 'I didn't grow up in a township or live in the rural areas for more than a month in my life so I think I'd be faking it if I tried to identify with that. I used to love rock music.

[5] Channel O is a South African music television channel that broadcasts all over Africa.

I was into Wham, Duran Duran, Depeche Mode and all that stuff. I
wanted to be a rock drummer.

'When we went to the States, I got into hip hop under peer
pressure, to tell you the truth. I was this African kid in New York
and I had to deal with all the stereotypes. Did you live in a tree?
How come you run so fast? Did you used to get chased by lions? So,
to me, I had no other way of connecting to those people without
getting into their medium.'

Mizchif came to South Africa in 1994, immediately after the
elections, clutching a demo he'd recorded in New York. He sent it
to Tusk, a local record label, but they said it was 'too American',
that no one would understand it let alone buy music like that by an
African artist. They told him he should come back to them in a
couple of years when he'd learned something about South Africa.

'It was good advice. Because there was a lot more culture here
than I'd thought, hip hop culture. People take hip hop more serious
here, especially in Cape Town. Even though I lived in New York
for six years, I didn't really begin to learn about hip hop until I came
back to Africa.' Nonetheless, Mizchif admits that he returns to New
York every year. 'Just to stay in the game, man,' he says. 'Just to stay
in the game.' And his accent suddenly vibrates with that unmistakable East Coast hum.

Mizchif's debut EP, *Life From All Angles*,[6] was released in 2000.
He admits it didn't sell a lot, but claims, 'It drew attention to where
hip hop could go, to the possibilities of a South African kind of hip
hop.' He starts to get animated as he warms to his theme. 'Hip hop
to me? It's global music because we've all got something different to
say. I can't talk about Philly Blunts. There are no Philly Blunts or
drop-top Lexuses here. So I talk about the miners; the fact that a
miner's life expectancy is no more than forty-five. I talk about the
way emcees in the States wear platinum. I don't mind them wearing
it but don't glorify it because you don't know what your African
fathers have gone through to dig it up. You know, like, three
quarters of the platinum in the world comes from here in South
Africa. Americans are very arrogant and sometimes stupid. They

---

[6] *Life From All Angles*, Mizchif, 2000, Eargasm Entertainment.

want to talk about Africa when it suits them but they don't take time to understand it.'

Like Dead Prez. It's a story that's been doing the rounds since we arrived in Jo'burg. If anybody wants to explain why South African hip hop is different, it's the example they use. 'Like that whole Dead Prez situation,' they say.

Dead Prez are just about as conscious as US hip hop gets these days (and they're certainly not, in Kenyatta's terms, 'Fort Green'); a duo from Virginia (Stic Man and M1) who have picked up the slack left by the likes of Public Enemy and KRS. Their platinum-selling debut album, *Let's Get Free*,[7] is an intelligent if raging assault on the racial status quo whose subject matter leaps from FBI involvement in the crack game to the foolishness of hip hop materialism via the merits of a vegetarian diet. It also, unsurprisingly, preaches a radical gospel of African identity. I interviewed them just after the release of *Let's Get Free*. This is the kind of thing they were saying.

Stic Man: 'We recognise Africa as including not just people born on the continent but citizens scattered around the world by colonialism. I met this black dude in Amsterdam. He was, like, "I'm Dutch." And I said, "What?" The truth is people have been assimilated, in mind and fact, by their colonisers.'

M1: 'When we say, "I'm an African," it means we recognise that our identity historically and presently is one and the same. All we are now is a consequence of what we've been. That sounds simple but it's important. It means, for example, that our roots are not slavery because that is only one part of the African experience and Africa was the cradle for a whole lot of important and positive shit.'

Of course, some kind of assumed African identity has been a key signifier of hip hop since time, whether simply an appropriated symbol or a key political or religious agenda. Generally, however, this assumption means little more than a romanticised notion that always reminds me of things like the poetry of the Harlem Renaissance (of Langston Hughes or Countee Cullen) or the

[7] *Let's Get Free*, Dead Prez, 2000, Loud.

literature of Negritude in '30s Paris.[8] For all the bluster, few of the big hip hop names have actually visited the continent. After all, even South Africa (the largest and most Westernised economy) isn't a staple of the international touring circuit and, more to the point, it's hardly a key market. Consequently, hip hop's so-called 'Afrocentricity' often brings to mind Wole Soyinka's scathing criticism of Negritude: 'A tiger doesn't proclaim it's tigritude; it acts.'[9]

Dead Prez, however, did choose to tour. They were here just a month or so ago and the city's still talking about it.

Mizchif explains: 'Dead Prez left so much conflict amongst heads, it was hectic. They had said that the cover of their album [a sepia-touched photograph of black women waving guns above their heads] was the Soweto Uprising.[10] But it wasn't. Actually, as a Zimbabwean, I know it was from the *chimurenga*.[11] No one had guns at the Soweto Uprising except the cops. So, before Dead Prez even got here, people had beef about that. Then they came on Yfm [a local radio station] and they were just preaching their revolutionary stuff – "Don't rely on the man", that kind of thing. At the time kids were calling in going, "Yeah, I feel you, man. Fuck white people." But the minute they left, everyone was saying, "Who are they to come to South Africa and tell us about our struggle?"

'It's difficult because there's already so much conflict between people here because the focus of the rest of the world has always been on Soweto. But there's been struggle all over; every township had struggles from Soweto to Guguletu.'[12]

I ask Mizchif what he thought, personally, and he laughs. 'I just thought it was funny because the Dead Prez show was half and half,

---

[8] The kind of thing I'm talking about is, for example, Nas's portrayal of himself as pharaoh on the cover of his 1999 album *I Am*; one example among many.

[9] *Myth, Literature and the African World*, Wole Soyinka, 1976, Cambridge.

[10] On 16 June 1976, 15,000 black students walked out of their Soweto schools to protest against apartheid in the most significant demonstration since the early '60s. Up to 100 students were killed by police trying to forcibly quash what was initially a peaceful demonstration.

[11] *Chimurenga* is a Zimbabwean (Shona) word meaning struggle. It is specifically used to refer to the war of independence.

[12] Guguletu is the largest black township of the Cape Flats outside Cape Town.

white and black. Because who has the money and the transport to get to a show like that?'

I think back to the Mos Def gig in London; a performance to the self-consciously conscious. I mention it to Mizchif and he shakes his head and smiles.

'Really, it's just typical of Americans. They have such a stereotyped view of Africa. When I was at high school in New York, my father ended up coming to teach our Social Studies class because, when I took the worksheets about Africa home, he was absolutely disgusted. Yes there's a rural Africa and a poor Africa and Aids in Africa but there are modern and urban and rich sides too.'

We're staying with Dylan; it's a palatial apartment that boasts a view of the whole city. The only trouble is, it's in Yeoville and this neighbourhood's developed quite a reputation. It used to be the very heart of Johannesburg nightlife; Rockey Street buzzed with clubs and cafés and restaurants and bars. But, like Hillbrow before it, crime chased away the white wealth to the suburbs. So Melville's the hot spot these days.

Dylan wants to buy his place but the area's mortgage blacklisted and nobody will front the money. White South African friends say we must be crazy to stay in Yeoville. They say they used to hang out on Rockey Street five years ago but they haven't been back for ages. Dylan claims that there's not much crime right now; not since the money left, anyway.

We eat at Supper Club, a Yeoville staple where a few rand buys you a plate of top-notch home cooking and the company of whoever's knocking about. The usual open-door policy has just been replaced by a membership scheme after an attack on another joint nearby. Last week, Sunday night, there was a stick-up at Tandoor (an Indian restaurant-cum-club and Yeoville institution) and all the punters were robbed at gunpoint.

After eating, we play pool with a couple of the regulars and this story is repeated, reprocessed and refined. What time of night was it? What kind of guns were they packing? How many of them were there? 'They were the famous five,' someone suggests. No. There were more of them than that. 'The dirty dozen,' he tries and everyone nods and laughs and the story is complete.

Monday Night Blues at Times Square on Raleigh Street is a spoken-word event and the small bar is packed. Poets and emcees and musicians wait their turn to take the stage. It's a mixed bag: a white Mozambican ska band (seriously) is followed by an old drunkard who scats over some lazy jazz. The audience is similarly diverse: predominantly black but a whole range of ages, fashions and manners. There are old dudes, laughing and getting toped on the sofas, skinny dreadlocks in red, gold and green, buff slickers in suits propping up the bar and feisty women with headscarves and attitude. I meet one of the emcees from Cashless Society,[13] one of the VJs from Channel O, a bubbly stand-up comic, and a white thirtysomething Londoner. I'm sure Dylan introduces him as something like 'the Admiral'. But he says his name's Andy. From Golders Green.

Most of the emcees and poets are women. While they sometimes preface their performance or crack a joke in Sotho or Zulu, their work is exclusively in English. It's a bizarre kind of scenario. Their subject matter and posturing and even accents smack of an American spoken-word circuit (that I've seen round Greenwich Village, say, or Haight-Ashbury in San Francisco) and, to me, the whole vibe seems kind of incongruous in the setting, irrelevant even. Dylan is cynical in his assessment. 'Everyone's got something different to say,' he remarks, echoing Mizchif. Then he adds, 'And nobody's listening to each other. Like that Fugees thing: "Too many emcees and not enough mics".'

A young woman called Miriam shyly performs some blank verse about sex with her boyfriend in a voice that lilts with American cadences. 'He sucks my breast like a real man should,' she says and the old dudes kill themselves laughing and I can't help but join in.

Later I'm chatting to Andy by the bar. He's lived here since 1994. He asks what I think of the place and I shrug because I haven't got it

---

[13] In 2001, Cashless Society actually released a track called 'Blaze Tha Breaks' on Bobbito Garcia's respected (and now defunct) Fondle 'Em label. This is the only time I know of a Jo'burg hip hop act getting an American release.

figured yet. He says he reckons South Africa will be fine when nobody considers it the West any more and everyone admits it's Africa. It's a throwaway comment, I'm sure, but it gets me thinking. I wonder what he means by 'Africa' and I wonder how many different answers you'd get to that question from the fifty million South African citizens.

In the aftermath of apartheid, in the fallout from democracy, and a step beyond the platitudes of 'Rainbow Nation', South Africans face new (or at least newly poignant) questions of race and class and generation and gender (in among the more basic ones of poverty and politics). Of course Thabo Mbeki's repeated calls for an African renaissance are largely framed within the laudable aims of speedy democratisation, developing technology, economic independence and forcing a reassessment of the way Africa represents itself and is represented worldwide. However, he has also been keen to stress the importance of an African philosophy and the vital role of young people.[14] These, too, are undoubtedly worthy concerns but they seem to deny the dynamic, interactive and, above all, international nature of popular culture.

Now this cultural osmosis is actually nothing new. Musically, the development of indigenous South African sounds throughout the twentieth century (from *marabi* in the '30s to *kwela* in the '50s to *mbaqanga* in the '60s) was made possible by the success of jazz in the USA. Politically, the South African nationalist movements of the '60s borrowed symbolism, tactics and philosophy from their coun-terparts in America's civil-rights campaign. These days, however, the stuff of popular culture is synchronously experienced by all con-tinents at once. This is not to say that popular culture is identically consumed (if Tokyo taught me anything, it taught me that); merely that it is consumed beyond nation and, in South Africa, a commu-nity like Yeoville is a prime example of this. Yeoville may be rough

[14] Check out two speeches from October 2000, for example. Speaking in Accra on the fifth, he described Western culture as denying 'the validity of our knowledge systems, our morals and ethics . . .' A couple of days earlier in Abuja he said the African renaissance meant 'channelling the energy and exuberance of the youth so that they who represent the future must begin to build that better future'.

but it's also cosmopolitan and therefore a significant boxing ring for this battle royale of national and personal character.

So for all my inner giggling at Miriam the poet's appropriated Americanisms I don't believe she's simply trying to say the same things as her Stateside counterparts. Rather she is using the tools at her disposal to authentically express her (African) identity and if this occurs at a symbolic rather than literal level of meaning then so be it. In Tokyo, I found hip hop culture that struggled against ascribed and homogenous identity. Perhaps here, hip hop can be a forum for reconciling seemingly conflicting definitions of who you are and this is necessarily an imaginative and associative process rather than an exact science.

Yfm is an extraordinary success story. A black-music radio station in Lorentzville, it was founded in 1997 and granted a broadcast licence for Gauteng Province. It is now the biggest provincial radio station in South Africa, attracting 1.5 million listeners every week, and it's made national superstars of its top DJs.

Tonight is the *Rap Activity Jam*, one of the station's most popular shows, and the poky building is packed with B-Boys. Some of them are in their best gear – basketball vests, trainers and baggy jeans held up by belts with Ruff Ryders buckles – while others are still in school uniform. I guess it depends on their age and how far they've had to mission to get here.

Every week, the *Jam* allows several unknown local hip hop crews to battle rhyme live on air and listeners ring in and vote the winners forward to a monthly final. It's tough competition even to make it on to the show. Outside on the wall there is some scrawled graffiti. 'I just want to freestyle,' it reads, and it's easy to picture a would-be emcee scribbling his frustration.

The DJs are a good-looking dread who goes by the name of Rude Boy Paul and a thick-set older guy called Oscar (Warona). Paul's the real hip hop head; Oscar's better known as one of the founders of the kwaito scene.

The MOP hit 'Cold As Ice'[15] is playing as a gaggle of kids cluster

---

[15] 'Cold As Ice', MOP, 2001, Sony.

around two mics, their heads bobbing to the heavy rhythm and their school ties pulled down to their chests or knotted at the waist. As he begins to fade the record, Paul asks them to introduce themselves. Trouble is, there are six of them and they all want to be heard and every time one of them speaks, his words are drowned out by a chorus of 'for reals' and 'no doubts'. Like Dylan said, 'Too many emcees and not enough mics'.

Paul cues up a Rawkus instrumental. It's an obscure Mad Skillz track – I don't know it and can't spot the revolving title – and an unkind choice, with skittering, irregular beats that don't suit the rhymes the emcees have prepared (of course, if they were genuinely going to battle, they ought to be freestyling anyway). They start off OK, each taking their turn to drop a couplet of indecipherable English sprinkled with *tsotsitaal*.[16] But then the shortest kid has to crane his neck to reach the mic and he loses his flow and, like falling dominoes, sends his boys reeling out of time. It doesn't help that the other competing crews are watching from the sofas that line the walls and they shake their heads and giggle as the emcees stumble to the end of the track.

Oscar sticks a microphone under my nose. 'This is a guy from London writing a book about hip hop around the world,' he says. 'Is there anything you want to ask them about South Africa?'

If he's caught me by surprise, the rappers are like springboks in the headlights and it looks like the short kid might bolt any second.

'So how long have you guys been listening to hip hop?' I begin.

One of them pipes up, 'About three months', and everybody in the studio packs up laughing.

Paul smiles, amused and tolerant: 'And you think you're ready to be an emcee?'

'Why do you rhyme in English?' I ask and even as I frame the question I feel a little guilty. None of them has an answer to this and Paul has to bluster some filler as they slope out of the studio.

Later Kanyasu has a dig at me. She thinks I was mocking them, though I didn't mean to. 'They're just kids copying what they see,' she says. 'What do you expect?'

---

[16] *Tsotsitaal* is township slang. It is derived from the word *tsotsi* meaning thief.

It's pretty much the same comment she made in Tokyo.

The next crew up is a four-man outfit who call themselves Optical Illusion. A little older and a little more savvy than the first lot, they ride the beats with easy confidence. Even if their rhymes are largely patchworks of soundbites and cartoonish phrases bitten from American emcees (the use of Wu-Tang's 'C.R.E.A.M.'[17] acronym or the rhyming of 'equator' with 'playa hater', for example), they're still the clear winners.

We catch up with them in the Yfm lobby. Romeo, who's twenty and looks the oldest by a year or two, does most of the talking. He says they've got some serious plans. They do all their own artwork, flyers and marketing, burn their own CDs and sell them where they can. Don't they want to get signed to a label? Romeo shrugs. They don't want to sell out, he says.

One of the other emcees, Genocide, chips in, 'South Africa's not ready for us yet.'

I ask them how they got into hip hop and what attracted them to the music in the first place, but it seems it's more than just lyrics they've borrowed from American rappers. Their answers could be lifted from any interview in *The Source*; they're all-purpose hip hop mantras that are trotted out by emcees the world over.

Romeo says, 'Hip hop is basically a lifestyle. It's about the people. The people make up hip hop. Without the people hip hop is nothing.'

Genocide agrees (I think): 'You look at me and you see hip hop. I am hip hop. My life is hip hop. Through hip hop I widen my thoughts. It's about the way I live. Like, this is my rhyme: "Words are seeds thrown on igneous rock, hard ground." Basically what I'm saying is that people rap stuff that doesn't mean anything. We're about the ghetto life of where we come from but other rappers are not as deep as the words they say.'

This seems like an unintentionally ironic observation. I try to push them to expand upon what they're getting at but I just get more of the same. Do they think their struggles are similar to

---

[17] 'C.R.E.A.M. (Cash Rules Everything Around Me)', Wu-Tang Clan, 1994, BMG.

American rappers'? 'No doubt. It's all one struggle.' But there must be differences too? 'Of course. But you just got to represent yourself, represent ghetto life. Hip hop gives me something to belong to.'

In my desire to elicit more personal answers, perhaps, I stop listening. Because it's only later, when I transcribe the tape of this conversation that I realise that, in this instance, this is the point: *belonging*.

Hip hop is a globalised medium that is locally adapted to articulate local concerns, no doubt. But it is also a source of potent and abstract symbolism. Are these South African rappers telling me what they think I want to hear? Possibly. Are they telling me what they think they ought to say? Sure. But in this case I reckon the meaning of each phrase is irrelevant compared to what the phrases signify. As the kids outside the Roots project in New York adopted talk-show truisms, as Dead Prez clung to an African identity, as Miriam the poet adopted the persona of black-American feminism, so Optical Illusion are using their hip hop soundbites as signifiers of their membership of a community. Just like the regulars at Supper Club creating fiction from the harsh realities of Jo'burg, these kids intuitively understand the importance of a good story. And that, as Appadurai expressed it, is a 'work of the imagination'.

I keep thinking back to New York: when a black kid uses Ebonics, he's down and alienated but a white record exec using the same is down with alienation. So which model do this lot conform to? Arguably both. Their appropriation of this language is a tool that allows them both to express the realities of township life and at the same time see beyond them. It sounds like a useful kind of tool to me.

Over the years, numerous hip hop artists have told me that hip hop is 'like a religion' and I've always thought that the genre has that aspect to it in its core rituals, symbols and rules that are both specific and oblique. Now I'm also coming to realise that the use of hip hop slang bears some resemblance to communal prayer, in that its significance is frequently in the context and act of its speaking rather than the meanings of the words themselves.

With the *Rap Jam* finished, Optical Illusion are heading out and we touch knuckles. Peace. One love. Suddenly, out of nowhere, there's another emcee on the scene who's spotted my microphone and wants to have his say. He's an ebullient little dude of about sixteen whose every overblown gesture is taken straight from a Hype Williams video. He lurches towards the mic: 'Yo yo! Listen up! My name's Gorgeous and I'm gonna be the first African rap superstar! I'm the African DMX,[18] y'all, for real!' His accent is a perfect gravelly pastiche of the Dark Man. As Romeo's heading out of the door, he turns and catches my eye. Just as hip hop is globalised and glocalised, so too are definitions of wack.

We're just about to leave Yfm when we run into Andy, the English guy we met at Monday Night Blues. It turns out I did hear Dylan right because he's also known as the Admiral and he's a DJ and recording artist who hosts the station's ragga show. Now here's a story. His parents were South Africans who fled apartheid. Working as a printer in London in the late '80s, Andy joined the ANC and helped out printing their leaflets and propaganda. Later, he decided to take his commitment more seriously and headed for Angola to train with the ANC's military wing, Umkhonto We Sizwe (Spear of the Nation) known as MK. After the 1994 elections, all of MK were promised jobs in the new South Africa so Andy moved with them. But he'd grown up in London going out to the ragga sound systems in Harlesden and Willesden and he'd always wanted to make music. And he did. It's a remarkable story but Jo'burg's that kind of place.

Even if you accept that authenticity of identity can be a creation of imagination and that local Jo'burg kids buy in to the language of (American) hip hop more for the metaphorical badges of membership than any more considered reasons, the older brokers of the local culture are certainly preoccupied with 'real hip hop'. Specifically they are quick to point out the failings of the current American scene and eager to develop ideas that will enable South African hip hop to stand apart and on its own.

---

[18] New Yorker DMX (a.k.a. Dark Man X) was the first artist of any genre to have his first three albums enter the Billboard chart at number one.

Blaze is a twenty-eight-year-old coloured guy.[19] Originally from Cape Town, he moved to Jo'burg a decade ago. One of the country's top DJs, he has a mix show on Yfm and plays at clubs and parties all over the city. Until the venue closed down last year, he also ran Metropolis at the weekends. It was a kind of hip hop Saturday school that ran workshops in the 'four elements' (one more time for you: breaking, rapping, turntablism and graffiti art) in the morning followed by a club all afternoon. A lanky dude with a seemingly permanent frown, Blaze is a considered character – which makes his voice all the more unlikely; a nasal Cape Flats accent is twisted by a strange slur that gives him a trace of something halfway between Jimmy Cagney and Elmer Fudd. At first he also appears to be suspicious of my questions and seems happier chatting to Kanyasu. But when he starts talking it's hard to get him to stop.

'You can't trust American hip hop any more. They know that seventy per cent of the consumers are white suburbans so they're just trying to make music that will intrigue them. Take "Move Somethin'".[20] You can hear that shit was made similar to Pharoahe Monch's "Simon Says".[21] The white kids liked "Simon Says" so Talib knew that shit's gonna happen. You see? American hip hop is cloned instead of artistically developed. It's all watered down. You can be, like, "Fuck the white man", but if you don't really understand it you'd better shut up. Although, to be honest, if you can influence a kid to think in a non-mainstream way then that's OK with me.

'That's why we've got to prove this shit works in Africa. We take conscious hip hop, we take the beats – because you know Africans got rhythm – and we challenge the way people think. What's hip hop about? It's always been about borrowing things from here and

---

[19] I'm using the word 'coloured' in a politically incorrect, 'when in Rome' kind of way to mean of historically mixed racial heritage. I know a lot of people find it offensive and pejorative but it is nonetheless still in widespread use in South Africa, partly because it means something different from the more palatable 'mixed race'.

[20] 'Move Somethin' ', Talib Kweli and Hi-Tek, 2000, Priority/Rawkus.

[21] 'Simon Says', Pharoahe Monch, 2000, Rawkus.

there and making the most of the material you have. You think South Africans don't understand that better than anybody?

'Let me tell you something: everything gets played out. Right now? The way I feel? I think American hip hop's played out. That's why it's our time to shine. Hip hop has to be shaped in an African way. I want to see hip hop cultures all over Africa that improve situations for their people. You only have to look at the world right now to know a change is coming and you gotta be ready. Hip hop is a common denominator. You can understand all youth cultures through this medium so maybe, in the future, we can use it to assist communities all over Africa and the rest of the world too.'

In some ways, this is typical hip hop bombast; big on soundbites and short on substance. He even includes the slightly millenarian 'change is coming' line that's a standard for American rappers (like, for example, the complete canon of Busta Rhymes albums from *When Disaster Strikes*[22] to *Genesis*[23] via *Extinction Level Event*.[24] An aside: I sometimes figure there's something slightly cargo cultish about hip hop – an overblown and almost ritualised materialism that sits side by side with doom-laden prophecies of Armageddon.) Blaze says hip hop can 'assist communities all over Africa' but, when push comes to shove, it's hardly surprising he can't illuminate how that might happen.

He admits that record companies in South Africa still don't understand the music, they're reluctant to sign hip hop acts and, when they do, they don't know how to promote them. More to the point, he also admits that the majority of the people who listen to hip hop in Jo'burg are more into the 'image' than the 'hardcore'. Nevertheless, he claims that the 'hardcore' (the heads, those who know their history and support every hip hop form) will always prevail.

Blaze has it figured like this: 'People who are into the clothes and the cars and the girls and the jiggy shit? They're temporary. Either they become hardcore or they get into something else. That's why

[22] *When Disaster Strikes*, Busta Rhymes, 1997, WEA/Elektra.
[23] *Genesis*, Busta Rhymes, 2002, BMG/J Records.
[24] *Extinction Level Event*, Busta Rhymes, 1998, WEA/Elektra.

the hardcore always comes out on top. Because they're stronger, deeper, more educated.' It's a comment that again takes me back to Stefano in Rome.

At this point, the guy's opinions start to get really interesting. He talks reverentially about 'old-school cats' like Public Enemy and KRS One as a source of information about black empowerment; how, as a kid, this music changed the way he thought.

I guess I know what he's getting at. We're about the same age so we can easily talk about the same music (even if our experience of it was very different). Nonetheless, I challenge him on this because when I listen to those old-school tunes now I realise that, even at their most lucid, Chuck D and Kris Parker were no more than polemicists. Blaze looks at me like I'm a fool and he addresses his answer to Kanyasu. 'People say hip hop is education but I don't see it like that. Hip hop is more like a religion to me that introduces me to other areas of study.'

The religion metaphor again and of course he's right. I know, personally, that it was my love of hip hop that led me to love its antecedents: soul, funk and jazz. And just as it was hip hop that first spurred me to read African-American writing – from Toni Morrison to Iceberg Slim to all the black thinkers I reference in this book – so, for Blaze, hip hop stimulated different interests: from reading about African history to reassessments of what it means to be a so-called 'coloured' South African to new understandings of Islam.

On reflection, I think this is often the way hip hop is most successfully 'glocalised'; it is the lens through which all sorts of other material is perceived and processed.

I am not claiming that identity is not still frequently prescribed. Of course it is. For many New York kids, a pastiche of gangsta thuggery doesn't represent a choice so much as its lack, and for every rebellious, dreadlocked Japanese B-Boy there are a hundred conformists. However, the point is that the assumption of an oppositional identity usually now takes place at an imaginary level. Let me give this idea a soundbite: you don't have to run away to join the circus when it pitches its big top in your living room every day beneath an MTV logo.

In the information age, mass media expanded and contracted at the same time. Global broadcasters pumped out homogenous material while niche magazines pitched to ever smaller demographics. But now we are entering the post-information age and information is not so much 'niche' as 'personal'. At a level that remains in the realms of sci-fi for most of us, this means information tailored to our individual mores. But, more practically and, for the moment, realistically, it means utterly individual consumption. Again, this is most easily understood by what it is not, so, to use a hip hop phrase, I'll bite from Nicholas Negroponte's book about bits:[25] 'Thinking of the post-information age as infinitesimal demographics or ultrafocused narrowcasting is about as personalized as Burger King's "Have It Your Way." ' Put simply: the plethora of information guarantees that your consumption is individual.

And identity? And hip hop? Well. As consumption is personalised, so too is the production of identity. And, because of both its global marketing and innate characteristics, hip hop has become a key tool in the production of that identity for young people worldwide.

I have continually reiterated the flexibility of hip hop meanings. However, what I've come to understand is that this doesn't just mean different interpretations by different people in different places. No. Rather, hip hop meanings are also often manipulated in the individual imagination. Imagined as opposed to ascribed identity is inherently fluid. So Blaze reasons, 'Africans have learned from their history that Westernisation is deceiving and, if we continue being subjected to Americanisms, our people will be lost.' And it is hip hop, a prime American form, that has led him to this conclusion.

This makes me recall a line that caught my imagination in Salman Rushdie's New York novel, *Fury*:[26] 'Even anti-Americanism was Americanism in disguise, conceding, as it did, that America was the only game in town and the matter of America the only business at hand . . .' In fact, I'd go further than that because, for Blaze and many like him, anti-Americanisms are actually articulated through Americanisms. Or, to put it in a more politically, morally and

---

[25] *Being Digital*, Nicholas Negroponte, 1995, Hodder Headline.
[26] *Fury*, Salman Rushdie, 2001, Jonathan Cape.

emotionally loaded way, America doesn't just produce 'its own gravediggers', these days it gives them the spade too.

The important thing to understand about a guy like Blaze, therefore, is as follows: in ever-decreasing circles of meaning, hip hop is a fundamental brand signifier appropriated by multi-national companies and the mass media; hip hop is an underground culture experienced through countless bedroom Web sites and obscure records from one-man independent labels, and hip hop is a suggestive influence that has led him individually to all kind of other resources and information. And, while this is undoubtedly ironic, I don't think it is unusual or contradictory. In fact, it is why hip hop 'works'.

Of course, this fluid and imagined identity is hardly unique to B-Boys worldwide: it's a phenomenon of our age. It is nonetheless a further demonstration of hip hop's inherent modernity.

Back in London, I'm idly browsing the Net when I chance across Alan Greenspan's report to the Congressional Financial Services Committee.[27] Scrolling down, I find the following comment about the collapse of Enron. 'The rapidity of Enron's decline is an effective illustration of the vulnerability of a firm whose market value largely rests on capitalized reputation. The physical assets of such a firm comprise a small proportion of its asset base. Trust and reputation can vanish overnight. A factory cannot.' What does this mean? Surely it means that Greenspan recognises that, these days, even corporate identity is imagined. So Enron was the business equivalent of Vanilla Ice: it failed to 'keep it real'.

This may seem like a spurious equivalence to note but for me it's a short hop back to Nike's emphasis on brand rather than product as the root of sales and from there it's a mere sidestep to Andre's comment about the kids shooting hoops in Brooklyn and the Bronx: 'The players on those courts have more cultural capital than anybody on earth. And less actual power than anybody on earth too.'

---

[27] Testimony of Chairman Alan Greenspan before the Committee on Financial Services, US House of Representatives, 27 February 2002.

These days corporate identity, brand identity, personal identity, hip hop identity . . . they're all fluid ideas to which value is attributed on a continuous, subjective and experiential basis.

We're sitting with Chubby (Sechaba Mogale), the twenty-five-year-old co-founder of Loxion Kulca,[28] a South African streetwear label that makes hip hop clothes with a nod to local fashion sensibilities. There are the typical baggy jeans and T-shirts to drown in but there's also a tailored look more appropriate to *pantsula*[29] style. Chubby is almost painfully polite and he won't start talking until he's served us Swiss roll and rooibos tea; fork and napkin for the former, coaster for the latter.

Five years ago, Chubby and his mate Wandi (Wandile Nzimande) were living on the streets, unemployed and broke. At the time, they wore their hair in dreads, piled high beneath the cheap woollen beanies sold by women on any street corner. Trouble was, these hats only came in dull colours so they approached the women with different materials and had new headgear custom-made. Soon, friends, acquaintances and then strangers were harassing them for hats of their own so they began to put in bulk orders. Then they came up with the name and had labels printed and sewn on to the front. Within three years, they launched their first full Loxion Kulca collection and their clothes are now distributed all over South Africa and they have their first international outlet in neighbouring Botswana.

Both in their mid-twenties, Chubby and Wandi are sharp guys with an eye for street fashion and, more importantly, an eye for a smart idea. Despite the ubiquity of Stateside hip hop gear in South African stores, they recognised a clear opening in the market. Because how many township kids can afford American trainers or a Hilfiger hoodie? So they approached selected Jo'burg hip hop crews to take to the stage in Loxion Kulca freebies, associating their products with hip hop's localised cultural capital and generating a

---

[28] 'Loxion' is township slang for location as in neighbourhood. 'Kulca' is just a corruption of culture.

[29] The *pantsula* are township gangsters. I get into this in more detail a little later.

word-of-mouth marketing plan worthy of Nike. Phil Knight himself would have been proud of these two for their recognition of the power of the brand (especially considering their lack of any formal background in the industry). Then again, I guess we're living in a brand-led, synchronously experienced, media-savvy world. So maybe guys like Chubby and Wandi are Phil's natural heirs.

They've got an astonishing and intuitive business acumen. Though the company has grown exponentially, they've kept their overheads to a minimum by out-sourcing all production. They are keen to bring through other South African fashion talent but, rather than employing more designers, they encourage individuals to set up subsidiaries beneath the umbrella of a parent company, Lokul Creationz. Most importantly, almost the entire range is locally produced (though even Loxion Kulca find it cheaper to have the soles of their trainers cut in the Free Trade Zones of Southeast Asia). As part of a South African economy where foreign exchange is ever at a premium, this is no small matter. Buy a Roc-A-Wear jacket and you're sending precious dollars out of the country. Buy a (much cheaper) Loxion Kulca number and you're supporting the nation's industry. Locally conscious as much as they are internationally aware, young, gifted and black, Chubby and Wandi are surely shining lights of Mbeki's African renaissance.

In some ways, however, they've also been hamstrung by success. On the one hand, they've been repeatedly criticised for making styles derivative of US hip hop gear. On the other, they are now in direct competition with the likes of Nike, a company whose marketing budget is many times their annual turnover. And, for all Loxion Kulca's considerable skill in gaining a foothold in such a competitive industry, their potential growth is always going to be limited by the financial muscle of the big boys. What's more, their original target demographic (black township kids) haven't got much money to spend and the fact is that, even if they buy Loxion Kulca, one suspects that the vast majority aspire to the American super-brands.

Chubby and Wandi's solution is to plan a limited-edition, more upmarket range at the same time as they try to secure distribution in ever more mainstream outlets. I find myself questioning this.

Because aren't they thereby abandoning the ethos (the brand identity, the hip hop identity) that was so successful in the first place?

Chubby laughs: 'But if we are going to grow as a company, the brand has to grow with us.'

From here the conversation drifts with seeming inevitability to the 'whole Dead Prez situation' and, from there, to Black August, a music festival organised by the American-based Malcolm X Grassroots Movement to coincide with the UN-sponsored World Conference Against Racism. Apparently Dead Prez are coming back to headline alongside Lauryn Hill. I say 'apparently' because the proposed line-up seems to change on an almost daily basis and a lot of the local hip hop heads are dubious about whether any of the international stars will actually pitch.

I suggest to Chubby that Black August could be an incredible showcase for Loxion Kulca. He wants the brand to grow and his original marketing scheme involved local crews bigging up the label, so why doesn't he approach Lauryn Hill to do the same? I claim it's just the kind of thing she'd go for: politically conscious and ethically sound. 'If she went on stage in Loxion Kulca and said, "This is what I wear in South Africa", maybe people wouldn't be so obsessed with American designers.'

Chubby's laughing again: 'It's a good idea but do you really think I'd ever get to meet with her when she's here?'

I concede that the answer's a pretty definite 'no'. Later, when I think about it, I remember that Lauryn is sponsored by Levi's; something that presumably prevents her from promoting other labels. So it wouldn't have worked anyway.

There are several ironies in all this.

It is ironic that Loxion Kulca are criticised for their 'Americanised' fashion style – something that surely reflects a yawning chasm between the pre- and post-apartheid generations – when an Americanised look is and long has been (among *pantsula*, for example) a staple of South African urban style. It is ironic, too, that the guys' attempt to shift their brand into the mainstream in some senses involves a shift in the opposite direction. Because if you take 'the mainstream' to mean 'the majority' then, unfortunately, the majority are too poor to buy the products. Most of all, however, it is ironic that Loxion Kulca – a company owned by two young black men from poor backgrounds – struggles to compete as a 'real hip hop' label against multinational public companies that mostly profit old rich white men.

Black August was organised by the Malcolm X Grassroots Movement to 'support the global development of hip hop culture by facilitating exchanges between countries where hip hop is a vital part of the youth culture'. But would it be possible to 'facilitate exchange' between Loxion Kulca and Lauryn Hill? The instinctive and correct answer is 'No chance'. This is not a criticism of Lauryn Hill (like Dead Prez, one of the few American hip hop artists to take more than a proprietorial interest in African identity), nor of Black August. Rather it is simply an example that illustrates the degree to which the corporate megaliths have appropriated hip hop.

In New York, where mainstream and hip hop culture frequently appear indistinguishable, I found this depressing as hip hop often seemed only to further alienate the very people who once used the form to express their alienation. But here? Maybe I'm dizzy with all the rhetoric of African renaissance but I can't deny the scent of possibility.

In the modern world, identity is imagined so a company like Enron's value lies in 'capitalized reputation'. I've come to understand that hip hop identity and value are no different. What does this mean? At a fantastical level, it means hip hop taking a successful stand against the organisations that appropriate its capital and exploit its symbolism. At a practical level, it means ensuring that, at some future point, Lauryn Hill or Dead Prez or any other American superstar takes to a South African stage dressed in head to toe Loxion Kulca. As a first step, it means real hip hop heads all reaching the same conclusions and realising the value of their own cultural capital. And that, of course, is merely a leap of imagination. So maybe Blaze was right after all: the hardcore will always come out on top.

I'm guessing that this sounds at best fanciful and at worst irrelevant: so hip hop reasserts ownership of its 'capitalized reputation'? So what? But I'm also guessing that your judgement depends on what you think hip hop is. Because if you still think that hip hop is simply a fad of popular music predominantly made by black men with foul mouths and a penchant for Christmas-cracker jewellery, then this won't make much sense to you. But I hope that you're beginning to see that hip hop is far more than the sum of its parts.

As I've already said, there are all kinds of definitions but, in this circumstance, let's use the analysis of one of the most respected hip hop academics, Tricia Rose, who highlights hip hop's role as a 'cultural form that attempts to negotiate the experiences of marginalisation, brutally truncated opportunity, and oppression'.[30]

Now think about it. In an era of 'post-democratic'[31] Western governments, aren't marginalisation, truncated opportunity and oppression pretty much the essence of issue politics? Whether it's young Anglo-Asians running riot in Oldham and Bradford or young anti-capitalists marching on the G8 Summit or young Palestinians blowing themselves up to show their rage at American support for Israel, these are the very issues that motivate them to take to the streets. However, from their positions outside existing power structures, none of these groups has much hope of changing jack. Protests are not going to make British Asians feel less marginalised any more than they're going to offer new opportunities to Indonesian sweat-shop workers or change oppressive American foreign policy.

Hip hop culture, though, is different. It is a worldwide cultural network with a flexible ethos that is global and local: glocal. It has long articulated Tricia Rose's core experiences and even sold them as symbolic tools of identity to young people across the planet. But, most of all, it has the power of 'capitalized reputation', a power that exists in the consumer choices of B-Boys as key players in brand semiotics. I find myself recalling Derek Walcott: 'I had no nation now but the imagination'.[32] Walcott was, of course, expressing the dislocated nature of Caribbean identity but, like De Bois's 'double

---

[30] *Black Noise*, Tricia Rose, 1994, Wesleyan University Press.

[31] I use 'post-democratic' to highlight the electoral apathy (among young people more than any other group) that afflicts most so-called Western democracies.

[32] 'The Schooner Flight', from *The Star-Apple Kingdom*, Derek Walcott, 1979, Noonday.

consciousness', doesn't the sentiment now ring true for disparate groups of young people worldwide? And hip hop is their nation of the imagination (in the heads of the heads). Hip hop culture (an admittedly diffuse phenomenon) is in a position of actual power that, I would argue, is unheard of for a pop cultural form. And it is a power that can be used for inclusion, opportunity and expression, if only it can reclaim its identity at an imaginary level.

You can't get to grips with hip hop in Jo'burg without getting to grips with kwaito.

In the early '90s, dance music in Jo'burg was almost exclusively what was called 'bubblegum', a style of South African disco popularised by the likes of Brenda Fassie. As apartheid began to crumble, though, so the commercial market began to be flooded with other musical forms, both imported and locally manifested. For example, reggae had long been a notable minority seller while Cape Town hip hop crew Prophets Of Da City were the first to gain national recognition. What's more, a nascent house-music scene (largely on the back of the UK's rave explosion) was starting to emerge. In this context, sales of bubblegum began to tail off until Don Laka, an experienced local producer, spotted a gap in the market for a novel style of indigenous dance music. He teamed up with Christos Katsaitis and Oscar (before his days at Yfm but already an established DJ) to found the Kalawa label. And they put together Boom Shaka.

In most ways, Boom Shaka were your average manufactured band, pieced together by wizened management, no different from, say, the Spice Girls. Following a tried and trusted formula, Kalawa teamed an emcee (Junior Sokhela), a dancer called Theo and a couple of pretty girls (Thembi and Lebo). Don Laka and Oscar made the beats (in the company of two other DJs, Madlala and Bruce), made Boom Shaka train their voices, made an image and made a plan. However, Boom Shaka's runaway success must have exceeded even their expectations. Certainly there aren't many manufactured bands that define a whole new musical genre ('girl power'? Yeah, right). Boom Shaka's 1993 debut, 'It's About Time',[33] was a massive

---

[33] 'It's About Time', Boom Shaka, 1993, Kalawa.

hit and kwaito was born.[34] Within a couple of years, it was the new sound of South Africa and had spawned several further superstars (Arthur, Bongo Maffin, TKZee, and the list goes on).

The origins of the word kwaito are disputed: some claim it's derived from the Afrikaans word *kwai*, meaning excellent, while others say the name was taken from notorious township gangsters the Amakwaito. But there is no disputing the music, which is instantly recognisable. Put simply, kwaito is a hybrid musical form. The rhythms are like house music in slow-mo, melodies and choruses are similar to bubblegum and mostly female vocals complement mostly male emcees dropping simple rhymes and chants in *tsotsitaal* (often with an unmistakable ragga sensibility). Throw a marimba[35] into the mix and you're just about there.

But, aside from the fact they're both expressions of youth culture, what's kwaito got to do with hip hop? Certainly no South African B-Boy, whether they loved or loathed kwaito, would admit an equivalence between the two styles. However, as an outsider, I can't help but notice the significance of hip hop symbolism in kwaito and the way in which both the interrelation and antagonism between the forms is arguably definitive of both.

To illustrate this, I'll draw a few polar comparisons (which, if nothing else, probably guarantee I'll never be welcomed back to South Africa): kwaito is slack where hip hop (in South Africa, at least) is conscious, female as opposed to male, for parties as opposed to politics, commercial as opposed to underground, and black as opposed to coloured (more of this later). These are, of course, stereotypes and don't stand up to close scrutiny. Nonetheless, for a brief overview of kwaito and hip hop, they represent a useful framework. What's more, even if such polarised themes would probably be rejected by the supporters of both musical styles, I've certainly heard such ideas alluded to, directly or indirectly, by kwaito fans and hip hop heads alike.

---

[34] For a decent and more detailed commentary on kwaito see 'Kwaito', Simon Stephens, *Senses of Culture*, Sarah Nuttall and Cheryl-Ann Michael (eds), 2001, Oxford University Press.

[35] A marimba is a kind of African rosewood xylophone.

Speaking on *Get Down*, an SABC documentary about the origins of kwaito, broadcast in April 2001, journalist S'bu Nxumalo said, 'The time was right. The youth was tired of the *toyi-toyi*.[36] They wanted something new. And Boom Shaka gave them "Thobela".'[37]

So kwaito emerged in the aftermath of apartheid and its development in Jo'burg reflected release from struggle in both actual and metaphorical ways. Practically, the new ANC government ensured SABC increased its black output, which brought kwaito to every TV screen and radio station. At the same time, access to foreign media increased and the price of electrical equipment (including stereos) fell. Symbolically, kwaito also expressed the potential new fluidity between the city and its surrounding townships. Perhaps too, most simply, it was party music coming out at a time when the black majority wanted to party. Zola, the latest kwaito superstar, expresses this neatly: 'As much as the children of the '70s and '80s had to be violent to make a point, the generation of the '90s had to deal with freedom and that is hard. Whoever says the struggle continues didn't tell us how. Kwaito came out of that.'

He's talking while we bomb around Jo'burg in an old Renault. I've been desperate to get to speak to Zola for a couple of days but he's proved a tricky man to track down. A short, skinny, blue-black dude with a *chiskop*[38] and a taste for silver, he's now a bona fide celebrity and he pinballs from meeting to meeting. His mobile's ringing, his manager's mobile's ringing, the office phone's ringing and Zola's expression lurches from bewildered to plain pissed off.

Luckily, Dylan's a good deal more resourceful than me and suggests to the guy from Zola's label (Ghetto Ruff) that we might deliver him to his next appointment at SABC. So Dylan's borrowed the guy's car – a deathtrap old rust bucket with no brakes – and

---

[36] *Toyi-toyi* is a South African mass battle dance which often featured in anti-apartheid demonstrations.

[37] 'Thobela', Boom Shaka, 1996, Kalawa.

[38] *Chiskop* is South African slang for a shaved head. A lot of *pantsula*, hip hop and kwaito stars shave their heads as a reference to time spent inside; just like the American (and now worldwide) hip hop fashion of wearing your baggy jeans low around your backside (because, in prison, you're not allowed a belt).

Kanyasu, Zola and me are chatting in the back. The conversation is punctuated with Zola's loose directions and the occasional expletive as we narrowly avoid ploughing into another lorry. Zola's got a sharp sense of humour and a nice turn of phrase: part South African, part American and part Victorian English. 'This would not be the most noble way to die,' he comments.

Zola takes his name from the notorious Soweto district where he grew up. He made his name in the groundbreaking SABC drama *Yizo Yizo*. Zola played the lead, a *pantsula* called Papa Action. Now, on the back of that fame, he's releasing his first album, *Mdlwembe*.[39] It's kwaito, sure, but the nods to hip hop are more pronounced than ever. The stand-out track 'Ghetto Scandalous', for example, opens with the line 'Even if I've got my own CD, I'm the same old G' before launching into the chanted hook 'Ghetto scandalous! / Don't fuck with us!'

Zola shrugs, 'The way I bounce around and move shows you I come from a hip hop background. But not everybody is like that. Just like there are divisions in hip hop, there are divisions in kwaito. There's violent kwaito, good kwaito and struggling kwaito. What I do, I call struggling kwaito. Whoever goes and buys my CD has to understand that this artist comes from a place where he sees a drunken father beat a mum on the street, where a friend died, where a friend got raped, where a friend got successful and went to college, where a friend died of Aids . . . and all of these things make him what he is today. He cannot tell one story and leave the other.'

In other words, for all the Americanisms, Zola is as keen as the South African hip hoppers to stress the authenticity of his music. 'I'm still struggling to find my identity within this situation,' he says. And, as with hip hop, this perfectly sums up the complex cultural negotiations that kwaito seems to encapsulate: walking the tight-rope between African and Western, continually redefining itself as it wobbles first one way and then the other. And this is evident at every level of production, consumption and symbolism.

Musically, some kwaito is obviously house-driven, some sounds very hip hop and some has a more traditional township flavour. But

---

[39] *Mdlwembe*, Zola, 2001, Ghetto Ruff.

it's all kwaito. Culturally, it is celebrated as indigenous South African music in opposition to the West; and yet Coke (who, unlike Pepsi, chose not to withdraw from South Africa in support of apartheid sanctions) now appropriate its local semiotics to sell their brand on the basis of a unified South Africa. But it's all kwaito. Its content is often overtly sexual and I've heard kwaito castigated both as typical of South African misogyny (a white South African friend goes so far as to say, 'Look at the sex-crime problems in this country. Kwaito doesn't help') and hip hop misogyny (as the videos are full of bootylicious babes draping themselves over this or that star). But kwaito artists also claim that the music is empowering to women in both the African and Western senses of what that might mean. In one interview, for example, Lebo Mathosa describes her stage performance like this: 'It's a Boom Shaka show, sweetie! What can I say? . . . There are two African women there and you know what African women are like – they really get down! If you don't like it, don't watch.'[40] She asserts individuality and freedom of expression as fundamental to the genre. How you choose to interpret such a comment from an artist who explicitly trades on her sexual appearance is up to you. But it's all kwaito.

However, the patchwork of Western and South African (both past and present) is arguably most obvious – certainly I find it most interesting – in the confusions of imagery. Watch a kwaito video on mute and you could be forgiven for thinking you were watching the latest US emcee as one or other dude, swathed in hip hop labels and festooned in chunky jewellery, fronts standard hip hop mannerisms and showmanship for the camera. But check out his footwear and, chances are, he won't be maxing a pair of fly Nike sneaks. No. More likely, he'll be wearing fresh All Star *tackies*. You know the ones, Converse-made canvas numbers that make you think of American high-school jocks in the '50s. And why Converse All Stars? Because kwaito has emerged from and reflects a *pantsula* lifestyle, that's why.

What is a *pantsula*? Roughly it's a long-standing term for a township gangster. But it's probably best to let Zola explain.

[40] 'Who's That Girl?', Maria McCloy, Rage Online, 2001 (http://www.rage.co.za)

'*Pantsula* have come from way back in the '50s right up to today. If you're a *pantsula*, you're what we call a *tsotsi*, or thug or hustler. It meant you were the man. You were known in every *shebeen*, you had the best women in town, the best car and the best clothing. Back in the day, it came from American gangsters like Al Capone and you wore chalk-stripe suits and two-tone shoes. Now, the real *pantsula* wear All Stars, Dickies[41] and a clean white T-shirt. *Pantsula* are rough and quick to hit someone but always clean and very much the charmer.

'Back in the day, they were popular in the townships because they were black and oppressed but successful. Stealing from a white person was acceptable because it was almost like you had a right to because white people stole so much from us. And if you wanted a car, you didn't want to shoot somebody's brains out to take the car. Back then it was art. You had to go and steal the most difficult car and when you came back everybody gave you respect and said, "He's the man!" You were like Robin Hood.

'But these days? Young boys have it wrong. They are very dirty, they don't take care of themselves and they will shoot somebody just like that.'

Pantsula style is key to kwaito's imagery and the lifestyle is key to its content (for example in Kabelo's massive hit, 'Pantsula For Life').[42] The notion of *pantsula* is very localised. However, as Zola points out, it has always been at least partially processed through American cultural references. These days, though, mafia style has been superceded by the video opulence of hip hop gangsterism. Are kwaito videos copying their stateside hip hop counterparts? No doubt. But that's not all that's going on.

And isn't it ironic that the evidence of this can often be found in the footwear of the performers? While the multinational sneaker manufacturers have done most to globalise the hip hop brand, the hip hop imagery is localised into kwaito via pairs of '50s-style Converse All Stars.

---

[41] Dickies is an old fashioned American workwear label popular with the *pantsula*; like All Stars, it's another American anachronism. Curious.

[42] 'Pantsula for Life', Kabelo, 2001, Prime Media.

As Zola remarks, 'All Stars are more at home in South Africa. Back in the day, they became the dress code of the people. I was amazed to find that Americans used to wear All Stars for basketball. Basketball has never been big in South Africa so how did they come here?' He shrugs and laughs.

But don't worry about poor little Nike. You can bet that, like Loxion Kulca, All Stars are already beginning to be swamped by the mighty swoosh.

Kwaito, then, like hip hop, is a significant battleground for young South Africans between Western and African culture. In fact, in his defence of his African-ness, Zola expresses exactly this in a funny and unconscious way. 'Listen to my English; this is pure South African English,' he says. 'But the Gs coming into the game now? The way they talk is American, their whole mentality is American.' Gs coming into the game?

But, as I've already suggested, kwaito is also opposed to hip hop. As the more successful commercial music, largely made by manufactured bands, often delivering slack lyrics, kwaito has taken much of the cultural space that might otherwise be regarded as hip hop's natural stomping ground.

The Rza, the mastermind behind Wu-Tang, has notoriously described R'n'B as 'rap and bullshit'; clearly delineating between hip hop and its flirtatious offspring. In the States, however, that distinction has become increasingly blurred as emcees, vocalists and producers eagerly cross-pollinate in search of commercial success.[43] In South Africa, I reckon kwaito fills the R'n'B role but, for the moment, the musical forms remain distinct. While kwaito is about money and nightclubs and sales, hip hop is ever more concerned with poverty and lyricism and authenticity. However, with the success of kwaito artists like Zola (for whom hip hop runs through his music like 'Welcome to sunny Durban' through a stick of rock), this may yet change.

I meet Zola again at Yfm. It's the night of the *Rap Activity Jam*

---

[43] The prime example of this is Jay-Z and R. Kelly's aptly titled recent collaboration *The Best of Both Worlds*, 2002, Jive.

and he's going to appear on the following show to promote his record. He's with the owner of Ghetto Ruff, a guy called Lance Stehr who's been in the South African music industry since time. Ghetto Ruff also puts out records by a Cape Town hip hop crew called Brasse Vannie Kaap (BVK) and they're currently in Jo'burg. After my brief appearance live on the *Rap Jam*, Lance takes a phone call and pulls me to one side.

He smiles ominously and says, 'Mr Fat wants to see you.'

I feel like I'm in a movie.

But if you can't get to grips with hip hop in Jo'burg without getting to grips with kwaito, then you can't get to grips with hip hop in South Africa without getting to grips with Cape Town. And when Mr Fat wants to see you? You go and see Mr Fat.

Part Four: Cape Town
I'm A African[1]

One of the most pernicious myths of apartheid propaganda was that
white and black people arrived in an empty South Africa at around
the same time. As Jan Van Riebeeck landed in Cape Town with his
party of Dutch settlers in 1652, so the Nguni[2] were making slow
progress south down the Indian Ocean coastline and the Sotho
occupied the high central plateau that towers above the tsetse belt.
That was the story, anyway.

In fact, Nguni people had already been in South Africa for at least
200 years, while the archaeological record shows Sotho occupation
of the Northern Transvaal stretching back a further millennium.
More to the point, however, it's notable that this propaganda didn't
even bother to reference the indigenous population first encoun-
tered by the white settlers when they landed at the continent's
southernmost tip. Because, by the time propaganda mattered, these
people were extinct in South Africa, wiped out by a genocidal
cocktail of murder, disease and virtual slavery.

The KhoiKhoi were nomadic herdsmen who lived on the
grazing lands of the Cape coast while their near relatives, the
San, were hunter-gatherers to the north and interior. With yellow
complexion and fine hair and features, they didn't look much like
their fellow Africans. Nonetheless there is plenty of evidence
(physical and linguistic) that the Khoi-San lived relatively
harmoniously alongside their neighbours (Xhosa, for example, is

[1] 'I'm A African' from Let's Get Free, Dead Prez, 2000, Loud.
[2] The Nguni are Xhosa and Zulu speakers.

punctuated by the distinctive clicking sounds that characterised Khoi-San languages). The arrival of the Dutch settlers, however, changed all that and, within little more than 200 years, the Khoi-San were gone.

Van Riebeeck arrived in the Cape under the authority of the Dutch East India Company rather than the government of Holland. So the original Cape colony was not an imperial frontier so much as a halfway house between Europe and the valuable Dutch possessions in the East; a stopover where the company's ships could take on provisions of fresh vegetables and meat. But it didn't take long for the settlement to start expanding. In 1656, after company cutbacks, I guess, nine free 'burghers' accepted what would these days be called 'voluntary redundancy' to take up twenty-eight-acre farms on the fertile banks of the Liesbeeck River. This was traditional KhoiKhoi grazing land and the occupation sparked the first South African war of resistance. After victory, Van Riebeeck claimed the territory by rite of conquest. It marked the beginning of imperial South Africa and the beginning of the end for the KhoiKhoi as their social structures started to disintegrate under this new pressure for land.

As the white settlers moved out to establish farms throughout the Cape Peninsula, so the need for labour became all important and slaves were brought in from Angola, Madagascar and the Far East. For more than a century, these farms (generally huge tracts of land because of the poverty of the grazing) existed in near isolation from Europe and even from Cape Town. Despite the apparent severity of master–slave relationships, sex between the races was as inevitable as it was taboo and it was in these communities that the foundations and contradictions of colonial South African society were first laid. Outside the boundaries of these farms lay the threat of black Africa while within their fences sat a mythologised homogenous white race (I say 'mythologised' because it's one of the great ironies of apartheid that few of the oldest white South African families could truthfully claim the label 'pure white'). Between the two, a new 'coloured' community was beginning to take shape; physically, socially and culturally squeezed into a no-man's-land of identity.

And the Khoi-San? The San were tracked by colonial hunting

parties and systematically murdered, wiped off the South African map. These days, the remnants of this once flourishing people scratch a living on the fringes of the Kalahari desert in Namibia and Botswana. As for the KhoiKhoi: stripped of their land, they were forced to work for the white settlers in a state of dependence that differed from slavery only in name. Their numbers were decimated by foreign diseases (particularly the smallpox epidemic of 1713) and they were gradually assimilated into the growing mixed population. So now this unique race can only be seen as a genetic shadow in the expression of a so-called 'coloured'; someone like Mr Fat.

So we're following Lance Stehr, who's driving back to his house with Zola in the passenger seat. He's a curious character, Lance; mid-forties, I guess, with that kind of cool, almost contemptuous indifference that I've found commonplace in South Africans of all races. In the Yfm studio, I was knackered and it was getting late so when he said that Mr Fat wanted to see me I suggested we might hook up the next morning. Lance looked at me with a barely concealed sneer. 'Just come and see him, man,' he said. His scornful manner reminded me of a conversation I had with some coloured guy I met in Cape Town a few years back. We'd been shooting pool in a city-centre bar for about an hour and he was stony silent throughout. He only started talking when he knew he was going to whip me. I remember he said something like, 'When people come from overseas, they always have an opinion about South Africa and they don't know shit and they don't actually give a shit.' Something like that.

We turn into Lance's driveway and the gate is opened by a bare-chested, wiry kid in a baseball hat. Dylan says, 'He's a breaker.'

'You know him?'

'Nah,' Dylan laughs. 'He's just got that elastic look about him.' Dylan's right. He's all limbs and sinew.

Zola ducks into the main house but we walk on around the back, following Lance to another building that acts as a dormitory-cum-office. I'm trying to set aside a tired headache and desperately hoping to recall everything I can about Mr Fat and his crew, Brasse Vannie Kaap.

Prophets Of Da City (POC) were *the* original South African hip hop collective and have a reputation that stretches back to the late '80s. Built in Cape Town around DJ Ready D and emcee Shaheen, they were an extended family of DJs, B-Boys, writers and emcees (who, in fact, produced kwaito stars Junior Sokhela of Boom Shaka and E'Smile). When Shaheen took time out from POC, Ready D formed BVK alongside DJ E20, Hamma (a South African hip hop legend in his own right) and Mr Fat and they released their eponymous debut in 1997.[3] And . . . that's about it. Come to think of it, I don't even know whether it's Mr Phat or Mr Fat.

It's Fat with an 'F'. We're shown into a back room and he's sitting on a lower bunk in shorts and T-shirt. He's a big guy all right; not tall, just dumpling round in a way that makes his hands seems too small for his arms, his head too small for his shoulders and his eyes too small for his face and gives a roll to his stride as he comes over to greet us. His manner is serious and his voice is soft and breathy as he waves us to a couple of plastic chairs. The name, the back room, his demeanour, my exhaustion: it all adds to the vague sense of meeting a mafia don. Until he starts speaking, anyway, and he talks with a gentle intelligence and apologetically prefaces every comment with 'I'm going to be mad honest with you' or 'I'm sorry but . . .'

'I heard you on the radio,' Fat says. 'What you said to those cats about rapping in English was cool, man. I'm sorry but, in Jo'burg, people are not prepared to go back to where hip hop came from. Here they think hip hop is just rapping. It's fashion not an art form. In Cape Town we try to teach the kids to go back to the basics. Our philosophy is emcee, turntablism, B-Boying, graffiti and our knowledge of self because without those five elements hip hop can't move any more than a man can walk with one leg. Those cats on the radio talking their lyrics about kryptonite and blah blah blah?[4] That's because they haven't got the basics. I'm sorry but if it's

---

[3] *BVK*, Brasse Vannie Kaap, 1997, Ghetto Ruff.

[4] I remember one of the emcees from Optical Illusion dropped a rhyme about kryptonite. Despite Fat's criticism, the kid is in good company. Ice Cube ('You Ain't Gotta Lie Ta Kick It'), Prodigy ('Bulworth (They Talk While We Live It)'), Big Daddy Kane ('Hold It Down') and Phife Dawg ('Award Tour') for starters have all, in their time, referenced Superman's least favourite element.

a one-on-one freestyle battle you can't come with your kryptonite stuff.'

Fat is quietly dismissive of Jo'burg hip hop. In fact, he's quietly dismissive of most hip hop (especially the current state of the scene in America). Because, for him, the whole culture goes back to his time growing up as a coloured kid in Bonteheuwel on the Cape Flats in the '70s and '80s. Hip hop is about way more than just music.

'I was aware of hip hop around 1984; Whodini, all of that. At school in Cape Town I wanted to be a singer until this guy bought a hip hop album, Run DMC,[5] and I realised I could say so much more in rapping. If you go into the deep roots of American hip hop, you find they rap about Africa. Why? Because they're looking for identity. I'm going to be mad honest with you, being from a – I hate this word – 'coloured' community, obviously you're seeking identity so, when you see people rapping over the TV that look like you, it grabs you. Damn! It's what you want to be!

'Hip hop has come full circle at present. Emcees are like the storytellers of the tribe, grafitti is cave paintings and the drums of Africa are like turntables: this is our ideology. We talk about the Khoi-San. I'm sorry but we are sitting in the cradle of man so why should we want to sound like Americans? Back in the day, if you'd told me that "you're bushman or you're Khoi", I'd have felt offended. But tell me now, man, and I'm proud. So that's what we're telling the kids: "You're bushmen. You're Khoi-San." See back to your roots and you see the beauty that comes from within.

'I'm going to be mad honest with you: to be coloured in this country is screwed because of apartheid. I'm not saying it wasn't bad for black people or any of that, I'm just saying it was bad for my people. It made us paranoid. White officials slide a pencil into a baby's hair and if it falls he's white and if it sticks he's coloured. What do you think about that? Families, whole communities, were divided like this. They [the officials] ask you some questions and if you answer in the wrong way or whatever they can take you and move you to a whole different area. I'm sorry but you can't even

[5] Probably *King Of Rock*, Run DMC, 1985, Def Jam.

imagine shit like that and it's not surprising cats on the Cape Flats make mistakes about what they want to be.'

It's humbling listening to Fat as he talks about hip hop and coloured identity with quiet and melancholic fervour and it's hard not to conclude that coloured society was truly the no-man's-land of apartheid. To take it back to De Bois, you could almost argue that these are people who were 'in' but not 'of' and 'of' but not 'in' all at once: a real dead-end kind of identity.

In his address at his presidential inauguration in Cape Town in 1994, Nelson Mandela said that the reconstruction and develop-ment of South Africa 'needs unity of purpose . . . It requires us all to work together to bring an end to division, an end to suspicion and build a nation united in our diversity.' Madiba was expressing a heartfelt and undoubtedly worthwhile sentiment (shared with most South Africans) that the time had come for the nation to move on. This sentiment, however, requires South Africa to tiptoe a tricky tightrope between past and future and it's a crossing that's certainly proved easier for some citizens than others. In all my time in this country, for example, I've met few white people who admit to having voted for the apartheid regime. Generally and with obvious motivations, they prefer to look forward (at least in public). Black people, too, are rarely prisoners of the past since they now have the satisfaction of victory and their recollections, however painful, are of a hard-fought, moral struggle that finally ended in triumph. But few coloured people are in a position to stride forward without one eye fixed firmly on history. Their very being is, after all, a product of apartheid (racially as well as emotionally) and so, in this context, I feel compelled to set the former president's unified ideal alongside Milan Kundera's famous assertion: 'The struggle of man against power is the struggle of memory against forgetting.'[6]

A typical and easy interpretation of the position of the coloured community in post-apartheid South Africa is as the meat in a flipped sandwich. Where once they were squashed between a tyrannical white minority and a potentially powerful black majority, they are now squashed between a tyrannical black majority and a still

---

[6] *The Book Of Laughter And Forgetting*, Milan Kundera, 1999, Harper Perennial.

powerful white minority. There are undoubtedly elements of truth in such analysis but, for the moment, I'm less concerned with the actualities of power than I am with the way colouredness is represented. Or, rather, the way it's not. An example: after the South African local elections in 2000, in which many coloureds voted for the Democratic Alliance[7] (and that's a poignant comment right there), the *Mail & Guardian* wrote, '. . . the DA's supporters – mainly whites and coloureds – turned out in large numbers, but . . . many black ANC supporters stayed home . . . the voting seemed to confirm Mbeki's statement that the country was one of two nations – one black and one white.'[8] In this instance, 'coloured' is thoughtlessly lumped together with white (as in other circumstances it is thoughtlessly lumped together with black) and the contemporary social text still strips this significant minority of any meaningful and realistic notion of self.

Of course, as a British outsider, I find this doubly poignant. At one level, I can't ignore the fact that in the racial politics of my own society, coloured people would be consistently (if thoughtlessly) regarded as black. At another level, I am suddenly and uncomfortably aware of my ignorance of both coloured history and contemporary experience. When I think of coloured South Africans, I'm forced to admit that there are only two images that have imprinted themselves on my mind via the crude filters of the global media: of Chester Williams sprinting down the Springbok wing in the triumph of the 1995 Rugby World Cup and of the notorious gangs of the Cape Flats. So I only know these people as sportsmen and criminals and I can't help comparing this to the most pernicious and stereotypical representations of black America.

Does Mr Fat actually look in any way KhoiKhoi? I don't really know; not least because the KhoiKhoi were gone more than a century before I was born. But I certainly understand why he chooses to reference this ancestry because such is the coloured

---

[7] The Democratic Alliance was formed as an alliance of the Democratic Party, the New National Party and the Federal Alliance in 1989. The New National Party formally withdrew from the alliance in 2001.

[8] Hugh Neville, *Mail & Guardian*, 7 December 2000.

struggle of 'memory against forgetting'. Of course, if this is about stories of the past, then current representation is equally important and Kundera's aphorism gives way to that of the South African poet Jeremy Cronin: 'Art is the struggle to stay awake'.[9] For Mr Fat, then, hip hop is both the cipher through which memory can be expressed (and, indeed, invented) and the art that keeps him awake. Apartheid stripped the coloured community of meaningful identity (even black people at least had the identity of opposition). When Mr Fat references the 'storytellers of the tribe', 'cave paintings' and 'the drums of Africa', he is using hip hop to say 'I'm an African'.

'I'm going to be mad honest with you, whites are our biggest audience. And you can see that I'm smiling. In order for our own people to accept that what we do is right, white people must first, because that's the nature of the slave–master relationship between white and coloured and at some levels it still exists. But it's OK because we are the CNN – the Coloured News Network – and we have to find a way to give the people the whole truth.

'The media come to the Cape Flats with their crap. Like, there was a BBC TV documentary and the opening voiceover said something like, "A boy born on the Cape Flats is destined to be a gangster." We got scared, man! Who are they helping saying that? There's all these ordinary people and you have to focus on the five per cent of violence? I live in Park Hill which is now apparently the number-one killing township on the Cape Flats. I know there's shooting but, damn, the way they go on!

'But we're not blaming the system no more, we're blaming our own people. So we have to take hip hop back into our hands. It was Ready D who said that if we're going to take back hip hop, let's do a whole album in the way we speak. That's how BVK came about. To hell with English emceeing! So all our lyrics are in our own Cape slang.

'It's the commercial media that pushes all that gangsta shit: rocks, ice, girls, all of that. I know that shit is hired because you see one girl in a Jay-Z video, then the next video, then the next. So I tell the kids that but I do it in gangsta slang. We want to help people and,

I'm sorry, but we've got to be on the same road as the people we're helping. So parents don't see rappers as gangstas no more. I still stay on the Cape Flats and the kids can know me and know I'm still the same person. You've got to go down, Patrick. See for yourself.'

I didn't really mean to head to Cape Town. It upsets my rigid plan for this book – one city in each selected country – and, what's more, I've been to Cape Town a few times before and, despite the beauty and whatever the guidebooks would have you believe, I've always found it a bit like Bournemouth, only not so funky. But even the heads in Jo'burg tell me it would be unforgivable to miss out on the Cape scene and, besides, my hip hop pilgrimage has all the mystery of following a star, so I can't just ignore my compass when it shifts its position in the night sky.

I've been talking about hip hop identity as 'capitalized reputa-tion', as a brand signifier appropriated by the oppressive mainstream. Well, Mr Fat for one is clearly a step or two ahead of me as BVK are already reclaiming hip hop's cultural capital for the benefit of the kind of people – alienated and disempowered – the culture was originally supposed to represent. What's more, whether he talks about the Khoi-San or the seemingly mystical links between hip hop and traditional African society, he's successfully locating himself in the 'nation of the imagination'. So I feel like I need to check this stuff out at first hand.

If those seem like two abstract motivations, I admit I've got more personal reasons too.

First off, I guess I'm intrigued by coloured identity. Appadurai has claimed that mass migration impels the imagination. Surely a mixed-race heritage is part of the same argument. In London, I often wonder at the number of mixed-race kids I see on my local streets at turfing-out time from the capital's schools. I recall the city I grew up in and I wonder if it's just skewed memory that casts it in terms of more homogenous communities: English, Irish, Jamaican, Nigerian, Pakistani, Indian and Bangladeshi. Certainly I know that in the States so-called 'ethnic minority' populations already out-number whites in many of the nation's urban centres. Certainly I know that current demographic patterns suggest it's not too long before the same is true in the UK and the majority of the majority will then be mixed race.

I have already suggested that many cultures are now synchronously (if not uniformly) experienced worldwide. I guess when most of us (or them, or you) are brown-skinned the synchronous cultural experience will have therefore taken human form and the need for successfully imagined (as opposed to ascribed) identity will be more pressing than ever.

In the second place, since arriving in Jo'burg, I've been reading voraciously about South African history and I remember my grandmother telling me that her father, a young Irishman, met her mother on his return from the Cape. I'm trying to figure out when he would have been here. It must have been around a century ago, with Rhodes recently dead, the Boer war concluded and the diamond and gold rushes long over. I suppose I wonder what he was doing here. But I know that South Africa was then still a land of opportunity for the British lower-middle classes as, in the space of thirty years, the Empire's control had expanded from its disputed Cape outpost to include all of modern-day South Africa as well as Zimbabwe, Botswana and Zambia.

As I wait with Kanyasu at Jo'burg's Jan Smuts airport (named for an Afrikaans icon) to catch my flight to Cape Town, therefore, I can't help but notice the distance between myself and a mere three generations of ancestry. I've always taken hip hop comfort in Rakim's great lyric 'It ain't where you're from, it's where you're at', but I'm realising, with the benefit of conversations in New York, Tokyo and Jo'burg, that 'from' and 'at' are more than ever these days mechanisms of identity that compete and complement. So the source material of even imagined identity is historical as much as present and has to be socially contextualised as much as it is individually constructed.

Blaze told me about the Nguni morality of *ubuntu*. As far as I understand it, *ubuntu* means something like 'humanity' although it actually expresses a whole lot more than that. There is a proverb that probably gets closest to its essence: '*Ubuntu ungumuntu ngabanye abantu*' – 'People are people through people'; a typically African ethos that stresses an individual's identity as part of society (with all the benefits and obligations that implies). As I come to realise that the most important identity is now, more than ever, one of imagination so I know that my identity within hip hop has always been so. But I also know that I can only truly imagine myself as a hip hop head with knowledge of people that have gone before. What's more I'm discovering that the contemporary society that makes people who they are is no longer, say, a small Nguni settlement. Rather it is a synchronously experienced global community.

One of the most striking things to emerge in the fallout from the terrorist attacks on the USA on 11 September 2001 was the international make-up of Al Qaeda: Moslems, sure, but Moslems from numerous backgrounds and nations united by a destructive idea, from their aristocratic Saudi leader to the disaffected, mixed-race Anglo-Jamaican 'shoe bomber'. It is apparent that imagined identity is now, therefore, inherently glocal and, to use the language of *ubuntu*, people – even people like me – are people through people worldwide.

'In Mitchell's Plain [on the Cape Flats] there are 1.2 million people and we have one police station manned by 120 police; that's a policeman for every 10,000 people. We have one fire station and a clinic that's only open during the day. The community is very sick; that's why we're so disappointed with this government and all its bitching and bullshitting. When's it going to change? Let me tell you something: an arms deal just went through for 43 billion rand. Who are we trying to protect ourselves from when we're at war with ourselves right now?'

This is Ready D, founder member of both BVK and POC. He was born in the famous Cape Town neighbourhood of District Six where, from the beginning of the twentieth century, all races and religions lived side by side in the very heart of the city. This neighbourhood, of course, flew in the face of the Nationalist Party policy of apartheid and, for about fifteen years after '66, the Pretoria government set about razing it to the ground and relocating its residents of colour to townships on the outskirts. Around 60,000 people were forcibly removed. It happened to Ready D's family when he was ten years old. So, for all my abstractions about glocalisation, it's no surprise that his prime concern is for the people in his own community.

The hip hop bush telegraph's proved itself to be in good working order. Just landed in Cape Town, I spent the afternoon trying to track down this guy's number. But I needn't have bothered. Turns out he heard some cat had just arrived who was writing about hip hop; so the social activist, philosopher, urban legend and, above all, B-Boy tracked down my number and called me.

We meet at seven p.m. in Bardeli's Café on Kloof Street in the centre of town. It's a swanky joint full of trendy young white people necking cocktails in London fashions. I've no idea why Ready D should have chosen this place to hook up and I'm beginning to wonder if I'll ever get to meet heads on their home turf.

Kanyasu and I are a little early but he arrives on the dot with a young dude called Nasief in tow. Ready D cuts a squat, muscular, ageless kind of figure – I guess he could be anywhere between twenty-eight and forty – in jeans, logo-free T-shirt and a red baseball cap with the word 'Osiris' embroidered in white. I reckon Nasief must be about twenty-five, though he could pass for eighteen. He's wearing a navy hoodie, 'Urban Gear' emblazoned across the front. He tells me that Urban Gear is his label. So it's not just Loxion Kulca tapping into the global, local, glocal hip hop vibe.

I call a waiter and order drinks. Beer? Spirits? They both take a glass of water.

I soon discover Ready D's a tough interviewee. In the past, I've interviewed all kinds of heads from superstars to wannabes and, when it gets difficult, it's generally because they're arrogant so-and-sos with more opinions than thoughts and egos matched only by the size of their bodyguards. But with Ready D it couldn't be more different; he's a spellbinding charismatic who carefully weighs his every word. Frankly there's not a lot of point asking him questions, better to just let him talk. And he starts pretty much where Fat left off: with the documentary the BBC made on the Cape Flats.

'I think it must have been '97. The BBC spent a year over here making a documentary called *Cape of Storms* about the HLs.[10] And

---

[10] HLs are the Hard Livings gang.

what happened? It gave them superstar status and fuelled the warfare because now all the gangs wanted to be just as famous and get into the papers. I'm not saying that was the makers' intention but that's what happened, you see?

'If you really want to understand gang culture in this country you have to understand it historically. Specifically, it has to do with the slave days, so to say, of deprivation and oppression. If you throw hundreds of thousands of people together into a very small space, they're going to get frustrated with one another. Then apartheid capitalised on that because a lot of the gang-bangers were informers to the previous government and in exchange they'd get drugs and guns. That's why all the hardware used in the gang warfare is, I would say, military hardware. For example, the Hard Livings broke into an army base. How do a gang break into an army base? They stole guns and grenades and bazookas and you can get anything you want on the Cape Flats right now. You can read this in the newspapers. This is documented fact.

'But when you start talking about the media you realise one thing quick. Poor people can't fight the propaganda. Look at what happened with PAGAD.[11] The community began taking action, people coming together against the gangs and drugs, and the media called it a "militant Islamic movement". But, I tell you, there were a lot of church ministers involved too; it was just a question of mobilising the community. The reason they [the media] said it was Moslems was because the Moslems were the most outspoken and, when people wanted to disguise their faces, they used a scarf, so the propaganda associated it with Hamas and the Gaza Strip. Not long after, PAGAD was infiltrated by the gangs, the police, even the FBI came over, until people were too afraid to speak. It's exactly the same as happened to the Black Panthers and the Nation of Islam. If you do your math and study

---

[11] PAGAD is People Against Gangsterism And Drugs, an organisation that grew up in Cape Town in the mid-'90s. It is, variously, a community group, a vigilante mob, a gang in its own right or a bunch of Islamic terrorists (closely associated with the extremist Qibla movement), depending on who you believe.

the history of this kind of movement, you can see this is what happens. You can't fight the propaganda.

'And, you know, this shit sold a lot of newspapers. One gang boss was assassinated live on television. They couldn't keep up with demand. And now the gangs are worse than ever.

'Back in the day, the gangs had certain codes you had to abide by: "the books". But now old gangsters are getting out of prison and they can't control the young ones. The young kids don't care any more about the books; the code of the streets is "kill for respect" and that's it, finished. I see kids as young as seven who can tell you about armour-piercing bullets, who can take a gun apart and put it back together in minutes. They're not afraid to die; that's the general gang sentiment right now.'

Ready D paints a bleak picture, explaining that the relationships between the gangs on the Cape Flats and the communities they come from are various and complex. The local communities are certainly the gangs' chief victims, whether caught in the crossfire or as the principal markets for the core business of drug dealing. Nonetheless, for better or worse, the gangs also act as a proxy power structure, filling in the numerous holes where state authority is inadequate, failing or absent altogether. Gangs like the Hard Livings, the Americans and the Mongrels can buy silence: they provide jobs, help with rent payments, offer loans, that sort of thing. What's more, in communities where 'mainstream' opportunities are so severely limited, the informal economy becomes paramount and so hundreds of thousands of people are indirectly tied into gang culture through money laundering (in the taxi industry, for example) or *shebeens* or handling stolen goods and so on and so on.

In such a context, I guess it's not surprising that gang leaders should sometimes be idolised by the disaffected. Just look at the example of the Staggie brothers, who ran the Hard Livings in Mannenberg throughout the '90s. Rashaad Staggie was lynched in 1996 during a PAGAD protest at his Salt River home. But his execution wasn't exactly welcomed by the whole community as some recalled how, only the previous month, he'd been handing out 50-rand notes to striking workers from the local garment industry: a proper Robin Hood. In 1998, his brother Rashied was charged in connection with the theft of weapons from a police base near Faure outside Cape Town. Crowds from Mannenberg gathered outside the magistrate's court chanting 'Viva Staggie! The people's hero!' Clearly, for countless alienated, angry or just plain bored young men on the Flats, the gangsters represent opportunity, physical and economic strength and, perhaps above all, glamour.

Against this background, the production, consumption and perception of hip hop on the Flats is inevitably schizophrenic. And it can be cleanly divided into a two-way struggle between the old-school heads who have been deep into hip hop culture since back in the day and the new breed of gang-bangers who enjoy gangsta rap music.

Ready D describes his first exposure to hip hop like this: 'I got into hip hop as we know it around 1982. The first stuff we were exposed to was, like, "Rappers Delight" and "The Breaks".[12] We knew exactly what those emcees were talking about back then. All that Scooby Doo stuff?[13] That's what our dads used to say to us back on the Cape Flats – "How are you, Scooby Doo?" – so we had that slang before hip hop.

'As time went on, the first hip hop video we saw was "Buffalo Gals" by Malcolm McLaren[14] and that really sparked us off. It changed our lifestyle in a big way because we could actually see the characters – the Rock Steady Crew and the kids in the video – and we could identify with them because they looked exactly like us kids on the Cape Flats.

'We started out as a dance crew but soon we were messing around with people's stereos, breaking their turntables, that kind of thing. We used to get music from pen friends and family who'd been forced to move out of South Africa. They'd send tapes, letters

[12] 'The Breaks', Kurtis Blow, 1980, Mercury.

[13] I guess he's referring to the line in 'Rappers Delight': 'A skiddlebebop, we rock, Scooby Doo / Guess what America, we love you'. Then again, he could be referring to rhymes in Rza's 'Unspoken Word', 'Alright Hear This' by the Beastie Boys, 'I Get Wreck' by Tim Dog and Krs One or even 'Scooby Doo' by Cypress Hill. I could go on. As cartoon dogs go, Scooby Doo is a surprisingly common reference point for emcees.

[14] 'Buffalo Gals', Malcolm McLaren, 1983, Mercury.

and magazines because you couldn't get the music here. If hip hop did come in it would only be one or two copies and we'd fight over them. One copy would circulate through the whole of the Cape Flats. If one crew got a tape from an aunt or cousin somewhere else in the world, that tape or a copy of that tape or a copy of a copy of that tape would circulate even if you had to press your ear to the speaker to hear what was left of the music beneath the crackling. I still have my tapes from back in the day, all the really shitty recordings. I treasure that stuff. It's part of my treasure chest.

'We recorded six albums as POC. Our early gigs all happened to be political- and community-orientated-type events because that's what was going on at the time, like rallies and anti-drug marches. That made us more conscious and then listening to hip hop from overseas added to the process. We knew we had to do research – about how we'd been divided up in this country, that sort of thing – because we realised we didn't know much about ourselves and we didn't get that type of education in school.

'Then a lot of material from our second album[15] was banned, our videos were banned, because of our political stance and the kind of statements we were dropping. These were the last hard days of apartheid. At the time, hip hop had started going towards black consciousness with groups like Public Enemy and X Clan. To be honest, we couldn't understand what these American rappers were talking about, being black conscious and African. They were over there so what did they know about Africa? But on our side we were quite ignorant as well. We heard Public Enemy rap about Elijah Mohammed and Minister Farrakhan and we didn't know who these people were and that really made us curious. Then NWA came on track with "Fuck Tha Police" – and we could immediately identify with that because we were going through the same thing that these guys were talking about.

'Back in the day, as hip hoppers, we used to be chased by the gangsters. A few of my homies wanted to kill me because when they saw me change my style of dress to tracksuit pants and *tackies* they thought I'd gone over to another gang. It was only when they saw

---

[15] *Boomstyle*, POC, 1988, Ghetto Ruff.

me practising breakdancing that they left me alone, you see? Hip hop got a lot of us out of the gang scene, out of the whole prison lifestyle. That's the main thing hip hop has done for the core players in this city.'

While hip hop may have kept Ready D out of the Cape Flats gangs, a lot of kids are not so lucky and their experience of hip hop is almost diametrically opposed. That is not necessarily to say the music actively encourages them to run with the gangs; only that, for them, its implications and impulses are very different. Rather than creating opportunities, hip hop helps only to limit them; instead of breaking down stereotypes, it reinforces them; and where the B-Boys have used hip hop as an imaginative tool of learning, so the gangsters imagine themselves to be gangstas. And that spelling is important. Because for the gang-bangers on the Flats, hip hop starts and finishes with gangsta rap.

'We've got probably one of the biggest gang cultures on the planet right here in Cape Town,' Ready D explains. 'So obviously gangsta rap had a very negative impact over here, adding fuel to the gang wars. If you combine our gang culture with the image of rappers like Snoop Doggy Dogg and Tupac? Of course it was so easy for gang-bangers to click on to that.'

It is hard to over-emphasise the symbolic connections between gangsta rap and the gangs on the Cape Flats; hard to do so without sounding like a Barbara Bush Christian conservative, anyway. For the moment one example is enough: one of the strongest youth gangs on the Cape Flats call themselves the Junior Mafias after Biggie's crew while another are known as the Westsiders (as in the West Coast of the USA). So young men who've never left Cape Town fight real turf wars over fantasy turf in mythologised places with names like South Central and Compton and Brooklyn and the Bronx that are conjured up by laser wands on countless stereos. Or, as Nasief puts it in a rare contribution, 'Everything Hollywood throws at us, we experience, and everything the movies exaggerate, that's what we live.' And the lines between hip hop 'drama' and hip hop 'reality' become ever more obscured.

So I guess it's no surprise that even a cat like Ready D who's tasted the rough cloth of a media gag sees it like this: 'People have got to be responsible and think about what they're saying and how it gets projected to the other side of globe. The record industry's got a lot to do with that and the media as well. OK, I know I'm talking about censorship to a certain degree. But you need to understand the kind of people who are listening to your shit.'

Ready D may be primarily concerned with the struggles of his own community but he understands the synergies as well as anyone. Because, like I said, these days people are people through people worldwide.

Nonetheless, there's little doubt that at least one side of the Cape Town hip hop equation remains a shining light of social action, both for the coloured community in particular and the city as a whole. And this comes down to the hard work and social con-science of the musicians and breakers from crews like POC, BVK, Black Noise and Moodphase Five and the local graf collectives like Word On The Streets, The Villainous Animatorz and Your Millennium's Best. The guys from BVK, for example, are involved in education projects and prison rehabilitation and take their philosophy of hip hop as a means for self-improvement anywhere that will listen, from the black township of Guguletu to the exclusive white suburb of Bishop's Court. 'When everybody's vibing together, it breaks down the stereotypes,' Ready D says simply.

While Ready D remains relatively optimistic about the potential of the Cape Flats, he is most revealing when he comes back to what he regards as the roots of the problems affecting his community. For all his distrust of the ANC government and disgust at the gangs, he repeatedly and scornfully returns to the media as the source of most of his bile and, at one point towards the end of his soliloquy, his usual eloquence and restraint gives way to an altogether angrier tone. 'Cultural oppression,' he spits. 'That's the right term to use. Because we've been trained to go after the latest fads and fashions and . . . it's . . . it's been rammed down our throats. It's the same thing as apartheid but coming with a new twist. They might have black faces on the television but it's the same cats from back in the day who hold the power. The media is still white controlled and they want to keep our consciousness to a minimum. Shit! Just look at the clothes we wear! That's got a lot to say about where we're going in this country in terms of culture or its lack.

'You want to know if I'm positive about where hip hop is going? I am. My only fear is when the record companies start getting hold of it and start to water it down; same as in the States. When the industry gets hold of you, you become a product of the industry. Hip hop should never be a product of the industry. In the case of BVK, it's very hard to steer us into the mainstream. We stick to our guns and rap in our own lingo but not in an up-in-your-face kind of way.[16] This is what we've learned. We're very revolutionary but difficult to ban. The media can think they're playing you as a pawn but we're smart. We have our own agendas as well. You know what? It all depends on economics at the end of the day. And the capital still lies in the hands of the wrong people.'

I've been so gripped by Ready D's take, his stories, that, from our little booth at the back, I've barely noticed the bar filling up. But now that he raises an eyebrow at me – 'We done?' 'Sure' – and it seems like he's got to cut, I scan the scenario. Since we sat down, Bardeli's has packed out and house music is pumping through the sound system and they're doing good business in Mexican bottled beer with lime quarters wedged in the necks. A brief handshake and smile and Ready D is gone, disappeared into the swell of bodies that seems to rise and fall with the regular thud-thud-thud-thud of the four-to-the-floor basslines. I still figure this was a weird place to meet.

A moment later the music fades and there's some guy speaking through a mic from a small platform at the other end of the bar. I shift my position and crane my neck. The dude's wearing a suit and tie and his hair's parted just so. He introduces himself as Martin from Red Bull and he says how proud they are to be sponsoring the Red Bull Home Groove search for the next generation of DJ stars.

He calls the 'local legend' to come forward and Ready D emerges

---

[16] Tracks from BVK's second album, *Yskoud* – meaning 'ice cold' – (Ghetto Ruff, 2000) illustrate his point. Take 'Afkoel' ('Alcohol'), for example. What at first seems to be a homage to drunkenness is, on repeated listens, a subtle attack on all the men who would rather drink than provide for their families.

from the crowd and takes the mic. It might just be me but he looks a little embarrassed as he tells several of the same anecdotes I've just heard; of growing up on the Cape Flats, of getting music from overseas, of running away from the cops. He talks for ten minutes or so before moving to the decks nearby. He then launches into an immaculate half-hour demonstration of the hip hop DJ's craft as he mixes funk breaks, old-school classics and recent floor fillers (almost exclusively, I note, American) into a musical cocktail that exceeds even its top-notch ingredients. Snatches drop in and out, rhythms are pulled apart and rebuilt, reversed and reworked, new melodies assembled beneath dextrous fingertips. For the most part, the crowd looks on nonplussed. Boys huddle around the decks but I figure they're more impressed by the dynamics of these unfamiliar skills than the music they're creating. To judge by their clothes, attitude and reaction, this mob are no hip hop heads.

When he's finished his set, Ready D takes another glass of water from the bar and stops by our table to say goodbye. Then he heads out. I guess at least I now understand why we met at Bardeli's; because even a living legend's got to make a living. And Red Bull are paying.

In the (hopefully temporary) absence of a laptop, I'm writing this on my handheld in my cheap hotel room near the Cape Town Waterfront. It's a tricky operation as my new gadget tries to translate my scribbles into text. It keeps turning my Ys into Gs and my Vs into Ns so the whole procedure is maddeningly laborious. Nonetheless, I'm keen to get down my thoughts while they're fresh in my head and, besides, I feel there's something appropriate in this awkwardness. If my thoughts and impressions were clear, I'd dump them wholesale on to a waiting hard-drive. But they aren't clear so the mental struggle to correctly signify these people, this *stuff*, is neatly counterpointed by the practical struggle to use the correct signifiers.

I've been wondering about the association in South Africa between hip hop and the Cape coloured community. I know it's hardly a precise correlation but it exists. Or used to, anyway.

There is no doubt (indeed they said as much) that the likes of Mr

Fat and Ready D have used hip hop to identify themselves as African within a social structure that, even now, tries to squeeze them out of the demographic landscape. However, such a conscious (in both the literal and hip hop senses of the word) and sophisticated understanding wasn't behind their initial grasp of the medium.

Under apartheid, because of the coloured communities' relative economic and political privilege (compared to black communities), hip hop was a relatively accessible cultural form (as Ready D freely admits). Coloured people on the Cape Flats may have had to fight over limited numbers of hip hop tapes sent by friends and relatives from overseas but they undoubtedly had more stereos and more connections outside South Africa than their black counterparts did.

These days, of course, hip hop music, movies and fashion are freely available to anyone with a full wallet. What sets someone like Ready D apart from the new breed of Americanised gangsters, therefore, is what he described as his 'treasure chest' of old recordings collected back in the day. This makes me recall something another legendary DJ, Bobbito, said to me in New York: 'Search and discovery is the most neglected element of hip hop.' I guess he had a point.

What's more, I'm fascinated by Ready D's recollection of seeing the 'Buffalo Gals' video for the first time; a video that included B-Boys of all races and skin tones. 'They looked exactly like us,' he said. And this was the primary reason to get into hip hop, and the politics (which are now central to his music) came much later. It's not hard to see why something as simple as familiar physiognomies on a TV screen should be powerfully affirmative for people marginalised by both white power and the black majority.

This fascinates me not least because I reckon the experience is diametrically opposed to my own first steps into hip hop. Like Ready D, I saw hip hop on TV. Unlike Ready D, I said, 'They look nothing like me.' And perhaps this was my primary reason to get into hip hop, and the politics (which are now central to my understanding of it) came much later.

I've already explained – in fact it's probably a truism – that the prosperity of hip hop in the US relies on its capacity both to articulate the black urban experience and to sell its otherness to white people. However, I haven't really considered the precise implications of this. Thinking about it now, it seems like an intuitive (if bizarre) contemporary pop-sociological truth that the majority's desire to associate with 'the other' is matched by marginalised groups' desire to unite with like. But, if this partially illuminates hip hop's success, it also partially explains why its meanings are so disparate. For all the shared love of hip hop – indeed, for all the shared political impulses that hip hop has stimulated – Ready D and I are coming at it from very different angles.

Last night, for example, when Ready D told me about the infiltration of PAGAD by the FBI, my immediate (if unspoken) reaction was one of disbelief. To me, it sounded suspiciously like one of those conspiracy theories so commonplace in hip hop. Would the FBI really be bothered with a small action group, however vigilante, at the toe end of Africa? Of course not. In fact, the story took me back to my interview with Dead Prez when they talked about the CIA's responsibility for America's crack problem: conspiracy theories both.

I said this to Kanyasu and was surprised when she disagreed. 'What makes you think you know best?' she asked. And I had to admit that I've no idea whether the FBI infiltrated PAGAD, the CIA import crack cocaine or the moon landing took place on a Hollywood sound stage. In which case, this is not about truth but about functions of culture. To be blunt, my background – born into a society where, at least superficially, Western capitalism seems to work OK – predisposes me to dismiss such notions as much as Ready D's predisposes him to give such notions credence. Like I said, we are coming to these things from very different angles. At least, though, hip hop has given us the context in which to have the conversations.

On my travels (mental as much as geographic), specific questions about hip hop have begun to give way to broad questions about identity. That's OK. Hip hop has been a significant part of who I am for more than half my life so I figure it's a logical expansion. I've come to realise that the nature of the world we now live in is such that identity (individual, group, national or transnational) is often produced glocally as much as locally, globally as much as glocally and contemporaneously as much as historically. This both stimulates and results in the production of imagined (as opposed to ascribed) identity. What I mean by this is simply that an individual's story of themselves can now be assembled from a seemingly endless array of resources.

The use of the word 'story' here is deliberate and important. You see, the idea of narrative provides a good model with which to examine this phenomenon because I'm beginning to understand that ascribed and imagined identity are not simply different means to similar ends but are fundamentally different processes with fundamentally different implications.

Look at it as this: ascribed identity is like a traditional novel; a mostly inflexible narrative on a single timeline from past to future in which cause and effect are clearly established. On the other hand, imagined identity is, appropriately enough, best compared to a more modern and interactive narrative medium: a Web site. It is a story that consists of numerous hot-linked subplots which can be fully pursued or utterly ignored, a pick-and-mix framework in which time and space are certainly less significant, possibly irrelevant; a model of self in which causality is ever obscure.

And hip hop?

In the creation of imagined identity, ideas or brands or images or, my preference, stories (essentially intangible associative media) are the chief international currency. And if the devil has the best tunes, then at the moment hip hop's got a monopoly on the best stories; partly because of its core attributes (like modernity and flexibility) and partly because of its appropriation by multinational brands and the globalised mass media. As pop cultural phenomena go, hip hop's got a swag-bag full of value. But who's turning that value to profit (real and metaphorical)? Despite being the source of all the ideas, brands, images and stories, it's certainly not hip hop's core constituencies of marginalised young people in cities worldwide.

I hope that by this point in the book, I've set out my stall of what I want. I want hip hop to be reclaimed by its key brokers for the benefit of these core constituencies. However, while listening to

Ready D prompted many questions, one stood out: if hip hop is to be reclaimed, to what precise end?

Ready D told me that you can't fight the propaganda, that at the end of the day it all comes down to economics. I know what he meant but I wanted to say to him that the propaganda is exactly what you can fight – in fact that's what he's doing in his work on the Cape Flats – exactly because it doesn't actually all come down to economics. And then I listened to him talk on behalf of Red Bull and I couldn't help but think that he was effectively collaborating in the appropriation of 'otherness'. Again, I know why and I certainly know Ready D's no fool and can see the ironies. But, unlike me, he's someone who has to deal with the pressing immediacy of local problems. And that's hardly something I can criticise.

If hip hop is genuinely to be reclaimed, therefore, it needs a big idea; something that makes sense in all its constituencies and all imaginations, a narrative device that fits in every hip hop story. This might sound like a fantasy but frankly the alternative – i.e., the status quo – is frequently too miserable to put up with whether, for example, it's African-American ghettoes creating dangerous fantasies out of reality or Americanised African ghettoes creating dangerous realities out of fantasy.

As I write this, the TV is on in the background. It's kids' programming on the South African satellite channel MNet. The presenter is a blond-haired, blue-eyed, chiselled teen pretty boy and, as he introduces the next cartoon, his affected slouch and exaggerated hand movements could have been borrowed from the manner of any rapper. Or, at least, borrowed from the manner of the likes of N'Sync, who borrowed them from any rapper. This time slot on MNet, the time slot for kids, is called 'Yo TV!' Very hip hop. MNet is pay television, not public access, but every day there's an hour or so called 'Open Time', a taster of shows that's free for everyone. I remember something else Ready D said, a passing remark about the Cape Flats. At the height of the gang violence, people flock to their doorsteps to watch the shootouts as free entertainment. This is known as 'Open Time' too.

If hip hop in Cape Town started out as a coloured phenomenon, it doesn't take long to figure that it's changing and fast. We head down to the Brainstorm hip hop matinee at All Nations in Observatory. It's Saturday afternoon and the joint's rammed with mostly black kids. It's a freestyle jam and the crowd's supportive of anybody who dares test their skills, even though a lot of the emcees are pretty hopeless. Only when a couple of little dudes with big attitude step to the mic does the reception change. 'Nigeria in the house, y'all!' they announce before rehashing some old lyrics by Jay-Z, Busta and Mobb Deep. It seems like these two must have spent more time practising their posturing than writing rhymes and the audience, who clearly share Mr Fat's attitude to Americanisms, are soon barracking them off the stage. But the DJs keep the beats kicking and the vibe is generally easy-going enough.

The punters who turn up to see Max Normal at The Jam in District Six couldn't be more different. Almost exclusively white and a little older, a lot of them don't look like hip hop heads at all as skate fashions mingle with indie kids and even the odd goth. Actually, this is largely explained by the band. Because Max Normal are a South African phenomenon and not hip hop as such, rather a four-piece hybrid of hip hop, funk and rock fronted by a white rapper, Waddy Jones, who wears a suit and tie beneath his faraway stare. Jones is a charismatic and deranged showman who lurches between stiff business persona and stage-diving nutter, all the while muttering, spitting or shouting his singular take on the state of the nation. They're not really my cup of tea but it's hard not to be engaged by the energy of the performance and the lyrical wit. 'So throw your spears in the air,' Jones rhymes. 'Cos this is Africa, baby, there's wild animals everywhere.' Then, later, he launches into an ironic sing-along anthem. 'I'm Max Normal,' he chants. 'Dress code strictly formal.' And he leaps into the ecstatic crowd.

While All Nations was predominantly black and The Jam predominantly white, I don't contrast the two to suggest that Cape Town hip hop is racially divided so much as to highlight the way hip hop manages to articulate different aspects of the racial spectrum and, therefore, different aspects of what it means to be South African (I suspect, in fact, that the salaryman angst of Max Normal's album *Songs From The Mall*[17]

---

[17] *Songs From The Mall*, Max Normal, 2001, Chameleon.

would touch a nerve or two in Tokyo). And, besides, I'm beginning to realise that some facets of the scene in this city demonstrate remarkable and heartening racial, cultural and economic integration. And, as I've already indicated, that's largely down to the efforts of a few key characters.

One afternoon at the Drum Café in Woodstock, two dozen teenage girls are going through their dance moves under the watchful eye of their choreographer-cum-mentor-cum-big-sister, Zinaida. She's only just hit her twenties herself – a slim, pretty young woman with a reddish complexion and natural Afro hair – but the girls are happy to listen to her and working hard. They're preparing for the second African Hip Hop Indaba, a now annual Cape Town event and the brainchild of the local Black Noise crew. The Indaba includes lessons in all the hip hop elements and worthy debates about things like 'Negative versus positive hip hop', 'How to build hip hop culture in Africa' and 'Are record labels in the USA destroying the diversity, ideals and objectives of hip hop?' Right on. There are studio demonstrations and freestyle jams concluding with the Battle of the Year for emcees, writers, DJs and breakers.

This time, though, the whole event kicks off with a day called Sisters in Hip Hop. The organisers have rounded up sponsorship from the likes of Lilettes and Rape Crisis and put together a programme of tailored workshops about hip hop and wider women's issues. These girls are performing at the opening and they're as skilful as they are dedicated; popping, locking and uprock-ing in complex choreographed routines to the live turntable skills of Cato, a rare female DJ. Most notable, though, is the racial and social mixture: black, white and coloured; rich and poor. There's Odelle, a coloured kid from Mitchell's Plain, dancing side by side with Elizabeth, a white kid from the exclusive suburb of Claremont.

That this should seem unusual, even to an outsider like me, is a little depressing. But the fact is that, for the moment, South Africa is still at best a manufactured 'Rainbow Nation', so Mandela wearing a Springbok rugby jersey or the quota for cricketers 'of colour' in the national XI are no more than Bandaids on the still raw wound of discrimination. But here? It's not about integration; just B-Girls getting down. So I guess even if the struggle really is one of 'memory against forgetting', it's still worth noting and celebrating kids whose memories barely tag the tail end of apartheid. This is, I figure, the first generation for whom social mixing is not an overt political statement.

Later, chatting to Zinaida, the ongoing pertinence of this becomes apparent. Born to a Zulu mother and a coloured father, she seems to personify many of the lingering confusions and prejudices and some of the new ones too. On the one hand she doesn't speak fluent Zulu; on the other her father is an academic who's spent the majority of her life in exile. He considered returning after the 1994 elections but, she says, 'Do you really think that he [as a coloured guy] would now get a position in an African Studies department? You're joking.' Zinaida herself, therefore, has grown up not so-called white, nor so-called black nor even, in fact, so-called coloured,[18] but in a position of constant racial otherness. In this context and in the context of my new understanding about the glocal nature of hip hop, her involvement in the culture doesn't surprise me.

Of course, I should have asked her what she made of this analysis herself but it never occurred to me while we talked. Nonetheless Zinaida did give me a copy of *A.F.R.O.*, the young black-consciousness/hip hop magazine that she edits and publishes herself, and I reckon the Alice Walker quote she's chosen to head her editorial supports my perception. 'Despite the pain I feel in honestly encountering the reality of life, I find it a wonderful time to be alive. This is because at no other time known to human beings has it been easier to give and receive energy, support and love from people never met, experiences never had.' I haven't been able to locate the source of this quote but I'm as sure that Zinaida was using it to refer to hip hop as I am that Alice Walker was not.

Zinaida tells me a story about the Drum Café. Apparently, yesterday, one of the (white) women who work there accused her group of stealing from the cash box. Zinaida's still fuming: 'She said, "You've got to stop this American shit, it's killing the country.

---

[18] What I mean by this is that Zinaida is of mixed parentage as opposed to mixed heritage. However bizarre that sounds, it is a noted distinction.

And, by the way, honey, you're not black you're yellow." I just thought, "Get on the boat and go back where you came from." It's bad enough hearing that shit from black people but it really made me think twice about the white people I know and what they might be thinking. Race here is becoming like a caste thing.' A caste thing? If that's true the value and meanings attributed to each racial group are situational and abstruse.

Outside the Drum Café, there is a sign trumpeting the venue's drumming workshops as 'the premier African interactive experience'. It seems they even run corporate drumming packages as 'team-building exercises' and the like and they've also launched in London and LA. In my mind's eye, I place this sign next to the comment Zinaida has just related. I set both against the group of B-Girls going through their moves inside and then consider the whole lot in terms of Thabo Mbeki's rallying call. So which can be seen to truly represent 'African renaissance': teenagers breakdancing or businessmen drumming up their profit margins? Which, in fact, truly reflects contemporary South Africa? Received American culture put through a local filter or received local culture packaged for capital's ends? Either, neither or both?

Inside, a young guy's taken over from Cato on the decks; messing around, dropping a drum break in and out and practising his scratching. Then, while the girls rest, he takes to the dancefloor and busts a few moves of his own; down-rocking into swipes, windmills and airplanes. He's a sixteen year-old called Marley. I try to tell him what we're doing in Cape Town but he already knows. Bush telegraph again.

He takes us for a walk around Woodstock to show us some of the nearby pieces by local writers. One in particular stands out: an extraordinary vibrant work by TVA that depicts a crumbling clock and several angelic figures; part Dali and part teenage poster.

Marley starts telling me about a recent beef between the TVA and WOTS crews that saw them repeatedly defacing each other's work. It's a long, convoluted and typical hip hop story so I try to change the subject by saying that I've never been that into graffiti anyway. Marley looks at me puzzled. 'But I thought you were a hip hop head?'

For all my repetition of hip hop's four elements (five if you count 'consciousness', six if you include Bobbito's theory about 'search and discovery'), I realise I've singularly failed to explain their key implication. I've plain forgotten to highlight hip hop's core principle: that it is *participatory*.

Sure, B-Boys may idolise this or that emcee just like rock enthusiasts idolise this or that lead-singer star. And sure, rock enthusiasts may practise their solos on cheap guitars just like B-Boys practise their mixing on cheap decks. However, for B-Boys participation isn't a dream, it's the point; in fact, as Marley's query demonstrates, it's what makes you a hip hop head. While other musical styles are driven by their consumption, hip hop is, at least in part, driven by the doing. So maybe hip hop is the 'premier African interactive experience'.

Narrow your eyes and you could think you were in South Central LA as you move through the Cape Flats districts of Mitchell's Plain and Athlone. Grids of seemingly endless roads criss-cross the dusty landscape past thousands of identical bungalows, concrete and symmetrical. There's graffiti on any unclaimed wall, young men in hip hop gear lounging on every corner and kids who pause in their games to stare as you pass. Old men glance up from their *stoep*[19] where they're killing time with their friends and drinking from super-sized bottles of beer.

I remember the first time I went to South Central. It must have been towards the end of '96. It wasn't for work (I was actually in LA to interview the original R'n'B supergroup, En Vogue), just tourism, I guess. Until then, my impressions of the place had been formed by the sets of movies like *Colors* and *Boyz N The Hood*: backdrops to urban nightmares of gangs and drugs. When I actually took the time to visit, therefore, I remember being surprised by how 'nice' it all seemed, idyllic even, as pretty, Toy-Town-style houses looked out over pristine lawns and apparently peaceful streets. Only when I opened my eyes a little wider did I begin to notice the number of stores that were boarded up or at least covered in security

---

[19] *Stoep*: Veranda.

measures worthy of Fort Knox. Only then did I notice that the
stores' trade seemed to be solely in alcohol and then I saw the drug
dealers on the curb and then the rags that flashed gang colours like
urban butterflies. So maybe it was just like the movies after all.

Open my eyes a little wider on the Cape Flats and I realise my
comparisons are superficial. For starters, there's a lot of overt
poverty here. Even in some of the best neighbourhoods, a closer
look reveals crumbling buildings and other signs of dilapidation.
What's more, many of the districts of the Flats are cheek by jowl
with shanty towns of tumbledown shelters built of corrugated iron,
scavenged wood, even cardboard. And, of course, the borders of
South Central are symbolic rather than physical. Here the districts
retain their apartheid boundaries, each being entirely surrounded by
broad motorways and railway lines: one way in and one way out for
easier control.

We're with Sky189 from the WOTS crew and Emile, the main
man in Black Noise. We're driving from spot to spot, checking out
Sky's work on the local walls. When they picked us up, I couldn't
help but be struck again by the peculiarities of race in this town.
These two are coloured guys and one of the first things Emile said to
me was, 'In England we'd both be black, right?' In fact, with my
received cultural experience, Emile – cropped hair, thirtysomething, slim and athletic – looks more Asian to me while Sky, who's
short and kind of nuggety-shaped with a long, straight ponytail and
slightly oriental eyes, could pass for a Polynesian. Why does this
matter? It doesn't. But spend enough time in Cape Town and you
find yourself always noticing this kind of thing as if apartheid's
gremlin was sitting on your shoulder and whispering in your ear.

Sky's a friendly, irrepressible character and another multitalented
B-Boy. Aside from the graffiti, he featured as an emcee on the last
Black Noise album.[20] And now WOTS have set up as a graphic-
design company from his mum's Athlone home. But Emile? He's a
lot more circumspect, difficult to read. He used to be a secondary-
school teacher but, like Ready D, has been involved in Cape hip
hop since the very beginning. 'I remember performing at the Mardi

[20] *Circles Of Fire*, Black Noise, 2001, Gimba Music.

Gras at the Cape district soccer field,' he says. 'This is way, way back. We had one really fucked-up turntable and everybody was just rhyming over it. We were doing one song that was really explicit, real 2 Live Crew type of thing. Then, as I'm walking off stage, this kid comes over. "Hello, sir!" It was one of my pupils and I thought, "Shit! I've got to start being careful." ' Emile is cynical, like he's seen and heard it all before. I'm sure he has.

Sky: 'Imagine we started the Universal Hip Hop organisation. It works like this: your track record is my track record, your reputation is my reputation. You're not competing against each other any more because nobody can sign any graf writers, B-Boys, emcees or whatever without the organisation's say so. They're all Universal Hip Hop.'

Emile: 'It's a good idea but it's never going to happen. I agree that there are people worldwide who are now willing to put things into communities that record labels would never do and I agree that we have to take back control of what is happening. But we are constantly battling just to survive. We're fighting with our own community, which always wants to jump on the bandwagon. It's much, much easier to be part of the system than to fight the system.'

We pass a long row of 'Mandela houses'. The ANC swept to power in 1994 with the promise of a million new homes and these are some of them. They're unimpressive one-room structures no more than a few metres square. For all the good intentions, I wonder if the locals regard them as a promise fulfilled.

Emile, I realise, is more than used to showing outsiders around the Cape Flats. He's seen charity workers, film crews, journalists, academics and, indeed, authors come and go. He's more than used to good intentions and more than used to unfulfilled promises, too.

Emile has developed a new interest: capoeira. Just like Ready D and Fat, Emile talks about hip hop's connection with Africa in almost metaphysical terms (at one point he remarks, 'There are forces at work beyond your comprehension'). But Emile has extended this connection to include this Brazilian cultural form that is part game, part dance and part martial art.

Capoeira, it is said, is based on an ancient African style of combat that was resurrected by Brazilian slaves. So that their masters didn't realise they were learning to fight, the slaves disguised the form as a dance and surrounded it with music and drums and song. Part dancing and part battling? The connections with B–Boying are clear. What's more, capoeira often even *looks* like breaking with its athleticism and floorwork and whirling limbs. Emile first came into contact with it a few years back when he saw the American B-flick *Only The Strong* ('Louis Stephens is a former Green Beret who isn't predisposed to take crap from a bunch of high-school punks').[21] More recently he was able to attend a capoeira *batisado* (a kind of celebration-cum-graduation) when Black Noise toured Sweden. Africa to Brazil to Africa via Hollywood and Sweden? I'm figuring that this is the kind of bizarre cultural equation that works these days.

'Kids can learn a lot about Africa from capoeira,' Emile explains. 'I wanted to bring it here as another form of expression because not everybody wants to break. Ask anybody about the best time they have at parties and it will be when they're dancing in the middle of the circle. With capoeira, it's like B-Boying to a live drum. You're dependent on everybody else's energy. That's a similarity to breaking.'

What's more, Emile admits that he likes the way capoeira is structured and he sets it out for Sky like this: 'It's not a democracy. With your Universal Hip Hop, someone's always going to say, "fuck it, I'll rap or DJ or dance for cheaper." Because people always need work and that's a bigger reality than any global organisation. With capoeira, your position is not just about skill. It's about seniority and maintaining the right philosophy.'

By now we're driving through Guguletu, one of the four main black townships on the Flats. Sky says that there's 'a lot of development going on at the moment'. But it still looks pretty miserable to me; neglected and shabby, as if, after decades of being ignored, it's finally been forgotten altogether. Around fifty years ago urbanisation in South Africa reached unprecedented levels as millions of black people headed for the cities in search of work. In Cape Town, Guguletu was the apartheid regime's solution as, by

---

[21] From the Internet Movie Database plot summary at http://www.imdb.com

the principles of racial separation, thousands of blacks were forcibly removed from the neighbouring coloured districts and dumped right here. Occasionally you can still spot the old signposts that are yet to be changed. Each begins 'NY' followed by a number. Flippantly, I wonder aloud whether 'NY' stands for 'New York'. Apparently it stands for 'Native Yard'.

I've already been told by several people that the word *guguletu* means 'our pride' in Xhosa and every one of them's accompanied the comment with a wry smile and a shake of the head. A more appealing use of irony, though, is made by the kids who pronounce Guguletu in faux-French accents so it comes out '*Jeu-jeu-les-toi*'. One boy, his face a mask of mock seriousness, says, 'It's a bourgeois place these days.' It's a good joke.

Back in the car, Sky's telling me that he's got a lot of friends from overseas; always has done. In fact he's married to a Swiss graffiti artist (and fellow member of WOTS) who goes by the name of Smirk. Although they work from the office in Athlone, they've now got an apartment in Claremont, close to town. 'I got out of the ghetto,' Sky remarks, laughing at himself.

We pass a petrol station on our right. The pristine pumps and the neon lighting of the major oil company's sign seem out of place in this environment. Next to the forecourt, a small cross marks the spot where Amy Biehl, a white American student, was murdered in 1994. I remember reading the story. She'd been driving some local guys home when her car was caught up in a mob of militant PAC youth. At the time, the 'one settler, one bullet' slogan was still doing the rounds. They saw the one white face in the car and she was beaten to death. Her murderers were imprisoned but later released under the auspices of the Truth and Reconciliation Commission, with the approval of Amy Biehl's parents who went on to found the Amy Biehl Foundation in her memory.[22] Sky says he was one of the guys in the car with her when it was attacked, one of the guys who got away. At first I think he might be spinning me a story: 'Seriously?' 'Seriously.' We're quiet for a while after that.

---

[22] The Amy Biehl Foundation is a charity that provides educational, employment and recreational opportunities for young people in South Africa.

As we drive back towards Mannenberg, Sky starts talking again. He wants to give us his analysis of the state of modern hip hop. 'It's the "Fuck you, I'm king" theory,' he smiles. 'You see, kids these days who say "bitch" and "nigger", they're all just obsessed with the emcee, as if they think rapping is hip hop, so they're talking loud and saying nothing. They use big words that sound fantastic but what are they actually saying? "Fuck you, I'm king!" Every time. And then the next one says, "Fuck you, I'm king!" '

Emile shakes his head: 'They're just kids. If they're not taught, you can't expect them to learn.'

Sky pulls in for a moment and we all stare at the wall on the opposite side of the road. Here, the usual gang tags have given way to a single enormous mural of Tupac Shakur which was commissioned by the infamous Staggie brothers from the Hard Livings. I ask Sky if he knows the guys who did it but he shrugs. It's been there a few years now and the paint's beginning to fade and peel. I wonder if it looked out of place when it was brand new because now it seems curiously fitting, just another part of the landscape.

A few kids have started checking out the car. Sky kicks it into gear – 'Let's go' – and pulls away. He looks at Kanyasu in the rearview mirror and his eyes are twinkling. 'So. Are you guys together then or what?' Kanyasu nods. 'And Emile's girlfriend's Swedish!' He exclaims. 'So this whole car's got jungle fever!' Emile is laughing as Sky launches into some karaoke Stevie Wonder: 'I've got jungle fever / She's got jungle fever / We've got jungle fever / We're in love!'

I'm looking out of the back window at the receding wall. I wonder what the New York-born, LA-raised, Vegas-murdered Tupac would have made of 'thug life' on this side of the planet. I wonder what he'd have made of this iconic representation of himself in a place he'd never been to and, I guess, was never likely to go to. I wonder if he'd have thought, 'Fuck you, I'm king!'

It's late on a Friday night and Woodstock is pretty much deserted. Bush Radio (Cape Town's community station) is empty too and would be silent but for the banging hip hop and deranged laughter that shake the walls of the small studio. It's the weekly *Headwarmers* show and the two DJs, the lead guy and his straight man, are having a gas. One minute they're gently mocking some kid who's rung in to freestyle live on air, the next they're dead serious as they extol the importance of a good education. Then they crack up again. They drop that Common Sense 12 on Rawkus,[23] then they decide to interview me but get no further than taking the piss out of my accent and sticking on a tune by Bristol DJ Skitz[24] – ostensibly in my honour; in fact to cover their giggles. Next up is KRS One but even the maestro doesn't meet their approval and they start to banter before the end of the intro.

'What's he *talking* about?' asks the lead guy. 'You have any idea what he's talking about?'

'I have no idea,' says his straight man.

'You have no idea?'

'No idea.'

'I mean, Kris, love and respect and all that because you *are* the man. But, down here? You've got to speak our language because we don't know what you're talking about.'

'He *is* hip hop.'

'What's that?'

'KRS One. That's what he said. "I *am* hip hop." '

'I am hip hop. You are hip hop. He is hip hop.' He reverts to his London accent and addresses me. 'What 'bout you, geezer? You hip hop?'

'Umm. Yeah,' I mutter.

'So we're all hip hop!' he announces, starts laughing again and sticks on a track by Dilated Peoples.

In this exchange, the straight man is Big Dre, one of Cape Town's most respected DJs, a mild, light-skinned coloured dude who never seems to stop smiling. But it's his compadre we've actually come to see. This is Shaheen; one-time Prophet Of Da City, some-time clown, full-time hip hop head.

In his way, Shaheen is the perfect counterpoint to his POC partner Ready D. Where Ready D is all quiet intensity, Shaheen

---

[23] '1–9–9–9', Common, 1999, Rawkus.
[24] 'Twilight Of The Gods', DJ Skitz, 2000, Ronin.

chats easily and laughs a lot: at himself, at me, at hip hop. Where Ready D seems to weigh each word, Shaheen blabbers them out with 'fuck it' unselfconsciousness. Where Ready D is cynical, Shaheen has wit like a whip.

Even physically, they're complete opposites: Ready D solid and squat, Shaheen a skinny character with wispy beard and cartoon features that animate all at once when he talks. He's wearing a cap pulled low at a skewed angle and a pair of original Adidas shelltops. 'Check out my cultural capital!' he laughs.

He uses language like that a lot. A couple of years ago he decided to go back to studying and now he's completing a degree at the University of Cape Town. Again, this is an interesting contrast with his former partner. BVK's decision to rap in *gamtaal*[25] was about reclaiming coloured identity on the Cape Flats, standing their metaphorical ground to document their own culture in their own language. Shaheen, on the other hand, has taken the opposite approach. His decision to go back to college was all about learning a different language; of academia, politics, power. It's a dialectical equation that brings to mind a Tricky lyric from *Pre-Millennium Tension*: 'I'll master your language and in the meantime I'll create my own'.[26]

'If you want change, you need access to certain things,' Shaheen explains. 'And you probably have to sacrifice a couple of years to do the academic shit. I mean, I read bullshit about hip hop in South Africa all the time. But what am I going to do? Whatever I might think, it's still in a library somewhere. I can tell our story right but how am I going to do that? OK. I've got to learn the language.'

This makes me think back to the whole Ebonics debate in the States; that people can be disempowered simply by their use of a particular phrase, slang or dialect. However, this dynamic can, of course, work both ways and that's a dilemma Shaheen understands better than anyone.

You see, we start talking about the appropriation of hip hop by mainstream media and multinational companies and the negative

---

[25] *Gamtaal*: Cape slang based on Afrikaans.
[26] 'Christiansands' from *Pre-Millennium Tension*, Tricky, 1996, Mercury.

impacts this has had on the culture's core constituencies worldwide. I feel like we're rhyming, Shaheen and me, like we're on exactly the same wavelength. But then he smiles and starts to shake his head. 'Trouble is, what you're saying is academic. You know how sceptical people are about academics?'

'Sure . . .' I begin but he's not done.

'It doesn't matter whether I agree with you or not. Because people are mad suspicious. Like, you know the jazz clubs down here in the '50s and '60s? White people come and take photographs and bring their friends and whatever. They take their pics, write some shit up, publish books and get permission to go all over the world talking about it. But the cats who actually do jazz? They're on the street fucking dying of TB! That's what I'm explaining to you. People are extremely cautious and cynical. To be honest, I totally understand that.

'Like the course I'm doing: Contemporary Popular Culture. They talk about hip hop in this city. I'm looking at the stuff and thinking, "This is such a lot of bullshit!" Here I am, a first-year student because I've decided to go back to school. And here they are, talking about shit I've been involved with for twenty years. Some of the stuff? It's so fucking limited. You think white people are ever going to get the inside scoop?'

'Would you want them to?' It's Kanyasu asking the question.

'To be mad honest? I just want to get the tools I need. Otherwise I don't give a fuck.'

Right. Shaheen's staring at me. I think I must be looking a bit forlorn because he suddenly packs up laughing, leans forward, playfully punches my arm and adopts his mock Cockney accent again: 'It's awright, geezer! You keep doing your shit. You do what you gotta do, know what I mean?'

'Look,' I begin. 'I understand what you mean about getting the tools you need but you're not actually thinking about trying to change the world on your own, are you? You need other people and hip hop automatically provides a worldwide network. And now, because hip hop's got more cultural capital than any other popular form, there's actually the possibility of doing something. That's all I'm saying. It's not academic.'

'Doing what?' Shaheen's still grinning.

'What?'

'You said there's the possibility of doing something. Doing what?'

'I don't know. In the first instance just getting people talking about the same issues; showing people that they have similar struggles and empowering them to identify with something bigger that offers them support.'

'And you're going to do that?'

'No!' I'm getting flustered. 'I'm just pointing out that the network exists already. The potential is there but nobody's tapping into it.'

'I talk to guys overseas,' Shaheen sighs. 'That's *exactly* what I do. If I go down to Brooklyn, I see it's exactly the same situation as in Mitchell's Plain. I meet guys from Puerto Rico who use hip hop to protest about American bomb testing.[27] That's really encouraging.

'I know that it's about more than hip hop but it's hip hop that allows me to see clearly. If you look at developing countries, globalisation is fucked up. Look how it's connected to colonialism and expansion; all the countries that have been under-developed by economic slavery and colonialism for fifty years and now they're forced to develop at the rate defined by G8 or the WTO or whoever. So the rich get richer and the poor get poorer. I see it daily on the streets right here and it breaks my heart. Speaking to other cats overseas, I'm beginning to realise that they think exactly like we do because this shit's happening all over the world. But . . . But talking about organising globally . . .'

Shaheen pauses and fiddles with his cap. He turns it back to front and then the right way round again. Eventually he holds up his hand, spreads his fingers and counts them off one by one.

'I say five things to you. First: you've got to know who you're up against. Even KRS One advertises Sprite. He advertises Nike as well, I think. Maybe he gives all the cash to NGOs and maybe they spend it right and maybe they don't. But going up against the

---

[27] He is referring to US testing in Vieques and tunes like 'Viequez' by Shanghai Assassinz (1999, Shanghai Records).

multinationals? You really think you can win? Second: a lot of us feel comfortable being in victim mode. Because we don't want to take responsibility for our situations and I understand that. But a cat who doesn't like things the way they are? He has to get out of his comfort zone and move from complainer to activist; from finger-pointer to fucking soldier. And that's hard because you're talking about people whose sense of self-worth is completely fucked up.

'Third: don't expect too much. I know I'm not in a position to do shit yet but I can taste it. That doesn't mean I'm sitting around waiting; we're working with kids, making our little contribution. But I know I need access to certain things before I can do more. If you're talking about global connections? Fucking hell! You know, I just want to connect to people overseas so that we can share information or share materials or even share pencils. You've got too many pencils? Send them over here because we'll put them to good use. Too many T-shirts? Send them over here because we'll wear them. Too many coconuts? Send them. Just create that global vibe of helping each other.

'Where am I? Four? OK. Fourth: you've got to be cautious and you've got to be humble. If a global network is the way to do things, better keep quiet about it. A lot of people will be against it because everyone has their own agenda. You need to create, like, a hip hop illuminati if possible! And that leads to the last thing: personal development. It's so bloody important because everything starts with the individual. I'm regarded as a leader because I've been in this for twenty years. But that creates its own pressure. To be a real emcee? You've got to remove the ego. It comes through you, not from you. Real hip hop? It's about the process. That's what I've learned.'

Shaheen stops talking and leans back in his chair. He yawns. It's well past midnight and for a moment he looks exhausted. He says he's got an assignment to write tomorrow. It must be knackering being a full-time prophet (of this or any other city), full-time student and full-time hip hop head. He cracks another smile. 'Listen to me! Even I'm talking like a fucking academic now. I'd better be careful.'

'But it's important, right?'

'What?'

'All this stuff. It's important to care about this stuff.'

'Sure. It's worth a shot, you know? It's worth a fucking shot. I tell you, hip hop is so fucking loaded with meaning. You need to understand I grew up in a community where the cops were shooting at you just for being you, know what I'm saying? For me hip hop was about self-worth, dignity, expression, allowing yourself to be wild and allowing yourself to develop your consciousness all at the same time. Of course it's important to care.

'But I'm going to be completely fucking straight about this: I love hip hop. I'm a hip hop head. I've been involved in this thing since 19-fucking-80. I've had death threats, police shit, I couldn't sleep at home, I've been shot at. All the bullshit you hear? All the struggle stories people tell to get credibility? I've been through all of that right here in South Africa. But – and this is the point – if it's not going to serve a purpose, if it's not going to allow people to develop in some way and make things happen to improve the lot of the people then . . . well . . . Fuck hip hop. I mean that, I really do. Fuck hip hop.'

Shaheen yawns again. Then he laughs. 'I never thought I'd say that.'

For all Shaheen's understandable frustration, of course, he is actually helping people to develop, to improve their lot; Ready D, Zinaida, Sky, Emile and many others in Cape Town too. In this city, hip hop makes a difference. While I may have found the scent of possibility in Jo'burg, here, like Shaheen, I can taste it. I can taste the same flavour that first attracted me to hip hop half my life ago and I can taste a future where this culture makes a difference glocally. Put simply, I now know that hip hop is capable of articulating positive struggle locally and I know there is already a network that can support such struggles globally. It's only a question of having the imagination to see it.

Does this sound like a pipe dream? OK. But I recall American social theorist Daniel Bell's famous dictum – 'The nation-state is becoming too small for the big problems of life, and too big for the small problems of life'[28] – and in my head this idea ties up with

---

[28] Cited in *Globalization*, Malcolm Waters, 1995, Routledge.

another from a very different source. There's a track from the '94 POC album *Phunk Phlow*,[29] called 'Neva Again' celebrating Mandela's election to the presidency. At one point Shaheen raps, 'I know those who supported the struggle locally / I support your struggle globally.' So I guess Shaheen had already got the picture the best part of ten years ago. Hip hop has always been small enough for the small problems but now I reckon it's big enough for the big ones too.

Perhaps it still sounds odd to you to talk about hip hop in such terms. After all, it's just pop music, right? Well. Even if I believed that to be true, pop music is important in these days when brands dominate ideologies and the medium is almost always the message. In the introduction to his analysis of modern imperialism, *The New Rulers of the World*,[30] John Pilger describes the death of social democracy in Western nations as 'the reduction of democracy to electoral ritual: that is, competition between indistinguishable parties for the management of a single-ideology state.' He goes on to describe the multinational media giants as central to this and the globalising process. 'They [the media conglomerates] provide a virtual world of the "eternal present", as *Time* magazine called it: politics by media, war by media, justice by media, even grief by media (Princess Diana).' He might, of course, have added 'culture by media' too.

In such a context hip hop, as the most successful American (and therefore worldwide) musical form and a significant global brand signifier, potentially has serious clout both as a voice of protest amid the monolithic, neo-colonial message and as a local catalyst for change. The multinational media giants can 'own' politics, war, justice and even grief but, by its very nature, they cannot own hip hop.

That said, of course, the global players (media, corporate, even political) have borrowed it very successfully. And while the majority of popular American hip hop may dress itself up in the paraphernalia of protest (when it rails against the police, pulls a gun or curses its

---

[29] *Phunk Phlow*, POC, 1994, Ghetto Ruff.
[30] *The New Rulers Of The World*, John Pilger, Verso, 2002.

mother), its core ideology – be ambitious, get successful, buy stuff and doesn't your wealth look pretty against the poverty of your peers? – is very much on message. But that's OK. It has all helped to globalise the hip hop brand.

Now, though, hip hop has to be reclaimed for its core constituencies. It might sound like a big ask but remember, hip hop retains its cultural capital (from the basketball courts of Brooklyn to the painted walls of the Cape Flats) and, to be blunt, there's always going to be a lot more ghetto kids than there are rap stars. It requires, therefore, only a leap of the imagination (and, perhaps, another reassertion of Bobbito's comment that 'search and discovery is the most neglected element of hip hop').

The first step is to recognise the global network and ensure it's communicating productively. It took a while to for me to realise it but, in fact, even for someone like me, such a network already exists. Before I went to the States, of course, it was friends and contacts in London who gave me introductions to the likes of Kenyatta (from Black L.I.B.) and Bobbito. In Japan, I found that Yuko knew Ameachi (from Ozone). As I leave Shaheen, I suddenly remember to pass on the number of a mate of mine, Bandit, from the Birmingham crew M.S.I. & Asylum. Those two hooked up a couple of years ago and Bandit's keen that they should get in touch again. When we get back to Jo'burg, Dylan shows us a documentary he'd made about African hip hop. This is Dylan who I was introduced to via a kwaito guy I knew in London; Dylan who used to emcee with a couple of Zimbabwean mates of mine, remember? We're watching the South African section and suddenly there's Bobbito on camera. Apparently he was down here three months ago. I didn't know that. Stranger still, when the documentary leaps to Nairobi, the audience is introduced to the city by the editor of local hip hop mag, *Phat*. He's a guy called Moses, one of Kanyasu's oldest friends. It's a small, small hip hop planet.

I'm not suggesting that all these connections are major players in global hip hop. That's not the point. All I'm highlighting is that it takes me less than five minutes to figure out my identity in my personal, globalised hip hop network. Imagine the kind of networks that could be figured out by the likes of Kenyatta or Ready D. Or, rather, figure out the kind of networks that they could imagine because '*ubuntu ungumuntu ngabanye abantu*'.

As for hip hop articulating local struggle, of course that's already happening too. I've heard it in the lyrics of BVK, maybe in Black L.I.B.'s cry of 'Play My Shit' as well, even in the anti-establishment rhymes of Tokyo's King Giddra. But I also know it's happening all over the world. Just as Shaheen tells me about Puerto Ricans rapping against America's military presence on the island, so I've met emcees from Dar es Salaam who address the Aids epidemic. I've hung out with Natural Desastro, a crew of Francophone Africans who live in Rome and write rhymes about the treatment of the immigrants who sell bootleg CDs on the city streets. I hear that in New Zealand there are Maori emcees who use hip hop to preserve their language and in Australia an aboriginal band called Blackjustis who talk about racism and land rights. Check out a track called '537 C.U.B.A.'[31] by the Parisian-based Cubans Orishas. It takes the traditional song 'Chan Chan' and transforms it into an anthem for expatriate Cubans worldwide who live with dislocation and aliena- tion. The title is taken from Cuba's international dialing code – 537. Recently, when I was in Paris, I caught up with Djoloff, a Senegalese band who mix hip hop with their local musical styles. It was during La Fête de la Musique[32] and I found myself chatting to Mbégane Ndour in the grounds of the French Foreign Ministry where they were due to play that night. 'They think we're good for their image,' Mbégane laughed. 'I'm sure nobody in the ministry has checked all our criticisms of French foreign policy.'

Hunched over my handheld in a Cape Town hotel room I wrote, 'If hip hop is genuinely to be reclaimed, therefore, it needs a big idea; something that makes sense in all its constituencies and all imaginations . . .' Reading Jeff Chang's *Village Voice* review[33] of Bakari Kitwana's excellent *The Hip Hop Generation*, I was intrigued to find him come to much the same conclusion. Chang writes: 'For Kitwana's Third World Press mentors, politics—specifically decades

---

[31] '537 C.U.B.A.' from *A Lo Cubano*, Orishas, EMI, 1999.

[32] La Fête de la Musique is the French music festival held on 21 June every year.

[33] 'Generation H', Jeff Chang, *The Village Voice*, May 2002.

of African decolonization and American civil rights activism—begat culture. Kitwana and the hip-hop intellectuals are faced with the opposite dilemma. In this generation, the culture must foster a politics.'

In fact, though, we find ourselves in a world where, as Pilger puts it, democracy is reduced to electoral ritual. This begs a flippant question – should hip hop concern itself with politics when politicians have long since stopped bothering? – but it also, I think, highlights a serious point. Hip hop's strength has always been in the diversity of its symbolism and meanings and that is one good reason for its global success. Even in its development, therefore, it needs to retain such flexibility. So, in the first place, the culture needn't foster any politics beyond its intrinsic ethos of protest.

In his decade-old book *Powershift*,[35] Alvin Toffler described post-national power in the hands of what he termed 'global gladiators'. Aside from the obvious corporate giants, he identified the likes of resurgent religions and radical NGOs as new brokers of transnational power. If he were writing today, I guess terrorist groups would be the first new boys in his equation. But I would argue that hip hop should not be far behind. Hip hop is and will continue to be a global gladiator for expression for the unexpressed, representation for the unrepresented and value for the unvalued; as simple as that. I've been looking for 'the big idea' when in fact that's exactly what hip hop is and has been all along.

Hip hop negotiates 'experiences of marginalisation, brutally truncated opportunity, and oppression'. That's its politics. Hip hop is four, five or six key elements. That's its politics too. Hip hop means participation, it 'comes through you not from you'. Participation is always political. Hip hop is a popular identity consumed by young people worldwide. In the era of globalised super-brands, consumption is more political than ever. Hip hop could capitalise on its reputation. That could be its politics. Hip hop should mean acting locally, connecting globally, thinking glocally. Surely that should be its first political manifesto.

---

[35] *Powershift: Knowledge, Wealth And Violence at the Edge of the 21st Century*, Alvin Toffler, Bantam, 1991.

Part Five: Rio de Janeiro
One Day It'll All Make Sense[1]

·Our last journey is to Rio via London. That's one hell of a schlep and I've got plenty of time to ponder why I chose Rio. In fact, the answer is simple enough. First, I have read a lot about hip hop in the city's slums and it seems to offer something different and interesting. Second, I heard a Brazilian proverb: 'Brazil is the country of the future – and always will be.' I liked the black humour of that and the sentiments seemed to make it an ideal place to finish up. Most of all, though, I wanted to go somewhere I've never been and about which I know next to nothing. I've visited New York, Tokyo and South Africa several times before so I need to head for a place with as few preconceptions as possible.

On the flight back to London, I get out my notebook with every intention of working but I'm knackered and I can't seem to string two coherent thoughts together. Unfortunately my head's too busy to sleep too so, on this leg of the journey alone, I manage to watch *Shrek* three times back to back.

We stop over in London and I head out for the night with a couple of my oldest mates. Maybe it's the jet-lag or maybe it's the *Clockwork Orange*-style indoctrination of spending eight hours with a mini TV screen at the end of my nose but, as the drink flows, I launch into a diatribe about the racist overtones of the movie I've just watched and watched and watched again.

You see, Shrek is a Negroid-featured ogre, right, who lives in a swamp. In the nearby city, the evil lord decides to clean up his

[1] *One Day It'll All Make Sense*, Common, Relativity, 1997.

neighbourhood and banishes all 'magical creatures' to Shrek's domain. The ogre's none too happy about this enforced exodus to his – what shall we call it? – ghetto because he won't be able to live his filthy life in peace. Sure, the ghetto is a fun-looking place where you can fart your life away if you so choose, but it's clearly a ghetto nonetheless.

So Shrek goes to see the lord ('Do you think he's compensating for something?' he asks when he sees the castle towers; a cheap dick gag for anyone who's missed the stereotyped racial subtext so far) and bargains himself a deal. If he saves the princess from the dragon, he'll be allowed to live in his slum in peace.

Shrek heads off to the dragon's lair and rescues the princess. Only trouble is, on the journey back, Shrek falls in love with her himself because, despite her noble background, she turns out to be totally streetwise. Maybe this shouldn't be so surprising because she too has a touch of magic about her and every night, when the sun goes down, she metamorphoses into an ogre.

Fortunately, hers is not a terminal condition and it transpires that when she kisses her one true love she'll assume her real form for ever. It has to be Shrek, we think. Go Shrek!

But Shrek delivers the princess to the evil lord. They're about to tie the knot when the sun starts to set and, hey presto, the princess is an ogre once more. For the lord, of course, the marriage is now a no go. After all, who'd want to marry an ogre? So Shrek rushes forward to kiss her and we expect her transformation back into a beautiful girl. Nothing doing. Turns out that, for all her daytime beauty, she is essentially magical (just as, say, an octoroon was essentially black) and so she returns with Shrek to his township where they live, we're guessing, 'happily ever ogre'.[2]

My friends are nonplussed. One of them points out that most of the stuff I'm talking about is in fact jibes directed by Dreamworks (the production company) at the typically whitewashed fare (*Pocahontas*, for example) churned out by arch rivals Disney.

---

[2] Trawling the Web, it's amazing how many articles you can find discussing race, identity and social morality in *Shrek*. I confess I've plagiarised this phrase from one of the best, by Eric Metaxas at christianitytoday.com

Another suggests that, by my interpretation, the whole movie actually sounds very politically correct. After all, the ogre/black guy/ethnic minority/ghetto kid wins the day and gets the girl, doesn't he? But I'm not having it. In the first place, Shrek only gets the girl when she turns out to have been an ogre all along, while, if she'd been a real princess, he'd never have got a look in. In the second place, I find it implicationally dubious that Shrek and his new girlfriend return to the swamp/ghetto/slum/township because, so the story goes, they'll only be happy in such (albeit romanticised) squalor.

Why do I recount this story? Partly because of the reaction of most of my mates, which largely consisted of bored shrugs and comments like, 'Even if you're right, so what?' Partly, too, because I reckon that my investigation of hip hop (a language of protest) has enabled me to question received culture like never before (a further example of Blaze's assertion in Jo'burg that hip hop fosters all sorts of critical thought). Most of all, however, I recount this story because of the singular reaction to my polemic of Francesca, one of my oldest friends, which relates to hip hop very well. She commented that the really interesting thing about *Shrek* is the way a traditional fairy-tale structure is turned upside down and she wondered what the implications of that might be. On reflection I see that she was on to something.

Shrek is not your typical fairy-tale hero. After all, he's an ogre for starters. So the fact that he gets the girl is a pretty obvious twist on the traditional. What's more, Shrek doesn't just get the girl but it's *his* kiss that turns her into an ogre too; this is like the heroine kissing the frog prince and turning herself into a frog. But these are just two minor examples of subversion (and ones obviously intended by the film-makers who seem to revel in the postmodern ironies) when compared to the main issue: Shrek's background. And this is where I start thinking about hip hop.

What are fairy-tales for? A standard explanation is that they socialise our kids, leading them on their journey to maturity by teaching them core social values like bravery in adversity and sacrifice. Most typically, however, they are about inclusion. They frequently take a character who, by force of circumstance or evil, is outside the mainstream and, as the plot unfolds, that character's merits (often with a magical catalyst) enable their integration (so Snow White and Cinderella, for example, get to marry their princes and Beauty redeems the Beast).

But Shrek? He's a grumpy so and so. He's an ugly outsider and he knows it and, what's more, that's the way he likes it. He's sympathetic, certainly, and he finds his redemption in true love, but then he wants to head back to his swamp (hardly surprising, given the representation of the city as a place of rules, regulations and oppressive conformity).

This, then, is a movie that celebrates not inclusion but alienation and isn't that, as I've already suggested, a very contemporary kind of celebration? Shrek is an antihero; not because of his character but because of his background. Kids think he's cool and funny and they may even want to be like him but that's never going to happen because he's an ogre. Shrek may even teach society a lesson through his actions but they still don't lead to his inclusion. For the mainstream, he is a charming (if dangerous) representation of otherness and exotica who we can cheer all the way back to the ghetto. He really should have been a rapper.

Another Brazilian saying goes like this: 'We don't have a racial problem because blacks here know their place.' In Brazil, that place is more often than not the swamp of poverty. In Rio, that place is generally the ghetto or *favela*.[3] And yet, despite the brutality of this proverb, the symbolism, representation and understanding of race in Brazil is a good deal more complex than in the USA or the UK (or, indeed, in *Shrek*).

At the time of the abolition of the slave trade in the 1850s, around half the population of Brazil were black slaves. Taking the number of freed slaves into account (around twelve per cent), this put black people in a clear majority over the whites and the mixed-race *mulattos*. Before the end of the nineteenth century, however, there was a huge wave of immigration from Europe which significantly changed the racial demographic until, by the '50s, only eleven per cent of Brazilians were classified as black. By the time of

---

[3] *Favela*. Shanty town.

the census of 1991, this had fallen to five per cent with whites now the majority of the population and *mulattos* a close second. At first glance, it seems an extraordinary turnaround; but all aspects of Brazilian culture require, I find, more than one glance.

I suppose my received cultural understanding of race is largely based on the dichotomised American model processed through the lens of typically British euphemism: i.e., a white person is someone of wholly white ancestry while a black person is someone with almost any amount (no matter how small) of African blood. Throw other races into the mix and I start to use the very British, catch-all term 'ethnic minority'. But in Brazil, it's very different. You see, race is not really about 'race' at all, but 'colour'.

Since the emancipation of the slaves in 1888, Brazilian society has actually been constructed on the idea of racial mixture. At one level, this has enabled successive generations of Brazilian intellectuals to look at the racial problems in the United States with smug self-satisfaction. At another level, though, the creation of a racially mixed society was less a question of choice than inevitability. The formalised preservation of a white elite was never going to be possible in a nation in which whites were in the minority (albeit a significant one; something white South Africa, of course, might have realised decades earlier). What's more, for all the rhetoric, the lack of segregation has done little to stop racism or promote opportunities for all. As Marshall Eakin points out in his entertaining introduction to Brazilian culture:[4] 'In 1990, just seven congressmen (out of 559) considered themselves black, and only six of Brazil's 362 bishops were black in a nation with a population of 70 million blacks and mulattos. Out of nearly 13,000 Catholic priests, only about 200 are black.'

I reckon the most intriguing phrase here is 'considered themselves'. Since race in Brazil is about colour rather than heritage (real or mythologised), there are (literally) countless descriptive terms for your complexion. The apparent drop in the black population in the last 100 years or so can, therefore, be partially explained by the fact that censuses require respondents to racially

[4] *Brazil – The Once And Future Country*, Marshall Eakin, 1998, Macmillan.

describe themselves. Apparently being 'black' is rarely an attractive option.

I have already talked long and hard about the modern phenomenon of imagined (as opposed to ascribed) identity and the possibilities of such an idea. I am nonetheless taken aback to find in Rio that race itself can be a creation of the imagination. I guess that in the London society in which I grew up race remained one of the few absolutes of definition (in contrast to for example, class or nationality). But now I'm beginning to see that even this may be an old-fashioned idea. Is someone of a particular race because you say so, because the majority says so or because they say so themselves?

Our first experience of the peculiarities of colour in Brazil comes within hours of landing at Rio. I call up this English guy, Luke, and he agrees to meet us at *posto* 9 on Ipanema beach.

Posto 9 is simply the number of the lifeguard tower but it doesn't take long to figure it's also much more than that as these stations punctuate this stretch of sand socially as much as physically. Eight, for example, is where gays hang out. Nine is for beautiful young *cariocas*[5] and the *gringos*[6] who like to watch them. Ten marks the seriously wealthy and beyond that you'll find the *favelados*.

What's this got to do with colour? Well, the social divisions on the beach can be seen as a microcosm of divisions in Rio as a whole. They are divisions of custom rather than law but, in practice, as the city prostrates itself on the sand to deepen its tan, the darkest complexions are always likely to be found as Ipanema gives way to the polluted section of Leblon and from there hits the mountainside where the Rocinha *favela* looks down across the beach idyll.

Of course there are light-skinned *favela* kids too. Often you can spot them as they cover themselves with the homemade white paste that bleaches their body hair as they sunbathe. Luke says that if you ask a *carioca* what colour they think they are, they will almost always give you an answer one shade lighter than the truth.

*   *   *

[5] *Cariocas*: residents of Rio.
[6] *Gringos*: anyone who's not Brazilian.

So who exactly is this Luke character, then? Here's a fairytale or something like it.

While, in the planning stages, the idea of pitching up in a strange city and hunting down some hip hop sounded like an adventure (even the point), now that I'm about to do it, the prospect seems altogether more daunting; especially when I haven't made a single contact, haven't booked a place to stay and don't speak a word of Portuguese beyond 'caipirinha'. Consequently, when out with my friends back in London, I ask if any of them have got Rio connections. At first I get nothing but shaking heads and blank stares but then someone says, 'What about Luke Dowdney? I heard he's in Rio.'

Luke Dowdney? It's a name I haven't heard in ages.

I was at school with Luke about fifteen years ago. He's a bit younger than me, and I remember only a couple of things about him. One: he was a some-time graf writer. Two: he was a mouthy little geezer who was badly picked on and ended up leaving the school.

I haven't seen him for more than a decade but it doesn't take me long to track down an e-mail address and drop him a line. He gets back to me almost at once. Sure enough he's based in Rio and, what's more, he knows most of the local hip hop heads. So it seems my personal hip hop network extends further than I even knew. He even promises to sort out a good, cheap hotel and find someone to pick us up from the airport.

Sitting by the pool on the roof of our Flamengo hotel (a pool on the roof? He was good to his word), it's strange to see Luke again as the scrawny adolescent I remember is now shaven-headed, about 6′1″ and built like an oak tree. I'd like to see the big kids at my school try and fuck with him now. What's more, when he tells me what he's been up to, it's quite some story.

Fed up with getting hassle, Luke started boxing in his teens. After sixth-form college, he took Social Anthropology at university and got the chance to do some fieldwork in Recife in the northeast of Brazil. It was his first visit to this country. He also began to take boxing more seriously and became damn good at it, ending up winning the British Universities middleweight title. When he finished studying, he considered turning pro and he flew to Japan to fight over there. After one bout, though he won easily, he felt nauseous and shaky and his vision began to falter. It turned out he'd had a minor brain haemorrhage and he was told not to box again.

He wasn't sure what to do next but he knew he didn't want to go back to England so he headed for Rio on a whim. Speaking passable Portuguese, he took a job with Viva Rio, a local charity, as an international fundraiser. He also went back into the gym. This time, while sparring with a local pro, he wasn't so lucky and a full-blown haemorrhage left him unconscious for a couple of days. He knew he had to give up boxing for good.

But Luke had an idea. Under the auspices of Viva Rio, he set up the Luta Pela Paz (fight for peace) boxing club in Parque União, one of the fifteen *favelas* that make up the Complexo Da Maré. The premise was a simple one: to keep the teenage boys who so typically become the *soldados*[7] of the *favela* drug factions[8] out of trouble by teaching them the skills and disciplines of the sport.

The project has been a real success. He has around fifty regular members and has already trained his first district junior champion. More to the point, he's brought in a youth psychologist who teaches the boys about citizenship and peaceful conflict resolution and he's managed to find some boys work placements and to encourage others back into school. Nonetheless, the gym's had its fair share of problems. For example, Luke intended to attract boys from different *favelas* which are under the control of different drug factions. But because the gym is located in a Commando Vermelho (the Red Command, the largest faction) *favela*, it's proved almost impossible to persuade kids from other neighbourhoods to join. Worse, Luke worries that the gym and he himself are beginning to be associated with Commando Vermelho. He's in something of a catch-22: while he knows he must not be associated with any

---

[7] *Soldados*: soldiers. The word generally used to describe the drug factions' personnel.

[8] I use the word 'faction' rather than, say, 'gang' mostly because it is both the term Luke uses and one they generally use themselves: *facção de drogas*. It is meant to show that these groups are distinguished from mere criminals by the extent and extreme violence of their activities.

particular faction, he also knows he can't even get into the *favela* without the tacit approval of the guys in charge.

As Luke talks about *favela* triumphs and disasters, I punctuate the conversation with a series of pretty vacant questions; mostly variations on the theme of 'Is it really as bad as all that?' And Luke relates a series of stories that convince me that it's not just that bad but worse.

He tells me about chatting to one of the boys in his boxing club, about how to get from one point in Rio to another. The kid's proposed route was a round-the-houses tour; a zig-zag movement across the city that ensured, for reasons of his own safety, that he never left Commando Vermelho territory. This kid wasn't a *soldado*. He had no connections with the faction beyond coming from the Complexo Da Maré. Luke claims that this kind of thing is typical. *Favela* kids' lives, he says, are so permeated by the factions that even their spatial awareness of the city they live in is as inaccurate as those Eurocentric mediaeval maps (or, indeed, the Eurocentric modern maps). They know that this street, mall or district is controlled by the faction that runs their *favela* and they can move freely in these areas. But the rest of the city is so out of bounds that it may as well not exist.

Luke gets to his feet and strolls around the hotel's peaceful pool deck and points out the different *favelas* in the distance. It's strange because I looked out over this view just a few minutes ago and I didn't seem to notice them. Now, at second glance, they're unmissable; cluttered shanty towns that stud the landscape on all sides.

Funny place, Rio; not least topographically with the rocky outcrops that punctuate the city and tower above the picturesque bay. In London, if you talk about slums, you might refer to 'the inner city' where poverty clusters in a vacuum of decent housing and amenities. In Paris, on the other hand, you'll talk about the *banlieues*, on the outskirts, as the location of the underprivileged. But in Rio, if you choose to notice them, the *favelas* are everywhere; cities within a city, no-go areas for the rest of the population, often looking down on the wealthy from the miserable hillsides they've colonised.

'They're places apart,' Luke says. 'What you've got to understand is it's war out there.' I soon come to understand that this is a loaded statement.

When he's not running his gym, Luke still works as a senior researcher for Viva Rio. At the moment he's working on a project to try and raise awareness of and change attitudes to the participation of children in Rio's armed factions and similar situations worldwide. In '96, Graca Machel published a UN report on 'The Impact Of Armed Conflict On Children' which had a profound effect on worldwide recognition of the plight of child soldiers in recognised war zones (more than ninety countries, for example, have signed the Optional Protocol To The Convention On The Rights Of The Child that sets eighteen as a minimum age for all combatants). However, for all the value of this report, it cannot encompass the problems of a city like Rio where kids' involvement in the violent, territorial struggles between drug factions is every bit as tragic.

You see, since the factions fight their battles within the boundaries of a legal state, they are still generally referred to in terms like 'gangs', 'crime' and 'delinquency'; terms that mitigate against a decent under-standing of the gravity of the situation let alone the formulation of an effective policy to deal with it. The aim of the project (run by Viva Rio alongside Instituto Superior De Estudos Da Religião, or ISER), therefore, is first to establish a globally recognised category of conflict which properly acknowledges the city's own 'child soldiers'. They've called it Organised Armed Violence.[9]

---

[9] Luke has written a paper for presentation to The Working Group On Children Affected By Organised Armed Violence which defines the phenomenon as follows: 'An intermittent armed conflict situation that involves over 1,000 deaths of combatants and civilians in a one-year period as the result of organised or semi-organised armed non-state groups with no political, religious, ethnic or ideological motivation, that are territorially defined and hold effective control over the communities which they dominate, utilise small arms and paramilitary organisation at the local level primarily for illicit economic gain, focus on children and adolescents as armed combatants and may confront the state through the use of armed violence if their economic advancement is threa-tened, yet have no intention of replacing state government or attacking government apparatus for political advantage.'

Is it really as bad as all that? Luke throws some stats at me and one of them shocks me into silence. Between December 1987 and November 2001, 467 minors were killed as a direct result of the conflict between Israel and Palestine. During the same period within the municipality of Rio de Janeiro, more than 3,000 kids were killed by small-arms fire in the drug factions' turf wars.

Once again I seem to have meandered off the hip hop track. But, once again, this culture has to be understood within contexts and, in Rio, hip hop (or at least its most interesting expression) comes from the *favelas*. What's more, to get a take on how the *favelas* work, you need a take on the drug factions that work them.

The city has a population of around seven million and at least twenty per cent of them live in one or other of about 600 *favelas*. The first appeared in the late 1890s on Morro Da Providencia (providence hill), overlooking downtown Rio. It was founded by Afro-Brazilian veterans of the military campaign against the supporters of the bizarre mystic preacher Antônio Conselheiro.[10] *Favelas* have, therefore, always been associated with black skin. It wasn't until the middle of the twentieth century, however, that the *favela* population really began to take off.

The *favelas* are not just poverty-stricken slums; they are historically unlawful settlements founded on undeveloped land. In the '50s, thousands of migrant workers were arriving in Rio each year, dislocated rural labourers in search of industrial jobs. Frequently accompanied by large families and unable to afford the rental prices of city tenement blocks, these migrants often had little choice but to build themselves illegal housing in the growing *favelas*. And the municipal government, recognising the need for this cheap labour, had little choice but to turn a blind (if disapproving) eye. Consequently for the next fifty years the *favela* population doubled roughly every decade. And yet, even as they expanded, these districts weren't included on any city map until the mid-'90s. They

---

[10] The campaign against Conselheiro was in Brazil's Northeastern Province. The word *favela* comes from a plant species common to that region.

are, therefore, both cities within the city and very much, as Luke put it, 'places apart'.

Given their history, I guess it's as unsurprising as it is unfortunate that *favelas* have little or no formal infrastructure; no running water, sewage systems, electricity and so on. What's more, since these neighbourhoods had no place on the city map, for a long time they made similarly little impact on local government that always had other constituencies and agendas to worry about. Even now, the provision of any social services within these communities is generally regarded (by politicians and community alike) as largesse rather than public responsibility. In the *favelas*, therefore, the growth of informal organisational, security and welfare structures starts to look kind of inevitable.

Forty years ago this meant the emergence of important local figures known as *donos* – typically, criminally connected strongmen who maintained social order with the threat of violence. It was a scenario that produced dichotomised *favela* communities of mutual reciprocity. On the one hand, there were the ruthless but 'necessary' criminals who ensured a relatively peaceful existence; on the other, there were the workers who provided a conspiracy of silence in which the *donos* could go about their business without having to worry about the cops.

Seen in this light, the *favelas* were fertile ground for the factions that emerged in the '80s as Rio became an important base for the export of cocaine to Europe and the States and large quantities of the drug also began to hit the city's own streets. At present, the local cocaine market is worth about US$170 million per year. Compared to the American market, which turns over around $US6.5 billion every month, this may sound like small beer. But when you realise that the monthly street sales of cocaine are five times the Rio State Government's annual housing budget, you're forced to take a second look.

The factions are highly organised and extremely well armed. To say they work 'against the law' is a pretty pointless observation. In *favelas*, the way they work 'instead of the law' is probably more relevant. The factions' activities are intricately interwoven with every aspect of *favela* life and there are, therefore, familiar patterns of mutual dependence (between the *soldados* and the community).

The original and still largest faction is Commando Vermelho. It was founded in the '70s in Cândido Mendes high-security prison on Ilha Grande, three hours west of Rio. Keen to squash popular dissatisfaction, Brazil's then military government eagerly locked up its opponents alongside hardcore criminals and some have noted the comparability of the faction's organisation with that of revolutionary political groups. Whatever. There is no doubt that the profitability of the new trade in cocaine sped its development just as there is no doubt that the nation's prisons remain the hub of the faction's activity – locked up and untouchable.

By the mid-'80s, capitalising on existing structures for selling weed, Commando Vermelho controlled Rio's cocaine trade and therefore the *favelas* too. The *favelas* were run by loosely affiliated *quadrilhas*.[11] Although each *quadrilha* was nominally under the auspices of the wider organisation, they in fact worked as near-autonomous businesses with varying degrees of power and profitability.

In the late '80s, however, the faction as collective began to splinter as the deaths of several important leaders produced an internal (and, therefore, inter-*favela*) power struggle. The prison model of mutual trust began to dissolve as younger players saw the potential to fulfil personal ambitions and so breakaway groups began to emerge. At the moment, Rio is in thrall to four competing factions – Commando Vermelho, Terceiro Commando (Third Command), Commando Vermelho Jovem (Young Red Command) and Amigos De Amigos (Friends of Friends) – with every *favela* under the totalitarian rule (more or less brutal) of one or the other.[12]

This fragmentation has seriously changed both the nature of the

---

[11] *Quadrilhas*: gangs.
[12] For a full explanation of the emergence of Rio's drug factions, see Luke's paper: 'Child Combatants in Organized Armed Violence: a study of children and adolescents involved in Rio de Janeiro's territorial drug faction disputes', Luke Dowdney, 2002, ISER / Viva Rio.

drug trade and, indeed, *favela* life. For starters, the whole business is more professionally run than ever with a rigid management structure as described in an International Labour Organization report for the International Program for the Elimination of Child Labour:[13] 'The trafficking hierarchy is organized as follows (from lowest to highest): watchman; dealer; packaging; security; product manager; general manager; owner.' What's more, where once the trade was essentially about shifting product, it is now a question of controlling territory and so distribution. The factions have to be able to defend their turf and this has meant the increased use of what Luke describes as 'war grade' weapons (with grenades and even bazookas and the like relatively commonplace). It has also accentuated the need for soldiers so the factions have recruited more and more kids to their cause and developed (or perhaps 'imagined') a culture of militarised glamour.

Favelas, therefore, have become protected garrisons, and when the locals describe conflict between factions they are less likely to use terms like 'battle' or even 'war' than 'invasion'. Even the untrusted and untrustworthy police use the same word for their occasional (and often bloody) incursions. So the *favelas* have become like island nations with imperial ambitions; robust in defence and attack, their boys on the frontline toting guns to signify their manhood.

Ironically, the *favelas* are pretty much crime-free. While your average *carioca* from the *asphalto* wouldn't dream of going into one, as an outsider, you're arguably safer in a *favela* than anywhere else in Rio since the factions rule with rods of iron and nothing takes place without their say so.[14] They are in the business of selling cocaine, after all, and the last thing they want to do is scare off potential custom. So you could probably walk the half mile from the well-to-do district of Gàvea up the hill into Rocinha and expect no hassle.

---

[13] *Brazil – Children In Drug Trafficking: A Rapid Assessment*, Dr Jailson de Souza e Silva and Dr André Urani, 2002, ILO.

[14] That said, of course, your safety in a *favela* depends on your business there, as evidenced by the horrific murder in June 2002 of TV Globo journalist Tim Lopes who was working on a report about drug traffickers in Vila Cruzeiro.

And yet the life expectancy in Rocinha is thirteen years less than that in its neighbouring suburb.

We head into Lapa, the former red-light district that's now a thriving centre of bars, clubs and Rio bohemia, fanning out beneath the famous aqueduct that once carried water into the city from the Rio Carioca. We're hooking up with a guy called Def Yuri, an emcee and DJ who's one of the original brokers of local hip hop. He's a mate of Luke's and works part-time for Viva Rio too. Yuri is a columnist on the Viva Favela Web portal that aims to bring Internet access and relevant information (news, job adverts, health education and so on) into the *favelas*. He's also got his crew, Ryo Radikal Rapz, and he's the mastermind behind one of the city's most important hip hop festivals, Hip Hop Pelo Rio.

We meet at Fundição Progresso, a kind of social centre-cum-disco which broadcasts a community radio station. Yuri's doing the hip hop show and familiar, East Coast-influenced beats ring around the warehouse-style space. I don't understand the Brazilian emcees' lyrics, of course, but Portuguese seems to lend itself to a hip hop flow; there's a softness to the consonants and some sort of natural funk in the rhythms of the language.

The station itself is a chaotic, bedroom kind of outfit. The turntables and CD deck seem to have been cobbled together with duct tape while the mixer looks like someone's school electronics project. Yuri and a few of his boys crowd around the single mic. Yuri's about my age, I guess, short, bouncy, excitable and permanently grinning from ear to ear. And racially? No idea. Brown-skinned with cropped hair, he just looks typically Brazilian to me but god knows what a *carioca* would say.

Yuri says he wants to interview me so I need Luke to translate. Yuri asks me what I'm doing in Rio. I explain about the book I'm writing and Luke tells it in Portuguese. He asks me what I think of Brazilian hip hop and I say I haven't had a chance to hear much yet. Luke wrinkles his forehead and tells me to say something else; something more interesting. Like what?

'Say something else about Rio hip hop,' Luke hisses.

'But I don't know anything.'

It's faintly comical as the Brazilians stare at the two London blokes stage whispering across the airwaves in a foreign language. So Luke decides to answer on my behalf and launches into an impassioned diatribe. I haven't got a clue what he says but it seems to do the trick because Yuri and his mates nod along and then pump my hand in agreement. When I look at Luke, he just shrugs and cracks up laughing.

I hand Yuri a CD to play as the last tune on his show. It's a track by Cape Town's Black Noise called 'Abada Capoeira' that uses Brazilian drum sounds and the capoeirista's traditional berimbau[15] over an old-school break. Yuri loves the fact that South Africans make hip hop let alone play the Brazilian martial art and he claps me on the shoulder. It's time to head out into Lapa, get a drink and talk hip hop.

The plan is that Yuri's going to tell us the history of the culture in Brazil, so we settle into the plastic chairs in front of a seedy pavement café. Only trouble is, Yuri's got quite a mouth on him. He's a cool guy and everything but, like most ageing hip hop heads, he's both thorough statistician and occasional philosopher and he insists on giving us every single factoid, nuance, personal implication and interpretation.

'The first contact with hip hop in Brazil was in the late '70s. It was really just a visual thing because we saw B-Boys on TV for the first time. It was the breaking that caught the attention because dance is always a big part of Brazil and that made me want to find out about the movement and get into the culture.

'But you can say that "year zero" was '83, when hip hop really broke into the media. In Rio, there were three proper hip hop TV shows: *BB Video Break*, which was on every day, *BB Video Clipe* and *Super Onda*. Of course, they weren't playing what we know as hip hop now; more stuff like Cameo and Break Machine. At the time, hip hop was really just Michael Jackson.'

Excuse me?

---

[15] The *berimbau* is a wooden stick, strung with a steel string to form a bow shape, with a gourd with an opening on one side which acts as a resonator.

'Sure. Everybody loved Michael Jackson in Brazil and everyone wore the white gloves and white socks.

'But the big moment came during carnival in '83. There was a TV presenter – an old, fat guy called Chacrinha – who did this breaking song.' Yuri gets to his feet to demonstrate. At first his mates protest his memory of how it happened and try to shout him down but, when he starts to rap the lyrics of this pop track, they kill themselves laughing – 'Break break legal! / Break break break para dançar no carnival!'[16]

'That was the most visible representation of hip hop's beginnings,' Yuri insists and he mock frowns at his friends. 'Now, a lot of people in the movement want to pretend it never happened. But it did.

'The LA Olympics was a big deal too. There were breakdancers at the opening ceremony so the Brazilian media thought it must be acceptable. After that, the first B–Boy bands to record were Electric Boogie and then Black Juniors. They were just dance records, happy music with no lyrical content, but they were huge and played in nightclubs everywhere. Then all of the TV stations held breaking competitions in every city around the country. I was part of a B–Boy crew back then and we went to these contests in all the proper gear. But the guys judging them kept throwing us out. They said it wasn't real breakdancing because it didn't look like Michael Jackson. I know it sounds strange now but that's the truth.'

Yuri's talking nineteen to the dozen and Luke is struggling to keep up. Luke tries to slow him down a bit but he bristles at the interruption and shakes his head. 'It's important to understand the beginnings,' he says. 'Because some people say the Racionais album in '98 was the first Brazilian hip hop when actually it's been here for nearly twenty years. In '93/'94, Gabriel O Pensador (Gabriel the thinker) was already selling huge numbers of records. Before him, Thaide e DJ Hum came out in '88. They never sold a lot but everyone knows them and they were the very first guys to start talking about racism and police violence. You see? You have to know where it all comes from.'

[16] Something like: 'Break, it's cool / Break, to dance at carnival.'

And then he's off again, leaving Luke floundering in the wake of his polemic. From what I can follow, a lot of what he says is fascinating. He describes hip hop in Brazil as 'dislocated'. 'Right now,' he says, 'hip hop is divided into lots of smaller cultures. There's gangsta rap, headbang rap, even skaters are into hip hop. But the most significant movement is always political.' He reminisces about a track Ryo Radikal Rapz put out called 'Foda-se A Policia' ('Fuck the Police') which accused the cops of being no better than the armed factions. He recalls getting banged up for a couple of nights in 1996 and stands up to demonstrate the way he was beaten. He also echoes sentiments repeatedly expressed by B-Boys from all over the world about what hip hop means personally: 'Hip hop lives and so has a living history. I'm thirty so I've had twenty years of this culture. If I don't preserve the history, I'm denying everything I've been involved in since I was ten years old. Hip hop is a contamination. Everything I know about the world came from this culture; it's my most important source of information.' Remember Japanese emcee ECD's description of hip hop as a 'flying spark'? Remember Blaze's comment that 'hip hop . . . introduced me to other areas of study'?

Unfortunately, though, despite Luke's prompting, we can't get Yuri to take his history beyond 1988. Not tonight anyway. So let me give you a brief run-down of the last fifteen years.

Nineteen eighty-eight saw the first significant Brazilian hip hop release, a compilation called *Hip Hop Cultura De Rua* (*Hip Hop Culture of the Streets*)[17] which included Thaide e DJ Hum, probably the movement's first architects. It was quickly followed by another, *Consciência Black* (*Black Consciousness*),[18] which was put out in São Paulo. This album had a track on it by São Paulo crew Racionais MCs who have since gone on, however reluctantly, to be the scene's biggest name. In 1993, their third album, *Raio X Do Brasil* (*X-Rays of Brazil*),[19] established them as the essential voice of the

---

[17] *Hip Hop Cultura De Rua*, Various, 1988, Eldorado.
[18] *Consciência Black*, Various, 1988, Zâmbia.
[19] *Raio X Do Brasil*, Racionais MCs, 1993, RDS.

peripheria,[20] the *favelas* that have for so long been excluded from mainstream urban life, and they supported Public Enemy on their Brazilian tour and played gigs to thousands.

Around the same time, a new voice emerged in Rio; that of a middle-class white student, Gabriel Contino, who renamed himself Gabriel O Pensador. His first release, 'Tô Feliz (Matei O Presidente)' ('I'm Glad I Killed the President')[21] caused a media storm, not least because his mother was a journalist then employed by President Fernando Collor. His self-titled first album shifted more than 300,000 units and the following four have been similarly successful.

A couple of days later, Kanyasu and me went to see Gabriel O Pensador live at Canecão, a cavernous, modern venue next to the Rio Sul shopping centre. To be honest, his performance bore little resemblance to any hip hop I know. Backed by a live band, the music is heavily rock-influenced and Gabriel – good-looking, long-haired and lanky – seemed to have attracted a bizarre mixed crowd of screaming teenaged girls and well-to-do Rio socialites. That said of course, we didn't understand his notoriously caustic lyrics that lay into everybody from the politicians to the police to the *lóraburras* (dumb blondes) representing the superficiality of Brazilian pop culture. What's more, for all his mainstream success, Gabriel has always allied himself to and supported the more marginal hip hop movement and always been happy to stand toe to toe with the establishment.

By the mid-'90s, hip hop had spread throughout the country with crews emerging in cities like Recife (Sistema X), Brasilia (Câmbio Negro, or Black Exchange) and Belo Horizonte (Black Soul). However, it was 1998 that saw the real emergence of hip hop as serious cultural broker (both musically and, arguably, politically) with the release of the Racionais MCs' album *Sobrevivendo No*

---

[20] *Peripheria*: Periphery. It's a word often used in the discussion of *favelas* that holds a sense of social as much as physical exclusion; in many ways comparable to the Parisian *banlieues*.

[21] 'Tô Feliz (Matei O Presidente)' from *Gabriel O Pensador*, Gabriel O Pensador, 1993, Chaos/Sony.

Inferno (Surviving in Hell).[22] To date, it has sold more than a million copies.

The Racionais are quite some phenomenon – and not just because of their sales figures. For starters, the content of their music is never less than incendiary. On 'Diário De Um Detento' ('Diary of a Convict'), for example, emcee Mano Brown lays out the anxieties of an inmate at São Paulo's notorious Carandiru prison over a cinematic, grungy funk worthy of the Rza. The date of the diary entry is given as 1 October 1992, the day before the infamous massacre in Carandiru in which 111 prisoners were shot dead by police.[23]

Furthermore, the Racionais' music has always gone hand in hand with social projects, including school and prison visits and lectures about drugs, racism, human rights and the like. Most interesting, however, has been the band's consistent hostility towards the mainstream media as they repeatedly refuse interviews and TV appearances. Similarly, their long-awaited new album (the follow-up to *Sobrevivendo No Inferno*) was slated to be distributed by Sony but negotiations quickly broke down and the band returned to their own label, Cosa Nostra, in association with the independent Zâmbia.

Put simply, the Racionais regard the corporate media as a significant part of the very system they're fighting and consequently refuse to engage with it. In Brazil, perhaps more than anywhere, their reasoning is understandable when the media landscape has been dominated for so long by the Globo empire. This media monolith runs the country's top radio network, its second-placed magazine group and the cable-television company Globo Cabo. But its real power comes from TV Globo (the world's fourth-largest commercial television network, ranked behind only the three US giants), which commands more than

---

[22] *Sobrevivendo No Inferno*, Racionais MCs, 1998, Cosa Nostra.

[23] Incidentally, the video for this track was MTV Brazil's Video of the Year in '98, though all the main perpetrators of the atrocity itself had still not been prosecuted. I can't help thinking that such an irony is somehow very typical of Brazil where corruption seems to be criticised, accepted and ignored all at once.

half the Brazilian audience share and three quarters of the advertising revenue.

Certainly it's hard to deny the Racionais' outlook when you consider, say, Globo's backing for the military dictatorship between 1964 and 1985, which led to the network becoming known as The Ministry Of Information, or indeed the partisan support given to right-wing candidate Collor in the '89 presidential campaign. After Collor's election, Globo's octogenarian owner Roberto Marinho was nicknamed 'the Kingmaker'.

There are, of course, obvious parallels between the Racionais attitude and that of BVK or Black Noise in Cape Town – lyrics that confront, the emphasis on social action and the distrust of the mainstream media. But there's also one outstanding difference: Racionais MCs shift some serious units and consequently their clout is proportionally greater. I don't point this out to claim that the Racionais have more control of their 'capitalized reputation' than the South Africans, let alone to suggest that they make qualitatively 'better' hip hop. Rather, if anything, I reckon the Racionais' success highlights the relative degree of politicised self-consciousness among Brazil's urban alienated compared to their South African counterparts.

Of course I realise that this is an enormous assumption and one which, even if correct, I can't explain. It is tempting to mention the Brazilian poverty gap (when five per cent of Brazilians own ninety-five per cent of the wealth and forty per cent of the population live below the poverty line), but gross disparities between the haves and have-nots are hardly something unfamiliar to South Africans. Perhaps, therefore, you need to look at the structure of apartheid that so successfully divided the disenfranchised. Or perhaps South Africa still has the optimism of a new democracy where the poverty gap is at least shrinking (however slowly). Or perhaps Brazilians are simply more culturally attuned to a dash of politics in their pop music.

Whatever. The real point of this comparison is simply to high-light a couple of things illustrated by the Racionais' success. Firstly, it opened the door for the new breed of politicised Brazilian hip hop (led by Rio's own MV Bill, for example). Secondly, it demonstrated the potential of this culture to make a profound social impact. And that's exactly what's happening . . .

One issue I've barely touched upon is hip hop's location. Across the world, hip hop is frequently identified by both protagonists and consumers with city more than nation and it's for this reason that I have so located each section of this book. In the States, this meant the decision to visit New York (as the culture's *alma mater*) with scant mention of LA, Chicago, New Orleans, Atlanta or any of the other places (arguably any American city) where hip hop now dominates. When briefly discussing the French scene, I wrote mostly about Paris and barely touched on the thriving (and very different) flavour of Marseille. I have sidetracked to Rome without even a nod to the other Italian hip hop strongholds like Milan and Napoli. And in South Africa, of course, I couldn't resist the fact that the scenes in Jo'burg and Cape Town advanced my thinking in different ways and therefore each merited a section of its own.

But in Brazil? Well. Not least because of the profound influence of the Racionais, there is no dispute that São Paulo is hip hop's beating heart. So why have I chosen to write about Rio?

If São Paulo is hip hop's beating heart then Rio is certainly Brazil's. When I started writing this book, I set it up as a journey and, like all the best journeys, I wasn't sure of the stops along the way, let alone where it would end. For better or worse, it has been a journey that has found urban alienation (to different degrees and in different ways) at every step. Now, I'm not saying that hip hop in São Paulo is not born from such alienation (indeed nothing could be further from the truth). But São Paulo *is* a heavily industrialised business capital with little else to attract a visitor. I was drawn to Rio, therefore, partly because it is a rough diamond of a city where opulence glitters among decay and one of the world's most beautiful settings cradles some of the world's most depressing urban realities. For an outsider, at least, the urban alienation seems all the more poignant in such a context.

But the most important reason I'm based in Rio is an altogether clearer one and it's as follows: this city is the birthplace of funk. I figure that to understand what Brazilian hip hop is, you have to understand what it isn't; and that's funk. As the States has R'n'B and South Africa has kwaito (and, I guess, the UK has UK garage), so Brazil has funk – a hip hop-influenced music where the party vibe counterpoints the 'real' culture's *gravitas*.

But Brazilian funk should not be confused with James Brown or George Clinton (though these are certainly its antecedents). If anything, it's more like Miami bass; an electronic, booty-bounce sound pulsing beneath nursery-rhyme-style choruses that are chanted, rapped or sung.

Head down to a Rio funk party (or *baile funk* – funk ball) on any weekend night and the atmosphere is one of almost orgiastic hedonism as the teenage girls get down in crop-tops and hot-pants and grind up against the teenage boys. The boys are dressed in Bermuda shorts (generally Nike or Adidas) and vivid shirts and I still can't get used to the fact that this is 'gangster chic', Rio style.

The flavour in the *baile* is consistently of tingling foreplay, of teenage testosterone and adolescent oestrogen gone haywire; a sense that, if you blink, you could suddenly find the whole nightclub fucking. In fact, the dancing is often as good as – like the euphemistically named *trenzinho* (little train) when couples simulate sex in a line and the *dança da cadeira* (literally, the chair dance) where the girls lapdance for their partners. A popular track generally gets the crowd joining in or acting out the basic lyrics. One record is a take on a tune I know as 'Who Let The Dogs Out?' But this one's called 'O Baile Todo' ('Everybody Party')[24] and the words of the chorus have been changed to '*Tirar camisa!*' ('Guys get your tops off!') and all the boys are happy to oblige, whirling their shirts around their heads. Another favourite is 'Tapinha' ('A Little Slap')[25] where an '80s electro beat underpins a gravelly male rap and a girl squealing the chorus '*Tapinha não dói*' ('A little slap doesn't hurt'). And, on the dancefloor, the girls pretend to slap their faces and backsides in a sexual manner that leaves little doubt about what they (pretend to) like. Frankly, the *bailes funk* make hip hop's notorious misogyny look altogether tame.

[24] 'O Baile Todo', Bonde Do Tigrão, 2001, Sony.
[25] 'Tapinha', Furacão 2000, 2001, CD Express.

Nonetheless, funk remains Rio's favourite music. And if the current scene as I describe it sounds a little feisty, that's nothing compared to its roots. I remember reading about the *carioca bailes* a few years back when their impact even crossed the Atlantic to the British press.

In the mid-'90s, funk was strictly *favela* music and as such it was inevitably and inextricably linked to the armed factions. The parties were soon notorious as settings for violence as kids from *favelas* under different factions vented their frustrations on their rivals. However, this was no ordinary nightclub brawling but was a form of well-organised, ritualised, often coke-fuelled combat.

A venue is divided into two. Even outside, kids from *favela* A queue one way and kids from *favela* B the other. They are thoroughly body-searched on the door by the numerous security guards because, for all the impending thuggery, weapons are strictly forbidden. Once in the club, the imposing bouncers form a human wall between the two groups and the *baile* can begin. Even from the early stages, when they're not dancing, boys from each side chant their own machismo and taunt the opposition. Then, at some point, the DJ decides that it's time for things to kick off and he announces 'Mortal Kombat' or '*15 minutos de alegria*' ('15 minutes of joy'). With that official blessing, the fighting can start and the guys begin to cross the line of bouncers into the *corredor de morte* (corridor of death). The aim is to invade the other side or, more likely, grab one of the opposition – *alemão* in *baile* slang (meaning, believe it or not, Germans) – and drag him back to your territory. There, if his mates aren't quick to rescue him, he can be beaten unconscious. Even to death.

Over the last couple of years, though, this kind of ultra-violent *baile* has fortunately become much less commonplace. The reasons for this are fairly predictable. By the late '90s, *carioca* funk had largely moved into mainstream popular culture. Consequently, when well-to-do kids from the *asphalto* began to get hurt, press, politicians and police started to take more of an interest. Once again, we come back to the idea of *favelas* as both 'cities within cities' and 'places apart'.

What's more, in March 1999, a fifteen-year-old called Julio

Miranda Cavalcante was beaten senseless at the Country Club (an infamous *baile* venue on the outskirts of Rio) and later died of his injuries. Though from Rocinha, his funeral attracted hundreds of mourners into the city itself and the city was forced to confront the reality of what was going on. So the police launched an initiative to crack down on the *bailes*, called Operation Funk. Estimates suggest that around sixty teenagers were killed in the *bailes* in the late '90s. The number may be many more as rumours abound of promoters paying the police to look the other way and bouncers dumping teenage corpses in shallow graves.

Perhaps the biggest reason for the drop in violence, however, is depressingly pragmatic; i.e., the success of the funk scene. With hundreds of thousands of kids going to the parties every weekend, favourite tunes climbing the charts and compilations selling in millions, the violence is arguably no longer the best way for promoters to make their bucks.

The most successful *baile* promoter is Furacão 2000 (Hurricane 2000) run by a guy called Rumelo Costa and, for those who'd like to ban funk outright, he's public enemy number one. From a *favela* background himself, he's been promoting parties for twenty years and he's loaded, with his kids in private school and a house in the up-and-coming neighbourhood of Barra da Tijuca. In the last decade, Furacão 2000 has become something of a media empire, putting out its own CDs and promoting them on its own TV and radio shows. Rumelo has twice been imprisoned for drug dealing but has never been convicted. His young wife Veronica (whom he met on a *baile* dancefloor) is a national pin-up and the Furacão 2000 TV presenter. She is also a *Vereadora*, an elected Rio city councillor.

If Rumelo is a hate figure for some, he's also a Robin Hood-style hero for the *favelas*; the poor boy made good. If many regard funk as a vehicle for the factions, drug dealing and violence, then many others see it as a legitimate expression of *favela* life that the terrified mainstream want to suppress and isn't that just typical? I guess your opinion depends on which city of Rio you're living in.

In person, Rumelo manages to be all you'd expect and nothing like it too. At first impression he looks every inch the stereotypical Hollywood drug dealer. He's in his early forties and wearing a black leather coat. His complexion is olive, eyes narrow and his hair, shaved at the sides, is tied back from the top into a thin ponytail. His accent is nasal, whiny, slurred and vaguely intimidating. In fact, his whole persona is not a million miles from the '80s baddies who Don Johnson used to chase in *Miami Vice*. But then he smiles and his face relaxes and he suddenly seems chilled and I start to question my initial judgements.

Nonetheless, for all his easy-going attitude, when Rumelo talks about the *bailes funk*, he is unsurprisingly cagey and weighs his every word.

'In the '70s, funk was the name given to international black music like James Brown, Isaac Hayes and so on. Ninety-nine per cent of the people going to parties in the suburbs were black so we started getting a lot of persecution from the federal police who said we were organising a racist movement against white people. Even the governor of Rio at the time said, "Why don't you play more national music?" But there wasn't any national, black music like that. So we started getting guys to sing over dub plates brought in from abroad.

'Sometimes it sounds like rapping but it wouldn't be right to call it rapping. Miami bass is definitely the best comparison. Funk is happy music. People don't want to listen to hip hop when they go out; they have enough reality in their own neighbourhoods.

'Funk, as we now know it, started in the early '90s. At Furacão 2000, we maintain it. The first big success we had was "Eu Só Quero Ser Feliz" ("I Only Want to be Happy")[26] in 1995. It was a really important song in the movement – "I only want to be happy and peaceful in the *favela* where I was born". It was the first national hit and it was about *favela* pride, with the message "I come from the *favela* and I'm glad I come from the *favela*".

'This is fundamental. A lot of artists that we started and produced have since gone over to the multinational labels. But when they leave us? They go and make pop music not funk and, of course, they never play in the *favelas* again.

'The violence? I don't want to talk about that. It's very com-

---

[26] 'Eu Só Quero Ser Feliz', Cidinho E Doca, 1995, CD Express.

plicated. It seems like the powers that be are very scared of organisations that bring a lot of people together. We have hundreds of thousands of kids coming down to our parties and it scares them.

'The whole city of Rio is divided into criminal factions; four big ones. The kids who come to the *bailes* are not part of these factions but they represent where they come from, so they represent whoever sends the orders where they come from. If you have a *baile funk* in one particular *favela*, it won't be just kids from the *favela* but from all over, you see? And they're thinking, "When I get in there, I've got to represent my area and my crew."

'It's important to know that funk now . . .' Rumelo sighs and, for the first time, seems to lose his train of thought. He's fiddling with his mobile phone, repeatedly opening the flap and looking at the small screen like it might show some answers. 'There's still some fighting at the *bailes* – north of Rio, places like that. But the Furacão 2000 parties have changed. In the last two years, we've sold so many CDs. We've become mainstream.'

So are you saying the violence was just because it was *favela* music?

'I don't want to talk about that. Samba was *favela* music and that has never had violence associated with it.'

So maybe it's funk's lyrics?

'I don't want to talk about it,' Rumelo says flatly and the conversation's getting a little tense. He checks the time and puts on a pair of shades.

But it's changing, right?

'Sure. People started to identify with the music because it was about personal happiness, you need to remember that. It's a light thing, not a heavy thing; so it's easy for the mainstream to get into.

'Yes it's come out of the *favela* to a certain extent but it's still *favela* kids making the songs in *favela* slang. A lot of the stuff that arrives at our door is pretty rough so we have to clean it up . . .' Rumelo starts laughing. 'Like, Bonde Do Tigrão are the national superstars of funk. Their name means Tiger Crew but originally they were calling themselves in *favela* slang something like Crew of the Macho Hookers. Or recently there's been a lot of fuss about "Tapinha não dói" but we actually cleaned up that song. When it first came to us, the girl wasn't saying "a little slap doesn't hurt" but "in the arse doesn't hurt". Funk might have become pop music but it's still got the *favela* at its heart.

'Personally, I stopped doing *bailes* in the *favelas* because it became too much trouble. It's always a difficult line to walk with the factions because we try not to divide young people. We want to unite them. You can hear it on our radio shows when we shout out to kids from every *favela* and every gang. But the biggest problem is politics. I went to prison for doing *bailes funk* in *favelas* so I don't do them any more. Twice they sent me to prison for being a drug dealer but they never had any proof. They just throw you in prison first and then investigate later. Forty per cent of people in prison are innocent like me. Why are they there? Because they have dark skin and they come from the *favela*. And, of course, they don't have the money to pay a good lawyer.

'I tell you, politics in this country doesn't work, that's just the way it is. My wife gets very depressed about it. It's a house of bickering. All the things she wants to do? She can never make them work. I don't have any politics. There's no point. But I am going to run for deputy next year because if I don't become a deputy they'll keep sending me to prison.[27] These days I need special protection and – I'm not stupid – you only get that by becoming political.'

Rumelo's phone rings. He's got to run and he stands up and picks up his car keys and starts to twirl them in his fingers. There is, I notice, something unusual in the way he walks. He hardly seems to lift his feet at all; kind of sliding them instead. It gives the peculiar impression that he's moving without moving. His parting shot sounds like a practised soundbite to me: 'Funk is happiness. It's the living spirit of young people. It gives them a space where they can forget themselves.'

Forget themselves? This phrase triggers something in my head; not least because I've heard it before.

It was a couple of days ago and we went to visit Luke's boxing gym in Maré. It's a good-size space on the second floor of one of the

---

[27] A 'deputy' is a representative in regional government. There are seventy deputies for the state of Rio.

few multistorey buildings on the edge of the *favela*. With a ring, heavy bags and even one of those timed lights that flashes out the length of each round, it's pretty well-equipped. There's a gap between the walls and the sloped, corrugated ceiling which has been largely plugged by some new concrete blocks. This is the handiwork of a few American soldiers, based locally, who Luke persuaded to come in and help out after the last time the *favela* was invaded. Bullet scars from that day's stray fire still climb one side of the gym. Nearby, a poster lists the rules of the club as agreed by its members; things like 'be honest', 'behave peacefully outside the ring' and 'receive guests to the club with respect and politeness'.

Luke's been caught at some meeting in town so the teenage boxers are messing around, ignoring the trainer's attempts to get started, play-fighting and showing off their latest dance moves. I get talking to a couple of the boys and it's one of them – I think his name's João – who says it: 'I don't mind listening to rap but it's too heavy for when you go out. When you're in a *baile funk*, you can just forget all your problems and go crazy.'

I'm not entirely sure what it is about this idea of 'forgetting' that sets me thinking but I find myself drawing comparisons between *carioca* funk and the state of American hip hop.

Before its adoption by mainstream Brazilian society, funk was very much the voice (albeit an incoherent and, arguably, negative one) of the excluded. In the last few years, the work of NGOs like, say, Viva Rio has been largely focused on trying to relocate the *favelas* (in both practical ways and the collective imagination) within the wider city. Theoretically, funk's success could be regarded as a part of that process (and certainly that's the kind of spin Rumelo would put on it). But doesn't the perception of funk – its connection to the factions, violence and promiscuity – actually widen the schism? To break it down, the kids from the *asphalto* might think it's cool to go to the *bailes* but their parents are more terrified than ever of the influence of *favela* culture.

Is that not similar to hip hop in America? It's a voice of the excluded that's achieved mainstream success and produced stars with fancy cars and nice houses. But it's also, arguably, reinforced that exclusion.

Of course, hip hop in America isn't to blame for the social sickness of alienation, discrimination and ghetto-isation any more than funk is in Rio. But in this area of culture – as often seems to be the case when discussing exclusion – if you're not part of the solution, there's a fair chance you're part of the problem.

Now, the *funkeiros'* desire to forget themselves at the *bailes* is totally understandable as they can forget grim realities to become dancefloor kings, warriors and lovers in their imagination just as American ghetto kids can use hip hop's symbolism to become players in each episode of their personal dramas. But I come back to Kundera once again; because surely 'the struggle of man against power is the struggle of memory against forgetting.'

Of course, it would be easy to push this comparison too far. After all, *carioca* funk never claimed to be about anything more than having a good time. American hip hop, on the other hand, did. But there's one fact about funk culture that seems undeniable and worth contrasting with the current situation in the States. If American hip hop is becoming (both culturally and, increasingly, musically) indistinguishable from R'n'B, the commercial success of funk has created artistic space for Brazilian hip hop to address serious issues seriously. And so it does.

MV Bill is probably Rio hip hop's best social critic. His name stands for Mensageiro da Verdade, or Messenger of Truth.

Bill cuts an imposing ogre of a figure. He's tall and broad, black and dark-skinned, with several gang tattoos as permanent reminders of a former life. His brow is thick, his cheekbones high and his jaw solid; he looks like he's been roughly hewn from a slab of onyx. There's a tightness to his mouth that suggests he doesn't suffer fools, and when he talks to you he'll look off into the distance for a moment or two before refocusing a needle gaze that checks you've been listening. He speaks with absolute confidence but no trace of arrogance. It's like he's sure of what he's saying and he knows it's important to tell it like it is; but he also figures that whether you get it or not isn't going to make the blindest bit of difference to his struggles.

In '99, he released the album *Traficando Informação* (*Trafficking*

Information),[28] a bleak portrait of *favela* life with Bill's brooding voice riding dark beats (some provided by Ice Blue of the Racionais). Track titles like 'Um Crioulo Com Uma Arma' ('Black Man with a Weapon'), 'Como Sobreviver Na Favela' ('How to Survive in a *Favela*') and 'Contraste Social' ('Social Contrast') should give you a fair picture of his subject matter.

He's best known, however, for the video he shot for the track 'Soldado do Morro' ('Ghetto Soldier'). He took a DV camera into the *favela* where he comes from and still lives, Cidade De Deus (City of God), or CDD, and filmed the local *soldados*, kids patrolling the claustrophobic alleyways, their faces concealed with scarves, their AR-15 assault rifles bouncing against their thighs or proudly brandished for the camera.

Bill was in trouble before the video was ever shown. The police heard what was on it, arrested him and threatened prosecution under all kinds of arcane laws. Unsurprisingly, the threats came to nothing. 'What were they going to charge me with?' Bill asks. 'I was just filming my own neighbourhood. They said I was glamourising violence. But if I thought for one second that the video was going to do anything but good in the *favela*, I'd smash it. The *favela* is my home.' He shakes his head and laughs bitterly. 'My mother was really upset,' he reflects. 'When I got into music she thought I'd never have problems with the Justice Department again.'

Jennifer Roth Gordon, an American anthropologist who has extensively researched Brazilian hip hop, has written, 'While it is important to recognize that Brazilian rappers critically engage with their hip-hop ancestors and do not import American rap in its entirety, Brazilian hip-hop has been fundamentally influenced by American racial ideologies.'[29]

Bill talks about race a lot and all his thinking seems to confirm the accuracy of this observation. Indeed he admits as much when he references the impact Public Enemy made both on him personally

---

[28] *Traficando Informação*, MV Bill, 1999, Natasha/BMG.

[29] 'Hip-Hop Brasileiro: Brazilian Youth and Alternative Black Consciousness Movements', Jennifer Roth Gordon; presented at the AAA Meetings, 18 November 1999.

and on his music. He adopts a typically American, dichotomised view of race both as a positive tool of identity and in opposition to the mythical, Brazilian racial utopia. It's not that he doesn't employ a sophisticated interpretation of Brazil's specific racial niceties when it suits but the dichotomised view enables him to engage in a different kind of argument. 'What's the face of the *favela*?' he asks. 'It's a black face. In Brazil, when you talk about helping black people, they say "Who's a black person here?" But they certainly know who's black when it's time to discriminate.'

He knows how to tell a horror story, too. When I start talking about crime in *favelas*, he cuts me off in mid-sentence. 'There's no crime in *favelas*. Because of the drug traffickers, you cannot commit a crime. For example, there were kids robbing buses just outside CDD. The gangs had to stop this because it was bad for their [drug] business. Look around the *favela* right now and you'll see a lot of kids with no fingers or their whole hands blown off.'

Though Bill talks eloquently about Rio hip hop, *favelas* and the future, it doesn't make for easy conversation. His every story, observation or soundbite is designed to confront, to make you reassess what he's saying and what you yourself think.

'Rap music isn't music, it's a form of free discussion. If I were a university intellectual or even a musician from the *asphalto*, nobody would question me. And if I made funk, I wouldn't ask any questions. But a black man talking about social reality? It's not seen as acceptable. Before I made this album, I had two songs that were often played in the *bailes*. So I used to try and sell them on tapes in the clubs but the security wouldn't let me in. In the end, I was selling the tapes like drugs. That's when I realised I'm an information trafficker.

'I'm not a musician or a pop star. I still live in the *favela* and I'm doing this on my own. I'm not linked to any political party, left or right. What can they offer me? I make changes in my own way. I want to better the lives of my people in the *favela*. I want to show the inability of the government and police to do their jobs. But when you start talking about equality and social inclusion, you can't expect everything to come to you. We have to start looking for our own answers too. We can't just look up for help, we have to look down. Trouble is, when you look down it often looks ugly.

'When I was a kid and I was given my first toy gun, I wanted to be a drug boss. So imagine how I felt when I got my first .38? I felt like the most powerful man in the world as I walked the streets with a bad-boy expression on my face. I tell you, for someone like me, it was the biggest feeling of power to get into a club for free. In a *favela*, if you have anything, it's because you've got a gun.

'But what you have to understand about this society is that questions of violence and crime are not just about guns and drugs. In Brazil, the only people who go to prison are those who steal a little. Those who steal a lot go free. Putting people into sub-human conditions in the *favelas*? When I show it I'm criticised but that's a form of violence. In Rio, there's still a lot of colonial influence. I heard of a black girl at a public school who suffered racism. She locked herself in a toilet and tried to cut off her skin to make herself white. But when we try to talk about racism, we're told we're neurotic. That's a form of violence. Kids from the *favela* always attend state schools but they have to work for their families too. Therefore *favela* kids never have a good enough education to get into public universities. They never have a chance. Those places go to middle-class kids from private schools. That's a form of violence too. You know . . . I'm talking about blacks but the same applies to Indians and whites who have nothing.

'People say hip hop is all about violence but they don't understand. Rap in this country is very anti-violence and does a lot of good. Of course it's not the only way to help young people, but I know it's helped me. Some people want to change hip hop to "I love this woman" and all that stuff. But we've heard that so many times in other music and, I ask you, do people really have that much love?

'As for funk, I don't really see a difference between funk and me because we're both the same colour and suffer the same problems. How can I curse funk artists? I need to bring them round to my way of thinking.

'A lot of people have died because of the *bailes*. They used to be like bloodbaths. Even today, "prohibited" funk still exists and it's a criminal life. I know because some of those guys are my best friends. But now, for the most part, the powerful media are able to say, "don't talk about that, cut your hair like this, wear clothes like that" and suddenly funk is everywhere. What can I say? It's just a bunch of failed actresses showing off their arses.

'I don't mean to criticise funk but I don't understand how someone can live in a *favela* reality and then only sing about sex and love. In my opinion, a funk producer doesn't want people to be educated because then they'll want to hear different music. So funk now means wealthy black people showing off their gold and this contributes to our problems because kids see them and want the same.

'The truth is that black people don't decide anything in this country. We don't employ and we're barely employed. You know what? A lot of famous artists have rung me to lend their support but they won't announce it publicly because they're scared they'll lose their record deal, their jeep and their blonde girlfriend. I don't give a fuck about the playboys. Nothing changes without sacrifice.

'I went to New York once and I was treated like a hero. But I refuse to be a hero there when I'm treated as a criminal in my own country. We've got nothing to learn from black Americans except their attitude. I've suffered a number of death threats but so what? Either they do it or they don't. Black people in Brazil have nothing to lose. We've never been involved in politics but now it's our time.'

I ask Bill what he means, how he thinks change will come about, and he looks at me closely. 'Why do you care?' he asks.

I try to explain about the book I'm writing. I say that it seems to me that different communities around the world are all using hip hop as a mechanism for social change and I'm trying to establish the connections. Bill is shaking his head.

'Caring doesn't change anything. When I talk to you, I know I'm representing the *favela* and you're interested. Fine. But I also know that social change will always come from the *favela*. An intellectual like you might have a wider understanding than the kids in my community but it's those kids that really need my information. What are *you* ever going to change?'

Sure. But I just figure it might be important for hip hop heads from excluded communities across the world to feel connected to a wider struggle.

Bill shrugs: 'Our preoccupation here isn't about hip hop or where hip hop's going. I don't really care about hip hop; it's just a form I've found that can help people. Sometimes in life you have to be a doctor and sometimes a bandit. Right now, I have to be a rapper.'

His niece comes over and starts tugging at his leg. She's a pretty little girl of about four or five with a pink dress and her hair in careful ringlets. Bill sweeps her up in one hand and cradles her in the crook of his arm.

'I'm sorry if it scares everyone but there will be a revolt in this city; a revolt where people from the *favelas* divide all the wealth. This is not because I rap about it or want it to happen and not because you decide to write about it; but because it's inevitable. I don't know the time or place but I know it's coming. It's like this: a father hits his stepson. He can hit him every day but it doesn't stop him growing. Eventually the boy won't take any more and, instead of just complaining, he will become violent and hit back. It's the way of the world. Write that in your book.'

Despite the power and passion of what he says, Bill's manner exudes a disconcerting calmness that gives him the manner of a prophet or, perhaps, a condemned man. As much as he dismisses my every question and supposition, it's done with weary melancholy more than any anger. At one point, as I'm telling him about my book, he says a single word – *ghetturista* – but it's less judgement than observation. I don't need it translated.

We leave Bill rocking his niece who's now sleeping with her head on his shoulder. I can't decide whether I feel inspired, depressed, or merely grateful that his life's not mine. A little of all three, I guess. And, for all Bill's stated lack of interest in any world beyond his own, I can't help but think that he and, say, Kenyatta and Shaheen would have quite some conversation.

We're driving through the suburbs of Rio where the *favelas* are divided by highways like Tarmac moats. The hazy mid-afternoon sun only seems to emphasise the sense of dusty dilapidation. I feel like we could be back on the Cape Flats.

Luke veers off and we mount a flyover that doubles back across the main road. The factions' graffiti is everywhere, showing that we're entering disputed territory. 'TC TC TC', roughly sprayed on to the concrete in green, competes with 'CV CV CV' in red. The *favela* of Vigario Geral is a battlefield in the ongoing war between Terceiro Commando and Commando Vermelho.

Vigario Geral is one of Rio's most notorious *favelas*. It has long been a focus for trafficking and, therefore, inter-faction rivalry. It is most infamous, however, for what happened here in August 1993. On the afternoon of the twenty-ninth, a group of heavily armed, masked men marched into the *favela* and opened fire. Two hours later twenty-one *favela* residents lay dead, including seven men who'd been playing cards in a bar and eight members of one family, slain in their own house. But these gunmen were not *soldados* from one or other faction. They were off-duty policemen gaining revenge for four previous murders of their colleagues by the traffickers. In fact, though, not one of their victims had any connection with the drug trade. They were just ordinary people going about their day-to-day business.

Rio was in shock. For all the city's seeming desire to ignore the *favelas*, nobody could ignore a massacre; especially when it followed the police killing seven street kids and one young adult outside the Candelaria church the previous month. It was these events that led, among other things, to the establishment of the Viva Rio charity.

Luke slows the car as we enter Vigario Geral. This is partly because the narrow streets are no more than potholed mud tracks and partly because of the man-made humps that halt your progress every few metres. You have to drive slowly through a *favela*; that's the rule. It's to make sure the lookouts can get a good view of who's in the car and check you're not a threat. There are stories of rich kids coming in to buy drugs and then, in fear, trying to speed their way out only to be shot to pieces by the *soldados*. I don't know if the stories are true but I don't need to find out. The lookouts are posted on roofs at every entrance to the *favela* so that they know exactly who enters and who leaves. If anyone's considered a risk – strangers who could be police or other factions – they let off firecrackers as a warning to their comrades. Unfortunately, firecrackers also announce news of a goal by the local football team, a party or pretty much any noteworthy event, so the bangs are a near constant soundtrack to the *favela*. This does nothing for my sense of well-being.

As we snail deeper inside, Luke drops his window and chats to the young dudes loafing on doorsteps and corners. He's keen to make us visible, let everybody know what we're doing here. He's got an easy manner and the guys laugh with him and shake his hand. I glance down a shadowed alleyway and there's a kid, maybe thirteen or fourteen, cleaning a gun. An AK47, I think.

We've driven as far as we can so Luke parks up and we get out. We turn down a narrow street, puddled and rutted, and we can suddenly hear a clash of drums. Fifty yards down, in the middle of the ramshackle housing, there's suddenly a solid, two-storey building, its walls covered with cheerful murals. This is what we've come to see. Because this impressive community centre in the heart of Vigario Geral is the home of Grupo Cultural AfroReggae.

In the early '90s, a guy called José Júnior (known simply as Júnior) was promoting *bailes funk* around Rio. When a *baile* in Ipanema descended into factional violence, however, the local government decided to take action. After all, fighting in the *favelas* was one thing but a fight on the main tourist drag? So they briefly outlawed funk in the city itself. Unfortunately Júnior had already sold a load of tickets for a *baile* of his own so, at the last minute, he had to change the style of music. He decided to play reggae. It was a disaster. But Júnior's a determined kind of guy and he set about planning another one. This time it was a huge success and Afro-Reggae, in its first incarnation, was born.

To complement the parties, Júnior and his partners began to produce a pamphlet that they gave out at each event. Eventually it developed into a full-blown newspaper but, back then, it was just a one-page photocopy. Aside from promotion, Júnior wrote about race, social issues and black culture and the material started to find something of a cult following.

Encouraged by their success, they decided they wanted to take this conscious ideal that they were developing into the *favelas* so they set themselves the task of finding the roughest neighbourhood in which to start. Then there was the massacre. At the time, Júnior didn't know anyone in Vigario Geral. But the massacre was a national tragedy so, in spite of the factions, it was relatively easy to get access to the community. He started workshops in drumming and dancing and, in 1995, formed Banda AfroReggae from local residents and former drug dealers.

Originally they played a kind of samba–reggae popularised by the Bahia band (and black activists) Olodum. But their recent album *Nova Cara*[30] shows a diversity of influences from reggae to rock. Is it hip hop? That depends, of course, on your definition. But I think so. It certainly uses rap, sampling and funk breaks to, in Rose's framework, 'negotiate the experiences of marginalisation, brutally truncated opportunity, and oppression' and it is certainly, in Chuck D's terms, 'black people's creativity'. Frankly, though, to describe the music as hip hop seems as limited as describing AfroReggae as a band. In fact, AfroReggae is now band, business, NGO and social services all rolled into one. It's an extraordinary story.

Today, there's a visiting group of *capoeiristas* in town from Bahia so AfroReggae are putting on an impromptu show in the social centre and the first-floor terrace is packed and expectant. Before the main band perform, however, it's time for the youngsters to do their stuff. One of the principles of AfroReggae is that every member takes responsibility for a junior group; it's 'each one teach one' at its most literal. There are, therefore, currently six groups of Afro-Reggae performers, each with their own style; from AfroSamba to the more prosaically named AfroReggae II. The kids are damn good, too; the steel-drum beats rattling beneath the melodies in a cacophony of sound and a circus of movement as even the percussionists (wearing heavy steel drums) throw themselves around with immaculately choreographed dance moves borrowed from samba, *capoeira* and B-Boying.

At the side of the makeshift stage, the members of the main band

[30] *Nova Cara*, AfroReggae, 2001, Universal.

are laughing and joking, cheering on their protégés. And there's Júnior himself, leaning against a wall with his arms folded, nodding gently to the music, his face shadowed by a baseball cap.

At the end of each set, the audience – locals, the Bahians, Kanyasu, Luke and I; only about forty strong, I guess – burst into cheers and applause. The band then return the compliment, applauding those watching and shaking everybody by the hand. One of the singers, a pretty little girl of about eleven with wide eyes and a dusty complexion, embraces me and plants a kiss on each cheek. Luke leans across and gestures to where Júnior's standing. 'He always makes sure the performers greet the audience,' he says. 'It makes them feel connected, part of the whole thing. When they performed for the American ambassador? He couldn't get his chequebook out quick enough.' I say, 'You're cynical.' But Luke shrugs. 'What's cynical? It's just common sense.'

It's AfroReggae's turn and they take their places: DJ, lead and bass, a line of three drummers behind LG, the vocalist, and Anderson, the emcee. LG starts to sing, a gentle Latin-soul melody over some simple chords: '*Tinha um som que imperava em Vigàrio Geral*' – 'There was a sound that reigned in Vigario Geral'. The DJ drops in a moody Wu-Tang drum break and Anderson's menacing voice raps back, call-and-response style: 'Explain the sound that reigned in Vigario Geral.' The melody fades out and the beat slows and dies. 'It was the sound of guns, my friends.' Suddenly, the live drummers kick in, their sticks cracking out the policemen's gunfire and echoing around the *favela*. 'Pow-pow-pow-pow!' LG howls, blowing away the audience with an imaginary weapon as the guitar screams and Anderson rattles out the story of 29 August '93, his voice taut with indignation: 'Twenty-one people assassinated because of the hatred and violence of the vengeful police!'

I can't describe this show and hope to do it justice. The music, the dance, the theatre, the passion of it . . . it's both awe-inspiring and deeply moving. Later Anderson tells me a story about the time they toured the Netherlands. After one performance in a particularly rough neighbourhood, a dozen kids handed in weapons. Anderson remembers one boy saying simply: 'I can't. Not any more.' I'm not surprised.

We're sitting with Júnior in his small, bare office adjacent to the centre. He's softly spoken but intense to the point of evangelical. He talks slowly, considering every word, pausing occasionally to check I've understood exactly what he's saying.

Júnior describes AfroReggae as a pyramid with the band at its apex. Below that, there are various bricks: charitable, business and co-operative. The NGO works in several *favelas*. Its core purpose is to keep kids away from the trafficking by giving them means to express themselves. AfroReggae runs workshops in music, dance, capoeira and circus; all backed up by social workers and medical care. As for the business part, it's essentially a production company. 'We are an NGO that makes our own money,' Junior smiles. 'We have great urban connections so we are able to stage shows for Brazil's biggest stars. All the people we work with know our cause so they charge us very little. So a show that would cost any other organisation 300,000 dollars, we can do it for a third of that and still plough 20 per cent of the money back into our work.' The third part is the co-operative, which handles all merchandising and creates employment opportunities within the *favela*.

So how many young people do you work with?

Junior shrugs. 'About 700 are directly involved in the pro-grammes,' he says. 'But it will be a lot more when we've built our new home.'

It turns out the building we're sitting in will soon be knocked down to make way for a new, bigger centre with top-quality sports facilities, an IT centre and the like.

Júnior is quite the charismatic and, when he talks about Afro-Reggae, he drops in quasi-spiritual references to destiny and his calling. I don't doubt his sincerity and, frankly, it's hard not to be utterly charmed. But there's no denying he's a sharp operator who manages to twist the stereotyped perceptions of *favelas* and tap the interest (and indeed wallets) of mainstream culture for the benefit of the organisation. Or, to put it another way, AfroReggae are fully aware of and eager to exploit their cultural capital to help the marginalised community they come from.

'AfroReggae has an ideology – to teach culture, social respon-sibility and creativity. These days, if you really want to change a situation, first you have to change the self-image of the people in that situation. That ideology and the structure of AfroReggae have already become topics for doctorates at universities here even though the people behind it – us – have no education. How did that happen?' He smiles enigmatically. 'It is our collective consciousness.

'What you've seen today . . . AfroReggae is talking of a war in which thousands of people have suffered. But this is not just a war that's happening in Brazil. We tour the world and we see the same war in many different countries. We represent the *favela* and we always come back here. But our show uses many forms – theatre, dance and music – many musical styles – rock, reggae, rap – and many cultures – African, Brazilian, American and European. In this way we are also truly global. You can say we are a positive effect of globalisation. After all, that is what music is for; to bring people together.

'Most people in this country find it easier to only deal with their own society; their outlook is very narrow. But if you are from a *favela*? If you are from a marginalised community? You are used to looking into shop windows where you cannot buy anything. You have to have an open mind to survive, to use the tools that you have. That is our great strength, you see?'

My mind is racing as Júnior talks. Maybe it's just that my thoughts are coalescing or maybe this is exactly what I've been looking for all along without knowing it. Put simply, that this is an oppositional voice that stands against exclusion with full knowledge of the possibilities of imagined identity and the value of its capitalised reputation; that truly acts locally, connects globally and thinks glocally. And, more to the point, it works.

But now Júnior's looking at his watch and his brow is furrowed in a worried frown. 'We must go.' We head outside and the narrow street is now bustling with people hurrying this way and that. It's early evening and the breeze is cool and the light is fading fast. Luke seems agitated. He's talking to Júnior in brisk Portuguese and his tone is urgent and irritable.

I catch Luke by the elbow and ask him what's going on. It turns out that there's an invasion planned for tonight so things are about to get hectic. Apparently Júnior met some of the faction leaders this morning but he couldn't talk them out of it. The local residents have heard the news and they're rushing to get home before things kick off. When the shooting starts, they'll shut themselves in, lie on the floor and hope for the best. We have to get out of here.

Although we're deep inside the *favela*, there's an exit by foot-bridge nearby. Luke says that we should walk over the footbridge with Júnior and he'll drive out with one of the local kids, someone the *soldados* know, who should guarantee they don't shoot him. The kid's mother kisses him on the cheek and tells him not to come back into the *favela* tonight. He's to go and stay with a cousin in another neighbourhood.

We walk briskly back towards Luke's car. It's now twilight and the streets are deserted. Luke jumps in and, with the little boy in the passenger seat, slowly pulls away. He turns on the inside light so that everybody can see inside.

Júnior, Kanyasu and me head for the footbridge. The silence is ringing in my ears. So, as we climb the steps, the building, urban hum of the highway traffic that rushes past below is as reassuring as womb music. I pause briefly on the bridge, in the no-man's-land between two worlds, and look back into Vigario Geral. Júnior is smiling. 'Always war,' he says in English. 'Always fighting.'

We meet Luke at a garage outside the *favela* twenty minutes later and we drive back into the other city of Rio.

Outro
It Takes More[1]

I started researching this book almost exactly a year ago. To get a non-fiction book accepted by a publisher, generally you submit a proposal and a fairly substantial chunk of sample text. In the case of this book, the sample I submitted was the Intro. Now, I'd be lying if I said I hadn't edited that section at all in the interim but it does stand almost exactly the same as when I first wrote it. I've just now re-read it for the first time in a while and I can't help noticing how naive I sound. I wonder, did my journey and research really change me that much? Maybe, in fact, this reflection is simply an inevitable part of the writing process, though I've never experienced it in any book I've written before.

The last part of the Intro framed two broad questions: why did I as a white, middle-class, suburban, English adolescent get into hip hop in the mid-'80s? And what was the essence of hip hop that so attracted me then and still holds me in its thrall? To be honest, the answers to both now seem absurdly straightforward.

Fortunately, in writing this book, its thematic scope broadened significantly. But therein lies the answer to the latter question. I genuinely don't think it is too extravagant to suggest that from the age of fourteen hip hop has opened more doors of enquiry for me than any other aspect of my life. Maybe I *was* just another white kid looking for a bit of appropriated alienation and I wouldn't claim that even the most intelligent and conscious rap lyrics have taught me a whole lot. But hip hop has been the catalyst that has led me to

[1] 'It Takes More', Ms Dynamite, Universal, 2002.

most of things I've learned to love, cherish and believe in as an adult. What's more, I've now met people from cities around the world who could truthfully say the same. Sadly, though, few of them were in New York and I remain convinced that, for all its success (or rather, *because* of its success), hip hop in the place of its birth is now too often a rod for black backs.

As for the first question? Well. In retrospect, I reckon I could have answered it right from the start with a little more self-awareness and no need for the globe-trotting.

I recently went on a radio show with the British writer and DJ Charlie Dark. 'What else were you going to get into?' he asked. Quite.

I'm writing this with MTV for company. At the moment it's a track by London boy band Blue, called 'Fly By'.[2] The chorus kicks in: 'System up with the top down / Got the city on lock down / Drive by in the low ride'. Lock down? Low ride? Check out the slang. The fact is that if white, corporate America (for all its degenerative diseases) still bestrides the world economically and politically, then black America bestrides it culturally.

On my London street, the local off-licence, owned by an Indian Sikh family with two teenage boys, has become a meeting place for the neighbourhood kids. They're all different races and from all different backgrounds and to hear them chatter is to hear a bizarre mélange of Jamaican, Asian and UK (garage) patois. But African-American slang predominates and they're all dressed head to toe in hip hop gear. And when I hear them refer to a girl as 'that bitch' (often stretched to 'be-yatch'), I'm tempted to get on my moral high horse and bemoan the misogyny. But that inclination is tempered by genuine pleasure at a sense of some sort of successful multiculturalism.

On my travels, this book metamorphosed into a search for some kind of 'reality'. What on earth did that mean? In fact, it meant coming to terms with all sorts of hard truths that were, at the same moment, very distant from my own life and crucial to my understanding of it; a fact that says a lot about both me and

---

[2] 'Fly By', Blue, EMI, 2002.

the world in which we live. But, paradoxically, the closest I came to concrete reality was in the realm of ideas. Because the truth is that hip hop is now a key imaginative resource for young people worldwide. In Tokyo, for example, it enables them to negotiate individuality, in Cape Town to negotiate with history and in Rio to negotiate a new understanding of race. And there are plenty more negotiations besides. What's more, in the coincidence of its own qualities, success, new technology and globalised media, it is frequently now a bridge between cultures. Recently I was told a good story to illustrate this. I met this guy called Burhan Wazir, a former journalist for *Hip Hop Connection*, who now works on the foreign desk at the *Observer* newspaper. Burhan is a Scottish-Asian by background and a hip hop encyclopedia. During the conflict in Afghanistan, he was sent to report on the Northern Alliance troops gathering on the Tajikistan border. Freezing cold, he was wrapped up in his favourite Puffa jacket. The first question he was asked by his Northern Alliance guide was, 'You into hip hop?' I tell that story mostly because it surprised me. I guess it shouldn't have done.

However, if hip hop is a bridge between cultures, then it also defines the language used at the meeting. I guess, therefore, there's a question to be addressed to black America. When those two foreign B-Boys meet in the middle of that bridge, how would you like them to greet one another: 'Word up, nigger' or 'Peace, my brother'?

Since I began researching this book, hip hop – American hip hop, anyway – seems to have changed very little. Creatively, it seems to be in one of those periodic troughs that have afflicted it throughout its history. Jay-Z's still the man, though to me his output sounds ever more lazy, while Nelly has gone from promising newcomer to fully fledged and unashamed pop star. I mention the latter mostly because he's next on MTV's line-up.

I interviewed Nelly about eighteen months ago, just before he blew up worldwide, and asked him what he'd bought with his record-company advance. He showed me the enormous pendant around his neck that spelled out his name in diamonds and platinum and cost more than $100,000. Watching his new video, he's still wearing it. God knows where hip hop will be by the time this book comes out but I hope and trust it's somewhere else.

One reason why hip hop has stagnated is, I'm sure, the current social climate in the States; the mood of a country that is still so profoundly affected by the terrorist attacks of 11 September 2001. Just after those attacks, I received an e-mail from Kenyatta. He remembered my commenting on the stars-and-stripes that hung in his next-door neighbour's window. 'Of course they're in every window now,' he said.

I was in Rio when it happened and some people greeted the news feeds coming in on CNN with unconcealed glee. I've spoken to lots of friends who were then in all different parts of Africa, Asia and South America and they can all tell similar stories. At the time, I was shocked almost as much by this reaction as by the news itself. But, considering the amount of time I'd already spent in alienated and excluded communities, I really shouldn't have been so taken aback. Because, broken down to the basics and ignoring questions of blame and responsibility, the facts are just two: the world is an unfair place; America dominates the world politically and economically.

In this context, I suggest that popular culture assumes a deeply significant role because, as I wrote in Jo'burg, these days 'anti-Americanisms are actually articulated through Americanisms'. And the dominant global popular culture is African-American. It's hip hop.

Joseph Stiglitz has written, 'Globalization today is not working for many of the world's poor. It is not working for much of the environment. It is not working for the stability of the global economy . . . To some there is an easy answer: Abandon globalization. That is neither feasible nor desirable . . . The problem is not with globalization, but with how it has been managed.'[3] Stiglitz is, of course, taking a wide, top-down view but, if you narrow the angle somewhat, his point is still pertinent.

Hip hop is now a globalised culture that is locally used to articulate protest. This is, in itself, remarkable and, indeed, more vital than ever in our post-democratic world where corporations

---

[3] *Globalization and its Discontents*, Joseph Stiglitz, 2002, Allen Lane.

exert undue influence over national and international political decisions and electoral processes are too often defined by apathy (in the West) or corruption (in the rest). However, I genuinely believe that hip hop can and should move beyond mere protest to effect global, local, glocal social transformation.

Let me explain how this might happen. And, if much of what follows seems addressed solely to black America, I'm sorry but, for the moment, I have to agree with Rushdie's assessment that America is 'the only business at hand'.

In the first place, as I've repeatedly stressed, hip hop must reclaim itself from the corporate giants that do neither the form nor its worldwide consumers any favours. However you choose to define hip hop, it surely should not be defined as a medium through which big business can further oppress the oppressed or exclude the excluded. And yet, in New York or the ganglands of the Cape Flats, this is currently a plausible definition.

In his book *The Mystery of Capital*,[4] the celebrated Peruvian economist and thinker Hernando De Soto tries to explain why 'capitalism triumphs in the West and fails everywhere else'. The core of his argument is that while, in the West, companies and individuals are able to put their assets to work as capital (through loans and so on), elsewhere the lack of formalised and enforceable property rights makes it near impossible for local entrepreneurs to raise money. At the moment, however, we find ourselves in a world where, as Alan Greenspan acknowledges, Western corporations have begun to capitalise not their assets but their reputations (and subsequently run into all kinds of problems as they fail to 'keep it real'). The irony of this is that, while the ability to capitalise assets has always been the privilege of the few, capitalised reputation is potentially a far more democratic process. Unfortunately it is a process which has thus far been fully exploited only by the same corporate giants. But now, surely, the secret's out.

Hip hop has unparalleled capitalised reputation; unparalleled cultural capital. This is, of course, in part because of its appropriation as an 'ident' by numerous corporations. However, while those

---

[4] *The Mystery of Capital*, Hernando De Soto, 2000, Bantam.

corporations may be able to copyright and fiercely protect their logos and brands, hip hop – arguably the most powerful brand of all – is not theirs to copyright. Hip hop, therefore, must be reclaimed.

So what form might this reclamation take? Ultimately it could mean reclaiming hard cash (and the model used by AfroReggae is one that could show the way) but, for the moment, I'm more concerned that it should take back its cultural capital at an imaginative level.

Despite the bad publicity often associated with rap superstars, several have set up organisations to benefit their communities, from the Wu Charitable Foundation to P. Diddy's Daddy's House Social Programs. But these operations, for all their good intentions, are pissing in the wind when big business still appropriates the superstars' cultural capital to exploit the very same communities. As a first step, therefore, this process at least needs to be acknowledged by everyone who cares; most of all the stars themselves.

Of course, if any of these rap stars don't want to make this imaginative leap (which, after all, amounts to a scathing criticism of their own lifestyle), we shouldn't be any more down-hearted than we are surprised. Hip hop is its own best marketing with B-Boys as the commercial foot soldiers. In his analysis of the wildfire spread of modern trends, *The Tipping Point*,[5] Malcolm Gladwell argues that ideas or products become successful less through mass advertising than through the actions of key players who have widespread influence because of their cultural capital. Isn't this self-evidently true of hip hop? Whether it's the players on the Brooklyn basketball courts or *favela* kids descending on Rio to party, they're the ones who define 'cool' and the mainstream follows. As much as if not more than the superstars therefore, the imaginative leap to reclaim hip hop needs to be taken by these guys, both in the States and worldwide.

The second thing to say is that America's hip hop generation must engage with the rest of the world like never before. The potential of hip hop as a tool for social transformation within America is something that has been discussed within hip hop for

[5] *The Tipping Point*, Malcolm Gladwell, 2000, Little, Brown & Company.

more than a decade but, let's face it, it's achieved very little. But outside America?

At a basic level, it's obviously important that America's rap stars understand the impact of their words and actions on the wider world. More than that, though, it's vital they understand the economic, political and social possibilities of the cultural power they wield.

Head into any slum (certainly any slum I've been to) in the developing world and you'll find young people who harbour enormous resentment towards the West in general and the USA in particular (whether informed by local or global situations). But these same young people express themselves through African-American slang and their heroes are rappers.

Since the end of the civil-rights movement, it is, I think, indisputable that the African-American community has not managed to (or has not been allowed to) punch its weight within its own country. But it is also currently indisputable that that same community now has the potential to be a significant player globally; not just on sports fields or in concert venues but politically too. And this situation is largely a product of hip hop's success.

At the very least this means American hip hop must make an effort to positively and intelligently engage with the wider world (unlike the platinum-selling rapper I once interviewed – I asked him where he'd been so far on his European tour and he replied that he'd been 'to UK, to London . . . and to England too'). It means hip hop stars touring the excluded communities that worship them, equipped with an informed view. It probably means lending their name and weight to local artists and enterprises that are so often squashed by the multinationals that pay these same rappers to sign to their company or endorse their product. It certainly means taking to the stage in a pair of Loxion Kulca trainers.

Even outside America, the cultural capital of B-Boys is often second to none; whether derived from hip hop itself or just the fetishisation of otherness. And this too should be reclaimed and exploited.

Cultural production from outside the West (whether it be of music or art or whatever) has long been perceived as 'cool' in the

West, now so more than ever. At the end of my road, there is a shop – one of a chain – that imports African sculptures, Mexican candlesticks, Indian rugs and flogs them on at twenty, forty, sixty quid a go. Frankly, I've always wondered how they get away with it. After all, what does the shop itself bring to the party beyond recontextualising the cheap goods? Well, what the English owners clearly do have is an understanding of the value of what they sell in both its original and London contexts.

In the past, it would have been reasonable to argue that this was a skill (albeit an amoral one) that set Western businessmen apart from the original cultural producers. Now, however, young people from excluded groups worldwide, especially the B-Boys, are as savvy as anyone when it comes to understanding ideas of marketing. Hip hop knows the value of a good brand; indeed, brand recognition has always been a part of the music itself. And this information is now increasingly recognised by cultural producers from non-Western situations, whether we're talking Loxion Kulca, BVK or Afro-Reggae. If American hip hop has largely conceded its cultural capital to others, then this new generation of savvy entrepreneurs seems to have learned from that mistake.

Of course, these worldwide cultural producers are rarely in a position of actual capitalised power. The third aim, therefore, has to be to establish international networks of contacts and distribution. Why? Primarily just to lend support and share experiences and information. But also to fully exploit their potential. The contemporary cult of otherness means that, for all their local cultural capital, guys like Black Noise can probably exert more influence internationally. For all their support at home, AfroReggae can most successfully sell their brand of exotica for the most possible money (charitable or not) in the West and pump that Western cash back into their local community. This is surely glocal thinking at its most effective.

At a personal level, one of the most significant repercussions of our travels was Kanyasu's decision to return to live in Zambia. She came to the conclusion, long considered if not articulated, that opportunities in the West are not all they're cracked up to be and, besides, Zambia is home. Kanyasu is currently setting up her own business making jewellery using craftsmen and techniques from all over Africa for sale in both local and Western markets. She is also organising to take a group of *capoeiristas* to tour East Africa. Later she hopes to bring over a hip hop crew from the States to run workshops in the local compounds (think townships, *favelas*, ghettoes). I must remember to have a word with Kenyatta.

I mention these projects for a couple of reasons. First of all, they seem like decent applications of my new mantra: act locally, connect globally, think glocally. For example, Kenyatta's cultural capital in New York is nothing compared to what it might be in Lusaka. After all, in New York rappers are a dime a dozen. But in Zambia? He could bring specific skills, thought and kudos to young people who would undoubtedly appreciate and learn from them.

More than this, however, these projects reflect Kanyasu's appreciation of the fourth point I want to make; one I only fully understood in conversation with Júnior from AfroReggae. He said, 'These days, if you really want to change a situation, first you have to change the self-image of the people in that situation.'

Throughout this book, I have repeatedly stressed the current importance and possibilities of imagined instead of ascribed identity. Even in excluded and impoverished communities, Kanyasu and I have met numerous people who have managed to imagine a positive sense of who they are that transcends their immediate circumstance.

However, the fact is that in most such communities this process has to be quite some feat of personal storytelling. Whether in the townships of Jo'burg or the *favelas* of Rio, people can only build identity from the materials at their disposal. Often, as expressed by Ready D or MV Bill, the available materials hardly extend beyond the negative stereotypes perpetuated by local and international media. But hip hop provides alternative building blocks. What's more, the blocks hip hop offers are not just imaginative but practical too, as the five elements can construct identity through action. And this is the point: hip hop can and must regard its elements as part of a political process to construct conscious identity in opposition to that the mainstream seeks to ascribe. So graffiti is artistic expression; but it's also as political as the socialist murals of Mexican, Diego Rivera, or the revolutionary calligraphy developed by the Beijing students in the late '80s. So breaking is about dancing; but it's also about the conscious reclaiming of social spaces, like the South African *toyi-toyi* or the worldwide carnivals of gay pride.

This thought process leads me back to my conversation with Charlie. As we chatted, the subject moved away from hip hop in particular to popular culture in general. The guy chairing the radio show started talking about the 'underground' but Charlie quickly retorted, 'There is no underground these days', and, again, I have to agree.

The appropriation of underground culture – hip hop included – by mainstream media, business and politics has surreptitiously robbed us of both the language of protest and even our consumer choice. This is, of course, an inherent function of global capitalism and stems from the relentless need to maximise profit. It's 'McDonaldisation', the realisation that the best way to make the most money is to sell more and more numbers of fewer and fewer products. Apart from fast-food restaurants, this is the philosophy of Niketown. As a writer, you can bet I've noticed it's the philosophy of the major chains of bookshops too. And the music industry? The major labels turn hip hop into pop, offer baubles to the few and systematically strip the majority of the excluded of their voice. And so the final point to make is actually Bobbito's: 'Search and discovery is the most neglected element of hip hop.' Or, as Blaze put it in Jo'burg, 'To be honest, if you can influence a kid to think in a non-mainstream way then that's OK with me.'

So let me recap this loose manifesto. Hip hop must be reclaimed at an imaginative level (as a first step) by its cultural brokers the world over. Rap stars must engage with the wider world to maximise their cultural capital just as the global cultural producers must connect and support one another to maximise theirs. At a local level, the expressive elements of hip hop need to be nurtured as a key resource of imagined identity. And, what's more, all these things must be done in the context of 'search and discovery', the conscious realisation that we are currently being fed a line that serves only profit.

Or perhaps I should just return to 'act locally, connect globally, think glocally', because that seems to sum it up well enough.

It's a year since I started researching this book but now, as I write the final few words, I'm wondering who will read it and, more to the point, whether they will care. Will it reach hip hop's power brokers; not the rap stars but the B–Boys worldwide? After all, hip hop, not books, is their cultural form of choice. Perhaps, therefore, it will be no more than a curiosity of passing interest to the growing numbers of middle–class, thirtysomething culture vultures and the reaction will be the same as that of my friends to my observations about *Shrek*: 'Even if you're right, so what?' I have a foot in both camps, you see, though these days I feel myself increasingly toppling into the latter.

I'm not saying that hip hop *will* change anything; I'm just saying it *can*. Frankly I'm with MV Bill on this one: I don't really care about hip hop; it's just a form I've found that can help people.

There is, however, one thing I know with absolute certainty, both because I have experienced it personally and because all the statistics say so. Worldwide – and these days you have to talk worldwide – the gap between rich and poor, powerful and power-less, mainstream and excluded is widening by the day and hip hop is one of the few cultural forms that successfully bridges that gap on a global stage. Hip hop has long talked about the possibilities for, depending on who you listen to, change, revolution or real social justice. Where once you might have been able to dismiss this as polemic, it now smells like prophecy. The time is now.

As I write this, the sound of MTV seeps back into my conscious-ness. It's a track by the current darling of the British music press, Ms Dynamite, called 'It Takes More'. An affiliate of the UK garage collective So Solid Crew, she's now struck out on her own with an album that mixes R'n'B and garage and hip hop, of course. Though I've heard this tune a hundred times before, as I sip my coffee I feel like I'm hearing the lyrics for the first time and they sound like a caustic attack on the state of modern hip hop. 'It takes more to amuse a girl like me,' she sings. 'You're talking like you a G / But you a killer killing your own / You're just a racist man's pussy.' So I just turn up the volume, sit back and revel in what I know right here and right now. It takes more and – you know what? – it's coming. No doubt.

A NOTE ON THE AUTHOR

Patrick Neate is the author of three novels, *Musungu Jim and the Great Chief Tuloko*, *Twelve Bar Blues*, which won the Whitbread Novel of the Year Award 2001, and most recently, *The London Pigeon Wars*. He is also a prolific and highly respected music journalist.

A NOTE ON THE TYPE

The text of this book is set in Bembo. This type was first used in 1495 by the Venetian printer Aldus Manutius for Cardinal Bembo's *De Aetna*, and was cut for Manutius by Francesco Griffo. It was one of the types used by Claude Garamond (1480–1561) as a model for his Romain de L'Université, and so it was the forerunner of what became standard European type for the following two centuries. Its modern form follows the original types and was designed for Monotype in 1929.